CIVIL PROCEDURE: THE ECONOMICS OF CIVIL PROCEDURE

by

ROBERT G. BONE
Professor of Law
Harry Elwood Warren Scholar
Boston University School of Law

TURNING POINT SERIES®

FOUNDATION PRESS
New York, New York
2003

Turning Point Series is a registered trademark
used herein under license.

COPYRIGHT © 2003 By FOUNDATION PRESS
                    395 Hudson Street
                    New York, NY 10014
                    Phone Toll Free 1–877–888–1330
                    Fax (212) 367–6799
                    fdpress.com

All rights reserved
Printed in the United States of America
ISBN 1–58778–172–7

TURNING POINT SERIES

CIVIL PROCEDURE

Civil Procedure: Class Actions by Linda S. Mullenix, University of Texas (Available 2003)

Civil Procedure: Economics of Civil Procedure by Robert G. Bone, Boston University (Available 2003)

Civil Procedure: Preclusion in Civil Actions by David L. Shapiro, Harvard University (2001)

Civil Procedure: Jury Process by Nancy S. Marder, Illinois Institute of Technology (Available 2003)

Civil Procedure: Territorial Jurisdiction and Venue by Kevin M. Clermont, Cornell (1999)

CONSTITUTIONAL LAW

Constitutional Law: Equal Protection by Louis M. Seidman, Georgetown University (2002)

Constitutional Law: Religion Clause by Daniel O. Conkle, Indiana University, Bloomington (Available 2003)

CRIMINAL LAW

Criminal Law: Model Penal Code by Markus D. Dubber, State University of New York, Buffalo (2002)

Criminal Law: Habeas Corpus by Larry W. Yackle, Boston University (Available 2003)

INTERNATIONAL LAW

International Law: United States Foreign Relations Law by Phillip R. Trimble, UCLA (2002)

LEGISLATION

Legislation: Statutory Interpretation: Twenty Questions by Kent R. Greenawalt, Columbia University (1999)

PROPERTY

Property: Takings by David Dana, Northwestern University and Thomas Merrill, Northwestern University (2002)

CORPORATE/SECURITIES

Securities Law: Insider Trading by Stephen Bainbridge, UCLA (1999)

TORTS

Torts: Proximate Cause by Joseph A. Page, Georgetown University (2002)

*For my wife Elizabeth and my son Josh,
the two people in my life who maximize my
happiness.*

*

About the Author

Robert Bone is Professor of Law and Harry Elwood Warren Scholar at Boston University School of Law. Professor Bone graduated from Stanford University and Harvard Law School. Following law school, he served as a judicial law clerk and then worked as an associate at a Boston law firm before joining the University of Southern California law faculty in 1983. Professor Bone has been a member of the Boston University School of Law faculty since 1987, and has also taught as a visiting faculty member at Columbia Law School and Harvard Law School. Since he began teaching, Professor Bone has specialized in civil procedure and complex litigation, and published extensively in both fields, including articles appearing in the Columbia Law Review, University of Pennsylvania Law Review, New York University Law Review, and Journal of Legal Studies. His articles employ a variety of theoretical approaches, both economic and non-economic, including decision theory, game theory, welfare economics, and theories of rights and justice. His most recent procedure publications examine the procedural rulemaking process and aspects of frivolous litigation, class actions, and judicial involvement in settlement.

*

TABLE OF CONTENTS

*

CIVIL PROCEDURE:
THE ECONOMICS
OF
CIVIL PROCEDURE

*

Introduction

> Nothing is of more immediate practical importance to a lawyer than the rules that govern his own strategies and maneuvers; and nothing is more productive of deep and philosophical puzzles than the question of what those rules should be.
>
> Ronald Dworkin[1]

To many readers, Professor Dworkin's characterization of civil procedure as posing "deep and philosophical puzzles" may seem strange—the irrelevant musings of a scholar too long out of touch with the realities of practice. Philosophy might have something to do with torts, criminal law, and contracts, but surely not civil procedure. The goal of civil procedure is essentially practical: managing a litigation system well. The field is a collection of technical rules that lawyers master in order to gain a strategic advantage over their opponents. None of this can raise philosophical puzzles, deep or otherwise. Or so the reader might think.

In fact, however, Professor Dworkin is correct. The design of procedural rules does present difficult questions of policy that at times implicate deep philosophical puzzles. The reason has to do with the

1. Ronald Dworkin, *Principle, Policy, Procedure, in* A MATTER OF PRINCIPLE 72 (1985).

1

close relationship between procedure and substantive law and the normative tradeoffs that a good procedural system requires. Substantive rights are only as good as the procedures available to enforce them. People can rely on others to use reasonable care, abide by their promises, respect privacy and avoid injury in large part because of the deterrent force of the substantive law, and effective deterrence depends on a properly functioning procedural system.

If we lived in a Panglossian "best of all possible worlds," our procedural system would enforce the substantive law costlessly and with perfect accuracy. But in our real world of scarcity and constraint, we have to settle for an imperfect system, one that creates its own costs at the same time as it reduces, though never eliminates, the risk of enforcement error. The challenge for procedural law is to find the right balance of benefit and cost, and to do so with less than perfect information about the likely effects. More extensive procedures can reduce the risk of error but also increase the cost of process and take resources away from other worthwhile social programs. As a result, any choice of procedural rule entails judgments of relative value and difficult tradeoffs that raise complex and controversial policy issues, and at times deep philosophical puzzles.

This book describes one way to make these policy tradeoffs: the approach of law-and-economics. The law-and-economics literature has devoted a good deal of attention to procedural issues and over time developed a powerful set of analytical tools. Indeed, economics is useful for analyzing virtually every feature of the procedural system, including burdens of pleading and proof, summary judgment, frivolous litigation, party and claim joinder rules, discovery, the class action, settlement, and alternative dispute resolution.

As I write this book, in the year 2002, procedural reform is a topic of political and public policy debate. In 1994, the Republican Party's "Contract With America" placed litigation reform at the forefront of the political agenda. Since that time, candidates for political office at all levels have included litigation reform in their campaign platforms, including such issues as how to handle frivolous litigation, when to employ class actions, and how much to encourage settlement and alternative dispute resolution. In fact, interest in procedure is more intense today than at any time since the opening decades of the twentieth century. Rule systems are in a continual state of flux, and critics challenge the most fundamental tenets of the adversary system, including litigant control and court-rendered judgment based on adversary trial.

In this dynamic climate, it is especially important for students of civil procedure to understand the policies that underlie the rules, and economics is central to such an understanding. The tools of economics can help practicing lawyers argue for rule interpretations favorable to their clients, help judges evaluate the arguments of counsel, and help legislative and committee-based rulemakers sort the merits of different reform proposals and select rules that serve the public interest well. Indeed, the future of the procedural system depends on knowledgeable lawyers who are equally conversant with the rules and the policies that support them.

0.1 POSITIVE VERSUS NORMATIVE ECONOMICS

Economics supplies two different kinds of policy tools: positive and normative. Positive economics is about prediction, and normative economics about evaluation. To make a judgment about any proposed rule, one must first have some way to predict its effects and then some way to evaluate those effects and decide on balance whether the rule has sufficient merit to warrant adoption.

0.1.1 Positive Economics

Positive economics relies on a theory of decision-making under uncertainty, known as the theory of rational choice. Roughly speaking, rational choice theory assumes that individuals have preferences over outcomes and that their preferences behave in certain regular ways; more precisely, that they satisfy the so-called "axioms of rational choice."[2] When

2. The axioms of rational choice state properties that a preference ordering must possess in order to assure that individuals will maximize expected utility. A description of the axioms is beyond the scope of this book. They include such properties as completeness (all outcomes can be rank-ordered according to preference), transitivity (if outcome L is preferred to outcome M

preferences behave regularly, individuals choose what maximizes their "expected utility." Expected utility is a complex concept. We shall use a relatively simple, though useful, version known as "expected monetary value," or "expected value" for short.

Positive economics is purely descriptive. It makes no claims about what people *should* do; it merely predicts what they *will* do. More precisely, it rests on the premise that reasonably reliable behavioral predictions can be obtained *if* one assumes that people maximize expected utility (or expected value). Therefore, positive economics is only as good as the predictions it generates. Not surprisingly, these predictions are hardly perfect. There is a growing empirical literature that tests the limits of rational choice, and we shall examine some of its findings in Chapter Three after we finish studying the basic rational choice models of litigation and settlement.

0.1.2 Normative Economics

Normative analysis belongs to a separate branch of economics known as "welfare economics." The distinctive feature of welfare economics is its aggregative approach. The basic idea is to choose the rule that maximizes social welfare. In the law-and-economics literature, it is customary to express social welfare as a function of social costs. In the procedure setting, social costs include the parties' private

and outcome M is preferred to outcome N, then outcome L is preferred to outcome N), and somewhat more complicated substitution and continuity properties. For a formal account of the axioms of rational choice and expected utility theory, *see* David M. Kreps, A COURSE IN MICROECONOMIC THEORY 71–81 (1990).

litigation costs, the public costs of the court system, and the error costs created by incorrect decisions. The aim is to choose a rule that minimizes the sum of all these costs.

One feature that makes welfare economics controversial as a normative matter is its aggregative approach. Suppose person A suffers a very large loss under a particular rule while person B enjoys a huge benefit. If B's benefit is large enough, it might exceed A's loss and create a net aggregate gain that justifies adoption of the rule. Some critics object that aggregating in this way does not take person A's individual circumstances seriously enough and can produce unjust results if A's loss is extreme. They argue, for example, that A might have an individual *right* not to be treated so poorly no matter how large the benefit to B, and that the idea of rights is inconsistent with the goal of maximizing aggregate welfare.

Advocates of welfare economics respond that concerns about rights and justice are perfectly compatible with an aggregative approach. Avoiding extreme losses and respecting individual rights are sometimes the best ways to maximize social welfare in the long run. Rights theorists disagree. But the important point is that welfare economics is not the only normative approach worth considering. Rights-based theories and theories of distributive justice also furnish important insights. We shall briefly discuss these alternatives in Chapter Six.

One final point. There is no necessary connection between positive and normative economics. One can use the predictive tools of positive economics without accepting the goal of welfare maximization. If protecting individual rights sometimes takes priority over maximizing aggregate welfare, for example, positive economics and the theory of rational choice are still useful ways to predict a rule's impact on individual rights. Indeed, prediction is essential to any normative approach that counts consequences in some way, whether that approach focuses on utility, rights, equality, or some other metric.

0.2 BASIC PLAN

This book is organized around a set of policy puzzles and problems. Rather than simply describe the various concepts and tools, the book motivates the discussion by situating the theoretical material in the context of practical issues of current importance. For example, Chapter One introduces the idea of expected value and the basic economic model of litigation by presenting them as tools needed to solve a concrete problem, namely, how to predict the severity of frivolous litigation.

There are several advantages to a problem-oriented approach. Motivating the analysis with legal policy issues highlights the power of economics in a particularly direct and immediate way. It also does a good job of conveying the central message, that economic analysis is much more than a collection of theories; it is a useful set of tools for solving practical legal problems. In the end, I hope that a problem-oriented approach will make the book not only more understandable, but also more exciting and more useful.

In a box at the beginning of each chapter, I highlight the economic concepts and tools that are covered in the chapter. This way the reader can keep track of what he or she is expected to learn. The main analytic chapters (chapters 1, 2, 4, and 5) also have a section at the end summarizing the main points.

This book assumes no special background in economics. Its purpose is to reach as wide an audience as possible. Moreover, the exposition avoids technical and mathematical detail. All the concepts are explained intuitively with relatively easy numerical examples. On a few occasions, a general mathematical formula is presented, but only when the formula is fundamental to the topic and takes a simple form. In all such instances, however, every effort is made to ensure the reader understands and can apply the analysis without using the formula.

0.3 CONTENT AND ORGANIZATION

This book is divided into three parts. Part One describes the tools of positive economics. The presentation is organized around two litigation puzzles, each of which is relevant to current policy issues. The first puzzle, discussed in Chapter One, is why a plaintiff would ever file a frivolous suit. Finding a solution is vital to formulating an effective regulatory response to frivolous litigation, and the analytic tools needed to solve the puzzle include the idea of expected value, the economic model of litigation, and the game-theoretic idea of an equilibrium.

The second puzzle, discussed in Chapter Two, is to explain why some lawsuits fail to settle and end up going to trial. A solution to this puzzle is critical to designing a sensible regulatory approach to settlement. And the solution requires an understanding of the economic model of settlement, the effects of hard bargaining and divergent expectations, and the impact of agency costs and attorney fee arrangements.

Chapter Three concludes Part One with a brief examination of the limits of rational choice. As we shall see, the insights of behavioral economics can be used to modify rational choice models of litigation and settlement in ways that improve the predictive power of those models.

Part Two describes the tools of normative economics. Chapters Four and Five focus on two policy problems, each of which has received a great deal of attention from policymakers over the past two decades. The first problem, discussed in Chapter Four, is how to design a pleading rule that provides fair notice and effectively screens frivolous suits. The analysis introduces the ideas of expected error and expected process cost and the distinction between false positive and false negative error. It also shows how to fold the positive analysis of frivolous litigation from Chapter One into an error and process cost framework.

The second policy problem, discussed in Chapter Five, is whether the United States should adopt the British Rule on attorney's fees. The discussion highlights the importance of analyzing multiple incentive effects, including effects on filing, settlement, litigation investment, and compliance, and also the importance of considering interactions among different incentives. Like Chapter Four, this chapter relies on the positive models of litigation and settlement developed in Part One for the predictions necessary to fill out the normative framework.

Chapter Six concludes Part Two with a discussion of the limits of normative economics and a brief description of some alternative approaches, including process-based and outcome-based fairness theories.

Part Three considers three additional procedural areas of intense interest today. The discussion applies an economic analysis to critique current doctrine and analyze proposed reforms. Chapter Seven focuses on discovery. Chapter Eight examines preclusion law. And Chapter Nine concludes Part Three, and the book, with an analysis of the class action. Although the discussion in these three chapters adds some new concepts, it mainly applies the concepts and tools developed in the rest of the book.

* * * * * * * * *

This book would not have been possible without the help of many individuals. I am especially indebted to my colleague at Boston University, Professor Keith Hylton, and to Professor Chris Sanchirico at the University of Virginia School of Law, both of whom read drafts of the manuscript and provided valuable comments that improved the final version in many ways. I also wish to thank my colleague, Professor Susan Koniak, who read Chapter Nine and offered numerous helpful suggestions. In addition, I am grateful to my research assistants, Aravind Swaminathan, Peter Cancelmo, and Ryan Cunningham, for their hard work on this project, and to Iris Greidinger for her editorial assistance. Of course, all remaining errors are my own.

*

Part One:

THE TOOLS OF POSITIVE ECONOMICS

Consider the following simple question: Will litigation delay be reduced significantly by adding more trial judges to the court system? One might think the answer obvious. With more judges, the court system can process cases more quickly, reduce case backlog, and thereby reduce delay. However, matters are not quite so simple.

With shorter delays, litigation becomes a more attractive option, so more cases are filed and fewer filed cases settle. With more cases in the system, backlog increases and so too does delay. Thus, adding more judges has the direct effect of increasing the number of cases processed in any given period of time, but it also has the indirect effect of increasing the total number of cases that must be processed. The direct effect reduces delay but the indirect effect increases it. The result depends on which effect dominates.

There is another indirect effect that complicates the analysis even further. Reducing the time to final judgment increases the real value of a monetary remedy by putting money in the plaintiff's hands more quickly, and it also makes the defendant's loss greater by forcing an earlier payment. This means that the stakes are higher for both parties, and with higher stakes, parties usually invest more in litigating the lawsuit. They might spend more on discovery, for example, file additional motions and contest them more vigorously, or raise more complicated issues. A more intense litigation strategy is likely to consume a greater amount of litigation time, and more time means longer delays.

This example shows just how complex the task of prediction can be in the strategic environment of litigation and how important it is to consider indirect as well as direct effects. The tools of positive economics have the virtue of making complex problems more tractable and providing a systematic way to identify and measure all possible effects.

THE ADVANTAGES AND LIMITS OF MODELS

Positive economics relies extensively on models that abstract from the details of real life. Our brief analysis of litigation delay, for example, started with a model of the court system that assumed a fixed number of cases and settlements and a fixed level of litigation investment.[1] As we complicated the analysis, we added more contextual detail and more complexity. First, we relaxed the assumption of a fixed number of cases and settlements, and then we allowed litigation investment to vary with

1. It made other assumptions as well, such as that cases are evenly distributed and the productivity of trial judges is not affected by docket pressure.

the stakes. Even so, the analysis still ignored most of the real world details.

Some people object to models because they abstract from the real world. How, they wonder, can a model generate useful predictions when it ignores large chunks of reality? In fact, however, abstraction is a virtue rather than a vice. Indeed, it is an essential aspect of rational thought. The human mind cannot possibly process all the nuances and details of real life. By abstracting from context, models make it possible to perceive hidden patterns and to process decisions in a tractable way. Even as routine an act as changing lanes on a highway depends on constructing an abstract model of driver behavior and road conditions, a model that assumes, among other things, that drivers are rational, that they care about avoiding accidents, and that they have at least a basic understanding of the rules of the road. This model usually works well enough, but when it does not, accidents often ensue.

Therefore, the goal cannot be to replicate reality. Instead, it must be to approximate reality closely enough to assure reasonably reliable predictions but not so closely as to make the process of prediction impossibly complicated. The key is to include those factors that have the strongest influence on behavior and leave out those that are likely to have much weaker effects.

The models we use in everyday life are ad hoc and informal, while economic models are rigorous, systematic, and often mathematically formal. Both kinds of models are useful. But the formal model has an advantage for policy analysis: its rigor makes it more transparent so the analyst can see clearly which assumptions are necessary and how the different variables interact.

Modeling is not the only way to make predictions. Empirical studies and even informal experience can also be helpful. However, modeling is particularly important in procedure because the alternatives have serious limitations. Reliable empirical studies of the litigation process are extremely limited; funding for future studies is scarce, and effective research design faces substantial methodological obstacles. For example, ethical concerns limit the availability of controlled field experiments; selection biases distort case samples, and confidentiality frustrates access to settlement data and other types of information. Furthermore informal experience, while helpful at times, is often unreliable. Memory tends naturally to sift and distort details in the process of recollection.

In fact, modeling and empiricism can complement one another. Models identify relationships that can be tested empirically, and if empirical results bear out the model's predictions, confidence in the model increases. The relationship works the other way as well: empirical results (and even widely shared informal experience) guide model construction by identifying the most salient variables to include. In short, empiricism helps to verify and refine models, which in turn help to shape empirical research.

A FINAL POINT

Economists often express their models in the language of mathematics. They do so because mathematics lends a high degree of precision and supplies powerful analytic techniques for deriving predictions. Unfortunately, however, the use of mathematics also makes models inaccessible to the non-mathematician and sometimes even breeds hostility to the idea of modeling in general. This is unfortunate. The logic of a model can almost always be described without the use of formal mathematics or at least without mathematics beyond the level of simple arithmetic (and sometimes simple algebra). All of the models in this book are presented with a minimum of mathematical technicality.

CHAPTER ONE:

THE PUZZLE OF FRIVOLOUS LITIGATION, OR WHY WOULD ANYONE EVER FILE A FRIVOLOUS LAWSUIT?

CONCEPTS AND TOOLS

- Rational Choice and Expected Value
- Economic Model of Litigation and the Decision to Sue
- Sunk Costs
- Simple Game Theory
  - The Idea of an Equilibrium
  - Asymmetric Information and Pooling
- Risk Aversion
- Reputation Effects

Frivolous litigation is a matter of intense concern today. There is a widespread belief that frivolous suits are responsible for many of the court system's most serious problems, including huge case backlogs, long trial delays, high litigation costs, and excessive liability that chills innovation and impedes vigorous competition.[2] During the 1980s, the

2. One particularly famous example in the popular press is the "McDonald's hot coffee case," in which the plaintiff sued to recover damages for burns she suffered from spilling a cup of hot

federal courts responded by tightening pleading requirements, and in 1995, Congress codified strict pleading for securities fraud class actions in the Private Securities Litigation Reform Act.[3] In 1983, the Advisory Committee on Civil Rules revised Rule 11 of the Federal Rules of Civil Procedure to sharpen sanctions for frivolous suits.[4] And in 1986, the United States Supreme Court expanded access to summary judgment as a tool to weed out frivolous and weak cases before trial.[5]

Despite this strong interest, we actually know very little about frivolous litigation. Empirical research in this area is extremely difficult to conduct because most lawsuits settle and settlements mask evidence of frivolousness. In fact, the prevalence of frivolous litigation is quite puzzling. If a lawsuit is frivolous, then the plaintiff has little chance of winning at trial. So why would he hire a lawyer, spend money drafting a complaint, and invest in pursuing a losing suit?

coffee. *See* Liebeck v. McDonald's Restaurants, P.T.S., Inc., No. CV–93–02419, 1995 WL 360309 (D.N.M. August 18, 1994) (reporting the jury's findings, including compensatory damages of $160,000 and punitive damages of $2.7 million).

3. Pub. L. No. 104–67, 109 Stat. 737 (1995). The strict pleading provisions are codified at 15 U.S.C. § 78u–4(b)(2).

4. *See* FED. R. CIV. P. 11 (1983). A decade later, the Advisory Committee amended the Rule by stripping it of some of its harsher provisions. This amended version is the Rule 11 in force today. *See* FED. R. CIV. P. 11 (1993).

5. *See* Celotex Corp. v. Catrett, 477 U.S. 317 (1986); Anderson v. Liberty Lobby, Inc., 477 U.S. 242 (1986); Matsushita Elec. Indus. Co. v. Zenith Radio Corp., 475 U.S. 574 (1986).

The usual answer is that the frivolous plaintiff is looking for a settlement. But this answer simply poses the other half of the puzzle. Why would a defendant ever be willing to settle a frivolous suit? Conventional wisdom has it that the defendant is better off paying a nuisance settlement than spending money on trial. But why is this so? A frivolous plaintiff, after all, would never take his case to trial. So why isn't the defendant's best strategy simply to refuse to settle and force the plaintiff to drop?

Solving this puzzle is an essential first step in designing an effective regulatory response to frivolous suits. If the puzzle has no solution—in other words, if there is no reason why plaintiffs would file frivolous suits in large numbers—then it might be best to do nothing at all, given that any regulation is bound to generate its own costs. As it turns out, however, frivolous plaintiffs do have incentives to sue. To see why, we first need to understand why and when parties file lawsuits.

1.1 ECONOMIC MODEL OF LITIGATION

1.1.1 Expected Value and Rational Choice

Intuitively, the decision to sue should depend on at least three factors: the likely recovery, the probability of success, and the cost of trial. A person is more likely to sue the larger the recovery, the higher his chance of success, or the lower the trial costs. Positive economics supplies a model of litigation that gives a rigorous account of how these variables interact. This model is based on **the theory of rational choice**. The following discussion describes the core features of rational choice theory and then outlines the basic model.

In a nutshell, the theory of rational choice holds that individuals maximize **expected utility**. Expected utility is the utility one receives from an outcome multiplied by the probability that the outcome will materialize. The idea of "utility" is rather complex. Roughly speaking, utility measures the relative strength of an individual's preferences; larger utilities correspond to more strongly preferred outcomes. Fortunately, there is no need to develop the concept with care because there is a much simpler and more intuitive idea that will serve our purposes quite well. This is the idea of **expected value.**

Expected value is a particular version of expected utility that applies when the decisionmaker is **risk-neutral**. Risk-neutrality denotes an attitude toward risk. A risk-neutral party gets no special pleasure from the thrill of taking a risk and suffers no special anxiety. He gambles strictly for the monetary payoff. By contrast, a **risk-seeking** party enjoys taking risks partly for the thrill of the gamble itself, and a **risk-averse** party gets anxious when he faces a risky choice. Many people are a bit risk-averse and become more so as they gamble a larger fraction of their personal wealth. But some people love to gamble and get more of a thrill the more they put on the line.

Most of the economic literature on procedure assumes that parties are risk-neutral. Although this assumption does not hold in all cases, it simplifies the analysis and generates predictions that are approximately correct. Furthermore, performing the analysis first under the simple assumption of risk-neutrality helps to show how results might change when risk preferences are more complicated. So we shall assume risk-neutrality and use the concept of expected value.

But what exactly is expected value and how is it calculated? Let us start with two simple examples that have nothing to do with litigation. In the first, John invites Mary to play a game that involves the flipping of a coin. If the coin comes up heads, John pays Mary $1000, and if the coin comes up tails, Mary pays John $2000. If Mary is rational and risk-neutral, will she play the game?

Mary faces a choice under uncertainty: she must decide whether to play without knowing for sure what the outcome will be. If the coin is fair so that heads is as likely as tails, the rational choice is fairly obvious after a moment's reflection. Mary will not play. It is instructive to see why this is intuitively clear. The reason is that Mary expects to lose more than she expects to win. The probabilities of winning and losing are the same (i.e., a 50% chance of heads and a 50% chance of tails), but the potential loss ($2000) is much greater than the potential gain ($1000).

Now consider the same example, except this time with a weighted coin that makes heads three times as likely as tails. Whether Mary will play this game is more difficult to determine. We might analyze the problem intuitively in the following way. Although Mary still stands to lose twice as much as she stands to win, her chance of winning is now three times as great as her chance of losing. In a sense, the fact that winning is *three* times more likely than losing might be thought to compensate for the fact that the potential loss is *two* times as great. On the basis of this rough analysis, we might predict that Mary will play the game in this form, and, as we shall see, that is just what she will do if she is rational and risk-neutral.

The important point to see from these examples is that Mary's decision depends not just on the payoffs but also on the probabilities. A given gain becomes less attractive the lower its probability, and a given loss becomes more serious the higher its probability. Intuitively, it might seem sensible to describe Mary's decisional process in terms of discounting a gain or loss by the probability it will materialize. This captures the fact that the gamble becomes more desirable as the payoff from a win gets larger *or* the probability of winning becomes higher.

The idea of expected value formalizes these intuitions:

> The expected value of an outcome is the payoff from the outcome (positive for gains;

negative for losses) *multiplied by* the probability that the outcome will materialize. The expected value of an option with more than one possible outcome is the sum of the expected values of each outcome taken separately.

Now let us apply this idea in a systematic way to our two coin flip examples. In both situations, Mary must choose between two options: to play or not to play. The option of not playing has only one outcome—the status quo—and its expected value is zero since nothing is gained or lost by not playing. The option of playing has two possible outcomes: winning and losing. The expected value of playing is different between the two games, however, because the probabilities of winning and losing are different.

With a fair coin, the expected value of winning is $1000 (the payoff from heads, which is a gain and hence positive) *multiplied by* 0.5 (the probability of heads). The result is $500.[6] The expected value of losing is *negative* $2000 (the payoff from tails, which is a loss and hence negative) *multiplied by* 0.5 (the probability of tails). The result is *negative* $1000 (i.e., –$1000).[7] Adding the expected values of these two possible outcomes gives a total expected value for playing equal to *negative* $500 (i.e., a *positive* $500 plus a *negative* $1000). Comparing the expected value of the two options, it is obvious that a risk-neutral Mary is better off not playing. After all, a zero payoff is better than an expected loss of

6. $0.5 \times 1000 = \$500$.

7. $0.5 \times (-2000) = -\$1000$.

$500. (Note that if Mary were a risk-seeker, she might play this game, provided the risk of the game itself gave her enough additional utility.[8])

The following diagram shows this example schematically:

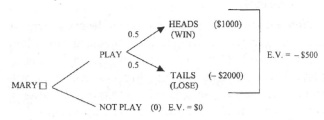

Now consider the example with the weighted coin. Since heads is three times as likely as tails, the probability of heads is 0.75 and the probability of tails is 0.25. Therefore, the expected value of winning is $1000 (the gain from heads) *multiplied by* 0.75 (the probability of heads), which equals $750.[9] The expected value of losing is *negative* $2000 (the loss from tails) *multiplied by* 0.25 (the probability of tails), which equals *negative* $500.[10] The sum of these two expected values, one for each of the two

8. In fact, risk preferences are often illustrated by using expected values. Suppose person A is asked to choose between receiving $100 for sure, or playing a game in which a fair coin is flipped and she gets $200 for heads and $0 for tails. If A is risk-neutral, she won't care which option she takes, since both have the same expected value. If A is a risk-seeker, however, she will strictly prefer to play the game, and if A is risk-averse, she will strictly prefer to receive the $100 for sure.

9. $0.75 \times 1000 = \$750$.

10. $0.25 \times (-2000) = -\$500$.

possible outcomes, gives the expected value of playing the game. This is $750 + (-$500) = $250. Since an expectation of $250 from playing is better than $0 from not playing, Mary will play the weighted coin flip game. Indeed, Mary will still play even if she has to pay a fee in advance (like buying a lottery ticket) as long as the fee is less than $250.

To generalize, rational choice theory holds that a rational, risk-neutral person will choose the option that has the highest expected value. To figure out what the person will choose, proceed in the following steps:

EXPECTED VALUE ANALYSIS

1. Identify all the possible options.
2. Calculate the expected value of each option as follows:
   a. Identify all the possible outcomes corresponding to each option. For example, the option of playing the coin flip game had two possible outcomes—heads or tails. The option of not playing had only one outcome—the status quo.
   b. For each outcome, determine its monetary value and its probability. (Be sure to use a negative sign for losses.)
   c. Multiply monetary value by probability and add the results over all the possible outcomes.
3. Compare the expected values for the different options. A rational person will choose the option with the highest expected value.

The idea of expected value makes a great deal of intuitive sense.[11] Discounting payoffs by their probabilities nicely captures the way a decision under uncertainty varies with risk and result. But people sometimes have trouble with the concept when they first encounter it. To see one source of confusion, consider the fair coin flip. We saw that the expected value of the game equals *negative* $500. But how, one might wonder, can this be the value of the game when a loss of $500 is not a possible outcome? There are only two outcomes: either heads comes up and Mary wins $1000, or tails comes up and she loses $2000. She can never lose $500. So what does it mean to say that this is the value of the game to someone who plays it?

The important thing to realize is that expected value does not measure actual outcomes. It measures the value of the gamble itself. Because a gamble, by definition, has more than one possible outcome, the value of the gamble must somehow take account of all the possible outcomes at once. A useful way to think about this is to imagine playing the game over and over again. Sometimes one wins; sometimes one loses. The expected value is the

11. In fact, a reader who is familiar with statistics might recognize expected value as the mean of the probability distribution of outcome values. In mathematical terms, let p_1, p_2, p_3 ,.... p_n be the probabilities associated with each of the **n** possible outcomes from choosing an option, and let v_1, v_2, v_3,.... v_n be the monetary values of each outcome. Then the expected value of the option is equal to:

$$p_1 \times v_1 + p_2 \times v_2 + p_3 \times v_3 + \ldots p_n \times v_n$$

average of all the expected wins and losses over multiple plays.

To illustrate, consider the fair coin flip. Mary has a 0.5 probability of winning $1000 and a 0.5 probability of losing $2000. This means that if Mary plays the game over and over again, she expects to win half the time. With each win she makes $1000, and with each loss she loses $2000. Adding all the wins and losses over all the multiple plays and dividing by the number of plays yields an *average* loss per game of $500. This figure, *negative* $500 (–$500) because it is a loss, is just the expected value of the game.[12] Because there is no way to know the precise outcome in advance, it makes sense to value the game in terms of the average over all possible outcomes. Put differently and less precisely, any particular play of the game can be treated as an average play and therefore assigned a value equal to the average over multiple plays.[13]

12. For example, if Mary played the game 100 times, she would expect to win 50 times and lose 50 times. Each time Mary won, she would receive $1000, for total winnings of $50,000. Similarly, every time she lost, she would lose $2000, for total losses of $100,000. Her net loss over 100 games, therefore, is $50,000 and the average loss per game is $50,000 ÷ 100 = $500. Affixing a negative sign to this figure to reflect the fact that it constitutes a loss, we have the expected value of playing the game once, which is –$500.

13. Actually, expected value is not expressed in dollar units; it's expressed in utility units. A payoff of 1000 dollars, for example, is assigned a utility value of 1000 and a loss of 2000 dollars is assigned a utility value of –2000. This is a technical point and not important for the reader to understand. I shall refer to expected value in dollar terms because it is easier to

The theory of rational choice is controversial. Many people bristle at the thought that they maximize expected value when they make decisions about love, marriage, and family. Furthermore, empirical research shows that people do not always behave in the way rational choice predicts. We shall examine some of these results in Chapter Three. Despite its limitations, however, rational choice is still a powerful predictive tool. Indeed, there are special reasons to believe that it suits the litigation environment in particular. Litigation is highly strategic and parties aim to maximize their own payoffs without much regard for the welfare of other parties. Furthermore, litigation decisions are usually made by trained lawyers with the experience and expertise to do expected value analysis reasonably well.

1.1.2 Modeling the Decision to Sue

A person deciding whether to sue faces a choice under uncertainty similar to the choice whether to play the coin flip game discussed in the previous section. In fact, a lawsuit is a kind of lottery. It is much more than a lottery, of course, but from the perspective of the parties and their attorneys it has many features of a game of chance. For the plaintiff deciding whether to sue, there are two options—file or not file–and two possible outcomes from filing— win or lose—with a range of possible remedies if she

grasp that way. The technical reader can ignore the dollar sign and translate into utility units (often called "utils").

wins. Neither the plaintiff nor her attorney knows for sure what the precise outcome will be.

The standard economic model of litigation based on the lottery analogy is sometimes called the Landes–Posner–Gould (or "LPG") model after William Landes, Richard Posner, and John Gould, who developed its main features during the early 1970s.[14] The simplest version of the model imagines an injured party deciding whether to sue. If she does not sue, she receives nothing. If she sues, she takes the lawsuit through trial and ends up winning or losing.

In real litigation, the parties proceed through distinct stages, such as dismissal motions, discovery, summary judgment, pretrial conferences, and eventually trial. The simplest model treats all these stages as a single unit. At the beginning, a prospective plaintiff has no idea how all the later stages will actually unfold in her case, nor does she care except insofar as these stages affect her chance of winning and obtaining her desired remedy. Thus, the litigation process is a random event for the plaintiff, similar to the flip of a coin. She (or more precisely her attorney) can estimate the average likelihood of winning and use this estimate to decide whether to sue.

14. *See* William M. Landes, *An Economic Analysis of the Courts*, 14 J. L. & Econ. 61 (1971); Richard A. Posner, *An Economic Approach to Legal Procedure and Judicial Administration*, 2 J. Legal Stud. 399 (1973); John P. Gould, *The Economics of Legal Conflicts*, 2 J. Legal Stud. 279 (1973).

To illustrate, suppose that Paul, the victim of a car accident, is considering whether to sue the driver of the other car, Diane. Schematically, Paul's choice can be diagrammed as follows, where p is the probability of winning:

SIMPLEST MODEL

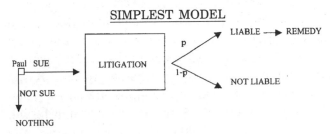

The model can be made more complicated by adding more decision points. For example, we might give the defendant, Diane, a choice whether to answer the complaint. If she does not answer, then she suffers a default judgment. If she answers, then she takes the case through the rest of the litigation process. The following is a schematic:

SLIGHTLY MORE COMPLICATED MODEL

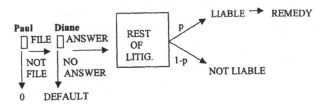

We can complicate the model even further by adding more decision points, such as a choice about whether to conduct discovery, whether to file summary judgment motions, whether to call one's own witnesses or cross-examine adverse witnesses, and so on. Which decision points one includes depends on which aspects of the litigation process one wishes to study. In the following section (Section 1.1.3), we examine one important consequence of treating litigation in stages: the interaction between sunk-cost and information effects. For now, however, we need only focus on the simplest model.

To illustrate the filing decision under the simplest model, suppose that Paul estimates his chance of success at 60% and his expected recovery if he succeeds at $100,000. He also estimates that he will have to spend $20,000 to litigate all the way through trial, win or lose. In schematic form, the example looks like this:

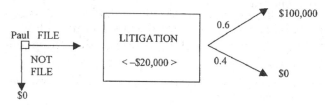

Will Paul sue if he is rational and risk-neutral? The answer is yes. We analyze the problem in exactly the same way as we analyzed Mary's decision whether to play the coin-flip game in the previous section. If Paul files, there are two possible outcomes: he wins with a probability of 0.6, in which case he expects to get $100,000; or he loses with a probability of 0.4, in which case he gets nothing.[15] Whether he wins or loses, Paul has to pay

15. There is a third possible outcome: Paul might get a settlement. We ignore settlement for now because, as we shall

$20,000 to litigate the case through trial. This includes the cost of hiring an attorney,[16] and paying filing fees, compensating expert witnesses, paying for copying, and so on. The $20,000 expense is like an upfront fee for a lottery ticket that must be paid no matter how the lottery comes out.

Let us apply an expected value analysis to Paul's decision whether to sue. Paul's expected value of suing is $40,000:

Probability of winning (0.6) *times* trial award if wins (100,000) *plus* probability of losing (0.4) *times* trial award if loses (0) *minus* litigation costs (20,000)[17]

His expected value of not suing is $0.[18] So Paul will sue if he is rational and risk-neutral.

We can generalize from this example. Let p be the probability that the plaintiff wins and defendant is held liable (so 1–p is the probability that the plaintiff loses). Let w be the monetary value of the

see in Chapter Two, settlement is a function of the expected outcome from going to trial.

16. In the United States, the so-called "American Rule" requires each party to pay her own attorney whether she wins or loses (subject to limited exceptions). For simplicity, we also assume that Paul hires his attorney on a fee-for-services basis rather than on contingency and pays all his other costs too. We shall examine the effect of fee-shifting and contingency fees in Section 2.4, *infra*.

17. $0.6 \times 100,000 + 0.4 \times 0 - 20,000 = \$40,000$

18. The baseline from which gains and losses are measured is the status quo at the time plaintiff makes the filing decision. This is why the expected value of not suing is zero. The plaintiff is left with the loss from his injury, of course, but this loss has already occurred. When the plaintiff chooses not to sue, he gains nothing and loses nothing *relative to his situation at that time*.

expected judgment if the defendant is found liable,[19] and let c be the cost to the plaintiff of litigating the case through trial.[20] In the Paul and Diane example, $p = 0.6$, $w = \$100,000$, and $c = \$20,000$.

With this notation, the expected value of suing is $p \times w - c$,[21] and the expected value of not suing is 0. Therefore, the plaintiff will sue when $p \times w - c > 0$:

FILING CONDITION
(assuming trial)

$$p \times w - c > 0$$

This inequality states the obvious. A plaintiff sues if he expects to gain more from suing ($p \times w$) than he expects to spend on litigating the case (c). When $p \times w - c > 0$, we say that the lawsuit is a **positive expected value** or **PEV** suit. When $p \times w - c < 0$, we say that the lawsuit is a **negative expected value** or **NEV** suit. Rational, risk-neutral parties will file PEV suits but not NEV suits if they expect to litigate the case all the way through trial.

19.   This is easy if the plaintiff seeks only money damages, but it is more complicated to measure the value of the judgment when the plaintiff seeks injunctive or declaratory relief. In that case, w is the amount the judgment is worth to the plaintiff in monetary terms. I shall focus on cases involving money damages for the rest of the book. However, it is possible to include other remedies as well.

20.   This analysis also assumes that the plaintiff hires his attorney on a fee-for-services basis and pays all his own litigation costs, including attorney's fees, whether he wins or loses.

21. $p \times w + (1-p) \times 0 - c = p \times w - c$

Although simple in structure, this basic model captures the essence of the filing decision. Lawyers decide whether to sue by considering the likelihood of success, probable recovery, and cost. To be sure, an experienced litigator is likely to rely on a heavy dose of intuition informed by experience, but the mathematical formulation does a pretty good job of modeling the basic thought process.[22] When a lawyer thinks about whether to take a lawsuit, she discounts the probable recovery by the likelihood of success and compares the result to the expected cost.

A reader might wonder how the numerical estimates are determined. The answer is that lawyers estimate these values by relying on a number of sources, including factual and legal investigations, personal experience, professional publications, and even computerized databases reporting the results of similar cases. The resulting figures are imprecise, of course. The lawyer in effect calculates rough averages over like cases. But averages work well for expected value, since expected value is itself an average over similar cases.[23]

For example, a lawyer deciding whether to take a medical malpractice case will interview the prospec-

22. In complicated high-stakes cases, lawyers sometimes hire economic consultants to do a more rigorous expected value analysis, especially at the settlement stage.

23. More precisely, the lawyer's estimates of the parameters, p, w, and c, are themselves expected values. For example, w, the trial award, is simply an expected value over the entire range of possible awards, or, what is the same thing, an average award for that type of case.

tive client and possibly conduct a preliminary investigation. She will then apply her knowledge of the
law and her own experience, as well as the experience of others handling similar cases, to estimate
likelihood of success (p). If the case is evenly balanced on the merits, she will estimate a probability
of about 0.5; if it is relatively strong, she might
assign a value of 0.6 or 0.7; if it is very strong,
perhaps 0.8 or 0.9. On the other hand, if she thinks
the case is weak, she might put the probability of
winning at 0.3 or 0.4, and if very weak, then perhaps 0.2 or lower. She uses a similar process, relying on experience with past cases, databases, and
the like, to estimate the other parameters—the
expected trial award (w) and litigation costs (c).
Experienced lawyers might not arrive at precisely
the same numerical values, but their estimates are
likely to be approximately the same if they have the
same information. Moreover, if the lawyer takes the
case, she will revise her initial estimates as the
litigation progresses and more information is obtained.

1.1.3   Sunk Costs

Before applying this litigation model to the problem of explaining frivolous suits, it will be useful to
introduce one more economic concept—the idea of
sunk costs. This idea is more relevant to later
stages of the litigation than to the filing stage and
we shall use it in subsequent chapters that focus on
post-filing events such as settlement and discovery.
However, the concept is also important in some

models of frivolous litigation and thus warrants a brief discussion here.[24]

"Sunk costs" are those costs that a party has already incurred and which, once spent, are gone forever and cannot be recovered later. According to economic theory, a rational party ignores sunk costs when making decisions about the future. This means that sunk costs are not included in an expected value calculation. For example, if a party has already spent money to investigate a potential claim and is deciding whether to sue, the cost of the investigation is a sunk cost and is not included in the filing decision.

The rest of this section illustrates the sunk cost idea with a concrete example. This example shows how sunk costs can affect litigating decisions at later stages of a lawsuit. In particular, it shows that a rational party might keep litigating even after learning that his suit is very weak on the merits. One might expect a party to drop under these circumstances, but if the party has sunk most of his litigation costs, it might be worthwhile for him to continue litigating.

The example involves a medical malpractice case brought by a patient, Pablo Prentice, against his surgeon, Doris Delano. Doris knows that she did nothing wrong. However, the patient, Pablo Prentice, was under anesthesia at the time and does not know for sure what happened. Pablo consults an-

24. *See* Section 1.2.3.2 *infra* (briefly discussing Professor Lucian Bebchuk's model).

other physician, who tells him that his condition was probably caused by Doris's negligence.

With the independent opinion in hand, Pablo estimates a 70% chance of establishing liability at trial. Suppose he expects to get a trial award of $300,000 if he succeeds and to spend a total of $80,000 doing so. From Pablo's perspective, the expected value of suing is $130,000 (i.e., $0.7 \times 300,000 - 80,000$). So Pablo files suit.

As Pablo litigates, the lawsuit moves through stages. For example, it goes through a filing stage and then perhaps a motion to dismiss stage, followed by a discovery stage, then a pre-trial hearing stage, and finally a trial stage. In the discovery stage, Pablo might first serve interrogatories and an initial document request, and then based on the response, decide which depositions to take.

Two things happen at each stage. First, Pablo spends a portion of his total litigation costs, which means that he has less he needs to spend in the future to get to trial. Second, Pablo learns something more about the facts and revises his initial probability estimate accordingly. In our case, we assumed that Doris in fact did nothing wrong, so Pablo should revise his estimate downward as he learns more.

The following diagram illustrates these two effects for our Pablo and Doris example. The dollar amount corresponding to each stage is the total expenditure Pablo makes at that stage, and the percentage at the end of each stage is Pablo's revised probability estimate based on information he receives at that stage and earlier stages.

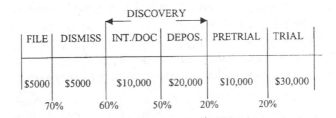

PABLO AND DORIS LITIGATION STAGES

For example, at the filing stage, Pablo spends $5000 to investigate, prepare and file a complaint and his probability estimate is 70% (since he learns nothing more from filing). During the dismissal stage, he spends an additional $5000 and learns adverse information that reduces his probability estimate to 60%. During the interrogatory and document request phase of discovery, he spends another $10,000 and acquires additional information that makes him even more pessimistic, reducing his estimate to 50%. Finally, when Pablo spends $20,000 to depose Doris and the other doctors and nurses in the operating room, he becomes convinced that his case is extremely weak after all and reduces his estimate to 20%.

Note that if Pablo had the same information at the beginning that he has by the time he completes the deposition stage, he would have estimated a 20% probability of success, assigned a *negative* expected value to the suit (i.e., 0.2 × 300,000 − 80,000 =−$20,000), and decided not to file. However—and here is the important point—after the deposition stage, when his estimate has fallen to 20%, he has sunk $40,000 of his litigation costs and has only $40,000 left to spend. Because he ignores sunk costs, this means that his expected value of continuing to trial is *positive*: 0.2 × 300,000 − 40,000 = $20,000. Therefore, Pablo will continue to litigate the case even though he would never have filed it originally had he known then what he learns later on.

In sum, as Pablo invests more, his expected value from continuing to litigate increases. But as he learns more, his expected value decreases. Thus, there are two opposing effects: the sunk-cost effect encourages Pablo to continue, whereas the information effect discourages him from continuing. In our example, the sunk cost effect dominates, and Pablo continues to litigate even after he realizes that he has only a slim chance of success. More generally, a plaintiff's choice depends on which effect dominates and that depends on how sunk costs and information interact. We shall use this idea in later chapters. For now, however, it is enough if the reader understands in general how sunk costs work in the economic model of litigation.

1.2 SOLVING THE FRIVOLOUS LITIGATION PUZZLE

Armed with the concept of expected value and the economic model of litigation, we can now turn to the task of applying these tools to the puzzle of frivolous litigation. The following discussion first develops a working definition of a "frivolous suit" and then examines positive expected value and negative expected value models of frivolous litigation.

1.2.1 Defining a "Frivolous Suit"

To solve the frivolous litigation puzzle, we first need to define a "frivolous suit." This turns out to be harder than it might seem at first glance. Although there is some intuitive appeal to equating frivolous suits with negative expected value (NEV) suits, this definition does not work. A lawsuit with a significant likelihood of success and substantial damages at stake—and thus a poor candidate for classification as frivolous—can still be NEV if litigation costs are unusually high. For example, a suit with a 30% likelihood of success and $500,000 in damages at stake is NEV if litigation costs exceed $150,000.[25]

Nor does it work to equate "frivolousness" with lawsuits that have a small likelihood of success. Some suits are very weak only because they seek to establish a novel legal theory at odds with settled precedent. For example, those who believe that test case litigation is vital to the development of civil rights law would object to classifying civil rights test cases as frivolous just because they have little chance of success.

25. $p \times w = 0.3 \times 500{,}000 = \$150{,}000$. Therefore, $p \times w - c < 0$ and the lawsuit is NEV whenever $c > \$150{,}000$.

As this example illustrates, a lawsuit is labeled "frivolous" not simply to say something about its merits, but to express a normative judgment that suit *should not* be brought. One of the main reasons it is so difficult to define frivolousness is that normative judgments of this kind tend to be controversial, partly because they implicate competing views about the proper function of adjudication. For example, someone who believes that the court system should be used to litigate a case only when the plaintiff's legal theory is supported by a reasonable construction of settled precedent might classify as "frivolous" a civil rights test case that tries to change the law. On the other hand, someone who believes that the court system is an appropriate instrument for social reform would be likely to classify most civil rights test case litigation as meritorious.

Despite this inevitable controversy, there are lawsuits that almost everyone would label "frivolous." The discussion in this chapter and the rest of the book focuses on two types of frivolous suits. In the first type, the so-called "strike suit," the plaintiff sues knowing facts that show the defendant is clearly not liable under any of the legal theories that the plaintiff alleges. This first type is analogous to an intentional tort: the plaintiff intentionally files a meritless suit, knowing for certain (or virtually for certain) that the defendant did not in fact do what the plaintiff alleges he did.

The second type involves a case in which the plaintiff files unaware that the defendant is not liable under the legal theories alleged. The plaintiff is unaware because he fails to conduct a pre-filing investigation under circumstances where the cost of investigating is reasonable. This second type of frivolous suit is analogous to a negligence tort: the plaintiff fails to use reasonable care, in the sense of conducting a reasonable pre-filing investigation, and ends up bringing a meritless suit.

In sum, my definition of "frivolous" has two prongs: (1) a suit is frivolous if the plaintiff files actually knowing facts that establish the complete (or virtually complete) absence of merit on the legal theories alleged; and (2) a suit is also frivolous if the plaintiff files without conducting a reasonable pre-filing investigation under circumstances where the suit would have been frivolous under prong (1) if the plaintiff had investigated before filing. It is important to bear in mind that this definition is not meant to cover everything that might be classified as "frivolous." For example, it does not cover suits that lack merit because of deficiencies in the law rather than the facts.[26] The idea is to identify a set of cases that most people would consider frivolous, in other words, to isolate a core of relatively uncontroversial meaning.

26. My definition also does not include factually and legally meritorious cases that are nevertheless labeled "frivolous" because the plaintiff is thought to be excessively litigious (the McDonald's hot coffee case might be an example of this). For a more extensive discussion of these definitional problems, see Robert G. Bone, *Modeling Frivolous Suits*, 145 U. PA. L. REV. 519, 529–533 (1997).

1.2.2   PEV Explanations

One reason a plaintiff might file a frivolous suit is that the suit has positive expected value notwithstanding its lack of merit. This can occur when trial error is very high. For example, suppose juries in a particular jurisdiction make mistakes 25% of the time. Suppose plaintiff's suit is frivolous and plaintiff knows it. Nevertheless, plaintiff's injuries are serious enough that he expects jurors to award $100,000 in damages if he can convince them that the defendant is liable. This frivolous suit has a positive expected value so long as expected litigation costs are less than $25,000.[27]

Another way a frivolous suit can be positive expected value is if the trial award is unusually high. For example, suppose juries award huge amounts in punitive damages, so a plaintiff expects a trial award of two million dollars if he manages to prevail. Under these circumstances, a frivolous suit has positive expected value even if its chance of success is only 5%, so long as litigation costs are less than $100,000.[28]

There are serious problems with these PEV explanations, however. For a suit to be frivolous according to our definition, the facts and evidence must be clear enough to establish defendant's innocence to a virtual certainty. But if the evidence is that clear, a judge or jury is not likely to make a mistake,

---

27. $p \times w = 0.25 \times 100,000 = \$25,000$. Therefore, $p \times w - c > 0$ and the lawsuit is PEV whenever $c < \$25,000$.

28. $p \times w = 0.05 \times 2,000,000 = \$100,000$. Therefore, $p \times w - c > 0$ and the lawsuit is PEV whenever $c < \$100,000$.

especially if the defendant conducts thorough discovery. Moreover, to obtain punitive damages, the plaintiff must show that the defendant acted with malice, which is a difficult and expensive undertaking, especially in a frivolous case.[29]

1.2.3 NEV Explanations

Because PEV explanations are not terribly convincing, we must look for reasons why a plaintiff might file a frivolous suit that is NEV. Positive economics offers tools that can be used to answer this question. The models are more complex versions of the simple litigation model developed in Section 1.1.2. Exploring these models in a general way teaches something about strategic analysis and introduces the basic concepts of **game theory** and, in particular, the core game-theoretic idea of an **equilibrium**.

1.2.3.1 Cost–Based Models

One reason why plaintiffs might file frivolous NEV suits has to do with litigation cost asymmetry. To illustrate, we shall examine a simple model developed by Professors David Rosenberg and Steven Shavell (which I shall call the "R–S model").[30]

Consider the following hypothetical. Suppose Paul Peters trips on his shoelaces while walking down

29. Also, the difficulty of proving malice will compound litigation costs and thus reduce the expected value of the suit even further.

30. *See* David Rosenberg & Steven Shavell, *A Model in Which Suits Are Brought for their Nuisance Value*, 5 INT'L REV. L. & ECON. 3 (1985).

the aisle of Diane Day's neighborhood grocery store and hits his head. Paul notices a puddle of water nearby and he decides to sue Diane for negligence alleging—falsely, of course—that he slipped on the puddle. He seeks $50,000 in damages for his head injury. Paul has no chance of winning and he knows it. Moreover, it will cost him $1000 to hire an attorney to file a complaint, and it will cost Diane $2500 to answer the complaint if Paul files. The following summarizes these facts:

Paul and Diane Trip and Fall Example

p=0   w=$50,000
Paul's cost of filing = $1000
Diane's cost of answering = $2500

With no chance of succeeding at trial, Paul will sue only if he thinks Diane will settle for at least $1000, an amount sufficient to cover his cost of filing. Paul reasons as follows:

It's worthwhile for me to file only if I can get a settlement for more than my $1000 filing costs. I know that Diane will not ignore the complaint because if she does, then it will result in a default judgment against her for $50,000. So Diane will either answer or settle. Since answering costs $2500, she should be willing to settle for anything less than this amount. I'm confident about my lawyer's negotiating skill, so I think there is a very good chance that we can get her to settle for more than $1000. So I should sue.

In settlement discussions, Diane's lawyer will bargain for a settlement as close to zero as possible and Paul's lawyer will bargain for a settlement as close to $2500 as possible. The actual settlement figure will depend on the relative bargaining power of the parties. If the two lawyers are evenly matched, Paul might expect a settlement of $1250, halfway between the two extremes. A settlement of this magnitude exceeds Paul's $1000 filing cost and makes suit worthwhile.

The R–S model is an application of **game-theoretic** reasoning. It is game-theoretic because it analyzes the strategic interaction between the parties. What Paul will do depends on what he thinks Diane will do, and vice versa. If Paul expects Diane to settle for more than $1000, he will sue; otherwise, he will not. Diane too chooses her strategy by anticipating how Paul will respond. She offers a settlement that she thinks Paul will accept as long as the settlement is less than her $2500 cost of answering. She does this because failure to settle will force her to answer and pay this amount.

This chain of reasoning, however, is incomplete. Why doesn't Diane threaten to file an answer? If Paul expects Diane to answer rather than settle, then he won't sue and Diane will never actually have to pay the $2500 to answer. An analogy to this strategy is a nuclear threat. One side threatens to use nuclear weapons if the other side attacks and the threat alone deters attack and avoids the need to use the weapons. So too, Diane threatens to answer and her threat deters Paul from suing and makes it unnecessary for her to follow through on the threat and file an answer.

The problem with this strategy is that Diane's threat is not credible. Paul has no reason to believe that Diane will ever follow through on it. Paul knows that when Diane actually gets to the stage of deciding whether to answer, she will actually choose to settle because she is better off *at that point* settling than answering. In other words, Paul knows that Diane's threat is a bluff, and Paul will call her on it. Under these circumstances, we say that the threat is **not credible**.[31] The point here is a simple one: when parties are rational, threats must be credible to affect an opponent's behavior.

Roughly speaking, the pair of strategies—Paul files suit, and Diane settles for $1250 (the halfway point)—forms what in game theory is called an **equilibrium**, or more precisely a **Nash equilibrium**.[32] "Nash equilibrium" is named after John Nash, a Nobel Prize winner for his work in game theory.[33] A Nash equilibrium is a set of strategies,

31. As we shall see in Section 1.3.2, *infra*, Diane's threat can become credible if Diane expects to face other suits besides Paul's.

32. This is not exactly correct as a technical matter. "Paul files suit and Diane settles for $1250" is actually a description of what happens in equilibrium rather than a complete specification of equilibrium strategies. A technically proper description of equilibrium strategies would require a more rigorous specification of the game, which is beyond the scope of this book.

33. And the subject of the book, "A Beautiful Mind," and the hit movie of the same name.

one for each party, that are mutual best responses to one another. "Mutual best responses" means that no party can guarantee a higher payoff by playing a different strategy when all the other parties play their equilibrium strategies. Thus, a Nash equilibrium has the property of stability: once the parties find themselves playing equilibrium strategies, they have no reason to deviate. For example, when Paul expects Diane to settle for $1250, Paul will file suit, and when Paul files suit, Diane will settle for $1250 (assuming equal bargaining power). In this sense, the two equilibrium strategies fit together and support one another; they are mutually reinforcing.[34]

34. This footnote is optional, intended for the reader interested in learning more about game theory. It can be skipped without any problem. The interested reader who has difficulty with the footnote might try again after reading Chapter Two on settlement. In game theory, a game like the Paul–Diane game is solved by a process called **backward induction**. *See* Douglas G. Baird, Robert H. Gertner & Randall C. Picker, GAME THEORY AND THE LAW 50–57 (1994) (explaining backward induction). Rather than starting at the beginning of the game and asking what the first player will do, backward induction starts at the end of the game and works backward through each stage, all the way to the beginning. At each stage, the analyst figures out which of the available strategies is optimal for the party who moves at that stage. The intuition behind backward induction is simple. When a party chooses what to do at any stage, he looks ahead and tries to anticipate what is likely to happen at later stages. Backward induction uses this same approach: it looks ahead to what will happen at later stages in order to determine what a player will do at any given stage. For example, in the game of tic-tac-toe, there are a finite number of possible moves, and each player decides where to place his "X" or "O" at each stage by trying to anticipate what will happen in the rest of the game (i.e., what the other player will do and then what he will do in response, and so on) if he chooses one versus another possible position to fill. By starting at the end of the game and working backward (figuring out what each party will do at each stage), backward induction replicates the player's way of thinking about his choice. By using backward induction, we know what will happen at each subsequent stage by the time we reach (through the backward process) any particular stage that we wish to analyze.

In our Paul and Diane example, Paul moves first by choosing between filing and not filing, and if Paul files, then Diane chooses between three possible strategies: doing nothing, filing an answer, or making a settlement offer. If she does nothing, the court enters a default judgment in the amount of $50,000. If she files an answer then Paul gets to move again and chooses between going to trial and dropping his suit. If Diane offers a settlement, Paul gets to choose between accepting, rejecting any possible settlement, or making a counteroffer. If Paul accepts, the parties settle for that amount. If Paul rejects, then Diane must decide whether to do nothing or file an answer. If Paul makes a counteroffer, then the parties enter into a bargaining process, which can be modeled formally as a bargaining game.

Backward induction instructs us to start at the end of the game and work backwards. We know the result if Diane does nothing—she loses $50,000 and Paul receives $50,000. We also know the result if Diane files an answer. Paul will choose to drop the suit and end the game because he has no chance of winning at trial; in game theory, we say that dropping **dominates** going to trial for Paul at this stage, or that dropping is a **dominant strategy** for Paul. Diane being perfectly rational and perfectly informed, can use this same analysis, so she will expect Paul to drop, and therefore concludes that if she files an answer, she will lose $2500 (the cost of filing an answer) and Paul will lose $1000 (the cost of filing a complaint). Therefore, as between filing an answer or doing nothing, filing an answer dominates for Diane, so Diane will file an answer if those are her only two options. But Diane has a third option: she can make a settlement offer. Obviously, she will not offer more than $2500 because that is the most she stands to lose by filing an answer. If she offers some amount less than $2500, the worse that could happen is that

1.2.3.2 Information–Based Models

The R–S model, however, has difficulty predicting a serious frivolous suit problem. For one thing, there is no obvious reason why the cost of answering should in general exceed the cost of filing, given that a defendant can respond with a simple "admit" or "deny."[35] Moreover, even when the R–S model predicts a settlement, the settlements it predicts are relatively small, at most equal to the cost of filing an answer. While nuisance settlements of any size can be frustrating to a defendant, it is not clear that

Paul would reject the offer and then she would file an answer and lose $2500. So Diane cannot do any worse by making a settlement offer than by filing an answer, and she can do better if Paul accepts an offer less than $2500. Therefore, making a settlement offer dominates filing an answer. So Diane will make a settlement offer for some amount less than $2500 if Paul files.

Now that we know what Diane will do if Paul files, we move backward to the first stage where Paul must decide whether to file. Being perfectly informed and perfectly rational, Paul can do the same analysis we just did. So looking ahead he expects Diane to offer a settlement if he files. He knows that he will either accept or make a counteroffer because these are better than rejecting outright (since he can always reject later in the bargaining process). (This model assumes that bargaining is costless for the parties.) So Paul will file as long as he expects to be able to get a settlement (either initially or after bargaining) in excess of his filing costs of $1000. Suppose that the rational outcome of settlement bargaining (i.e., the result of a bargaining game not specified in this footnote) is a settlement in excess of $1000. Then, for Paul, filing dominates not filing, so Paul will file. Putting it all together, we can predict that Paul will file; Diane will make a settlement offer for some amount less than $2500, and the parties will settle for an amount between $1000 and $2500.

35. And since the defendant knows the plaintiff's suit is frivolous, it should be easy for the defendant to deny the allegations.

small settlements create a serious enough social problem to justify the burden of legal intervention.

There is a more complicated cost-based model, developed by Professor Lucian Bebchuk, which *might* have more predictive power.[36] Professor Bebchuk's model is too complex to consider in detail. It relies on the principle that parties ignore costs they have already sunk in the litigation (see Section 1.1.3). The idea is that a plaintiff might be able to make a credible threat to litigate a frivolous suit all the way through trial, assuming positive trial error, if the suit goes through enough stages and the parties sink sufficient costs at each stage.[37] Several

36. *See* Lucian Arye Bebchuk, *A New Theory Concerning the Credibility and Success of Threats to Sue*, 25 J. Legal Stud. 1 (1996).

37. This footnote is for the reader interested in game theory and can be skipped without any problem. The interested reader who has difficulty with this footnote might try again after reading Chapter Two on settlement. The Bebchuk model is solved by the method of backward induction. *See supra* note 34 (describing backward induction). The logic can be roughly illustrated with the following simple example. Suppose that the plaintiff has a 30% chance of success and expects a $100,000 trial award if he succeeds. Suppose that he anticipates at the beginning of the suit spending $40,000 in litigation costs to take the case all the way through trial: $20,000 during the pre-trial stage and $20,000 for the trial itself. Suppose that both parties are fully informed and know all these facts about the lawsuit. This is an NEV suit at the time of filing: i.e., $0.3 \times 100,000 - 40,000 = -\$10,000$. But suppose that for some reason the plaintiff does file and spends $20,000 to litigate all the way to the eve of trial. On the eve of trial, the lawsuit is PEV. The plaintiff still has a 30% chance of winning at trial and expects a $100,000 trial award if he wins. But he has already sunk $20,000 of the $40,000 in litigation costs and need only spend $20,000 more to try the

conditions must be satisfied, however, including that the suit is positive expected value on the eve of trial (or whatever the final stage is), and these conditions are difficult to satisfy in the case of frivolous suits with a very small chance of trial case. Accordingly, the expected value of taking the case from the eve of trial to final judgment is positive: $0.3 \times 100,000 - 20,000 = \$10,000$.

We proceed by backward induction, starting at the end of the game. Since the lawsuit is PEV on the eve of trial, the plaintiff will be able to make a credible threat to litigate through trial and therefore the defendant should be willing to settle. Now back up to the beginning of the penultimate stage, the stage immediately before the eve of trial. (You might think of this stage as summary judgment.) Anticipating a settlement on the eve of trial, the plaintiff should be willing to litigate the penultimate stage as long as his litigation costs for that stage are less than the expected settlement. Given that the plaintiff is willing to litigate the penultimate stage, the defendant should be willing to settle at the beginning of the penultimate stage rather than litigate to the eve of trial (only to settle there).

Now back up one more stage to the stage just before the penultimate stage. (You might think of this stage as the last wave of discovery requests.) The same logic applies at the beginning of this earlier stage. If the cost to the plaintiff of actually litigating this stage is less than the expected settlement at the beginning of the next (i.e., penultimate) stage, the plaintiff can make a credible threat to litigate and the defendant should be willing to settle.

It should be obvious that this reasoning can be repeated stage-by-stage, moving backward until the very beginning of the lawsuit is reached. If total litigation costs are spread over the different stages so that no single stage is too costly relative to the expected settlement at the beginning of the next stage, the parties should be willing to settle at the beginning of each stage and thus at the beginning of the first stage; that is, at the outset of the suit. And it turns out the settlement can be for a substantial amount.

success.[38] As a result, the model is better at predicting NEV litigation—which is in fact Professor Bebchuk's objective–than it is at predicting truly frivolous litigation.[39]

There are, however, economic models that make much stronger predictions and do so in intuitively plausible ways. These models rely on **asymmetric information** rather than asymmetric costs. In all these models, only one party knows that the lawsuit is frivolous, and the fact that there is privately held knowledge encourages strategic behavior that produces large settlements even in frivolous suits.

In general, asymmetric information is an important source of social cost in economic models of litigation. One of the key elements responsible for the high costs is the incentive of some parties to "pool." After briefly describing two asymmetric-information models, the following discussion turns to a closer examination of the idea of pooling.

38. For example, if the frivolous suit has only a very small chance of trial success, it is difficult to see how it could have positive expected value on the eve of trial. Consider the example in the previous footnote. With an expected trial award of $100,000 and $20,000 in expected litigation costs left on the eve of trial, the probability of success would have to exceed 20% to make the lawsuit PEV at that stage. This means that for a truly frivolous plaintiff to be able to make a credible threat to try the case, the probability of trial error in a clearly frivolous suit must exceed 20%.

39. For a discussion of the limitations of this model, *see* Bone, *supra* note 26, at 539 n. 73.

1.2.3.2.1 *Plaintiff Knows Suit Is Frivolous*

The simplest asymmetric-information model, developed by Professor Avery Katz, covers cases in which only the plaintiff knows that the suit is frivolous.[40] The basic intuition underlying the Katz model is easy to understand. If the defendant cannot tell the difference between frivolous and meritorious suits, a frivolous plaintiff can masquerade as meritorious and "trick" the defendant into offering the same settlement he would give to a meritorious plaintiff.

For a concrete example, let us modify the hypothetical involving Paul Peters and the grocery story owner, Diane Day. Assume there is no way for Diane to know that Paul tripped on his shoelaces because there are no witnesses to the accident. To see what is likely to happen under these circumstances, imagine how Paul and Diane might think about their strategic options:[41]

> ***Paul***: I certainly don't want to sue if Diane will simply refuse to settle. After all, it's costly for me to file and I get nothing unless Diane makes a settlement offer. But there is hope because Diane doesn't know whether my suit is frivolous. Of course, if she believes that the vast majority of suits are frivolous, she might not be willing to settle. But if instead she believes that most suits are meritorious, she might be willing

40. *See* Avery Katz, *The Effect of Frivolous Suits on the Settlement of Litigation*, 10 Int'l Rev. L. & Econ. 3 (1990).

41. The dialogue in the text is taken, with some minor changes, from my article on frivolous litigation, *see* Bone, *supra* note 26, at 543–45.

to make a high offer in order to avoid the cost of going to trial against a meritorious plaintiff.

* * * * * * *

Diane: If Paul's suit is frivolous, I should refuse to settle, but if Paul's suit is meritorious, I should make an attractive settlement offer because settlement will avoid the cost of going to trial. Unfortunately, I don't know which type Paul's suit actually is. But as the owner of a grocery store, I have considerable experience with slip-and-fall cases and can estimate how likely it is that a slip-and-fall case in general is frivolous.[42] If that likelihood is small enough, it's better to settle all the time and for an amount that a meritorious plaintiff would accept. Of course, doing so gives a huge windfall to frivolous plaintiffs and encourages frivolous filings. But if there aren't very many frivolous suits, then there won't be many occasions when a settlement is wasted. On balance, I gain much more by paying off a few frivolous plaintiffs and saving trial costs in lots of meritorious suits.

However, this strategy is not good for me when the fraction of frivolous slip-and-fall cases is

42.   This probability estimate is not an estimate of the likelihood that a *filed* slip-and-fall case is frivolous; it is the likelihood that a *potential* slip-and-fall case not yet filed is frivolous. This distinction is important because focusing on potential suits allows the model to predict the effect of Diane's settlement strategy on Paul's filing incentives. This is a technical point, however, and is not strictly necessary to grasping the intuition behind the model.

large. For then settling all frivolous suits will encourage everyone to file and I'll end up settling too many frivolous suits. Under these circumstances, I'm better off refusing to settle at least some of the time in order to deter some frivolous filings.[43] I could refuse to settle all the time and deter all frivolous suits, but then I would have to pay for trial in all the meritorious suits. Perhaps there is a happy medium here—I could refuse to settle some of the time to deter many frivolous plaintiffs, but not so much of the time that I end up paying a lot for trials in meritorious suits.

* * * * * * * * *

As this narrative roughly illustrates, there are two possible equilibria. The first equilibrium obtains when the likelihood of a potential frivolous suit is *small*: defendants like Diane always settle (and for the settlement value of a meritorious suit), and frivolous plaintiffs like Paul always file. As a result, all frivolous suits are filed and all such suits settle for substantial sums.

The second equilibrium obtains when the likelihood of a potential frivolous suit is *large*. It is worthwhile under these circumstances for defendants to refuse to settle sometimes in order to deter

43. The reader might wonder how Diane is able to settle some of the time when she is defending only one lawsuit. The way to think about this is to imagine that Diane is sued repeatedly (or imagine lots of different grocery store owners facing similar suits). In that case, Diane adopts a strategy of settling some of the time and litigating the rest of the time.

frivolous filings. As a result, some (but not all) frivolous plaintiffs sue; some receive substantial settlements, and some (but not all) meritorious suits go to trial. The best way to interpret this second equilibrium is not as a prediction about what will happen in Paul's and Diane's particular suit, but rather as a statistical prediction about what happens over all the cases like theirs. Understood in this way, the equilibrium tells us in general how frequently frivolous slip-and-fall cases are filed and how often defendants settle.[44]

1.2.3.2.2   *Defendant Knows Suit Is Frivolous*

It is also possible for the informational asymmetry to be reversed, so the defendant is the only one who knows suit is frivolous. An example is a medical malpractice case in which the doctor knows exactly what happened during the surgery but the patient does not. An uninformed plaintiff will file a frivolous suit if he thinks there is a sufficient chance his suit might be meritorious. Such a suit is "frivolous" when the plaintiff fails to conduct a reasonable pre-filing investigation.

The model for this situation is too complicated for an extended discussion.[45] But the equilibrium results can be understood intuitively. Two factors affect the parties' strategies. First, the defendant in a meritorious suit has an incentive to try to "trick"

---

44. The mathematical tools of game theory can be used to construct a rigorous model and calculate precise numerical predictions.

45. *See* Bone, *supra* note 26, at 550–63.

uninformed plaintiffs into believing their suits are frivolous and dropping. The defendant does this by refusing to settle—which is the same thing that a defendant in a frivolous suit would do—and gambling that the plaintiff will (wrongly) infer from this refusal that his suit is frivolous. However, this ploy does not always work in equilibrium, and when it fails, meritorious suits go to trial, generating litigation costs.

The second factor has to do with plaintiff's incentives. Plaintiffs do not always conduct reasonable pre-filing investigations because they expect either to settle for an attractive sum or to learn about the merits from the defendant less expensively later in the litigation. When the plaintiff does not investigate before filing, she ends up filing frivolous suits and sometimes takes those suits all the way through discovery in order to verify whether they are frivolous. These incentives increase the number of frivolous filings and add wasted litigation costs.

1.2.3.2.3 *The Idea of Pooling*

The reason why frivolous suits create problems in these two asymmetric-information models has to do with what economists call **pooling**. "Pooling" is the term used to refer to the masquerading or tricking strategy that played a central role in both models—frivolous plaintiffs masquerade as meritorious to trick uninformed defendants, and defendants in meritorious suits masquerade as defendants in frivolous suits to trick uninformed plaintiffs.

The general idea of pooling is fairly easy to grasp. In these models, one of the two parties, the plaintiff or the defendant, comes in two different types (for example, frivolous or meritorious), and the opposing party does not know which type he faces. If the opposing party could tell the two types apart, he would give one type, the "good type," better treatment than the other type, the "bad type." In the Katz model, for example, plaintiffs are either meritorious (good type) or frivolous (bad type) and the defendant cannot tell the difference because he does not know whether the suit is meritorious or frivolous. If the defendant could distinguish the two types, he would treat meritorious plaintiffs (the good type) better than frivolous plaintiffs (the bad type)—by offering a high settlement to the meritorious and refusing to settle with the frivolous. Bad types know this, so they pretend to be good types in order to exploit the opposing party's ignorance and get the better treatment too. This strategy is called "pooling" because one type "pools" with the other in the hope that the opposing party will be unable to tell the difference.[46]

46. In the other model, the "bad types" are defendants in meritorious suits and the "good types" are defendants in frivolous suits. The labels can be a bit confusing in this situation, but the analysis is the same. If the plaintiff could tell which defendant he faced, the plaintiff would insist on a high settlement in meritorious suits and drop in frivolous suits (dropping being better treatment from the perspective of a defendant). Since the plaintiff cannot tell, however, defendants in meritorious suits have an incentive to pool with defendants in frivolous suits in an effort to trick the plaintiff into dropping so they will not have to pay a settlement.

Of course, the opposing party expects bad types to pool. Moreover, he can formulate rational beliefs (based on past experience, word of mouth, and other sources) about what fraction of the population are bad types and what fraction are good types. If he believes there are relatively few bad types (for example, only a small fraction of the plaintiffs are frivolous), he might be better off just letting all the bad types pool rather than trying to deter them, since deterrence itself is costly. In the Katz model, for example, the defendant offers everyone a high settlement when the fraction of frivolous plaintiffs is small because refusing to settle, the deterrence strategy, is costly when the plaintiff turns out to be meritorious.

On the other hand, if there are lots of bad types in the population, the opposing party is not just going to let them all pool. When there are enough bad types, deterring some of them is less costly than giving all of them undeserved windfalls. So the opposing party tries to punish bad types in order to force some separation. Punishment takes the form of withholding the better treatment. In the Katz model, for example, the defendant refuses to settle some of the time. But there is a rub. Because the opposing party does not know which type he faces, any punishment he metes out must be imposed on good types too and that turns out to be costly for him. In the Katz model, when a plaintiff turns out to be meritorious, a refusal to settle forces the case to trial and the defendant must pay the extra litigation cost.

Thus, it is the strategic interaction between informed and uninformed parties that generates social costs when pooling is involved. Bad types succeed sometimes with a pooling strategy and receive the better treatment that should go only to good types. This creates social costs. In addition, the uninformed party sometimes responds to the pooling threat by punishing good types as well as bad, and this also creates costs.

To crystallize understanding of the pooling idea, consider the following simpler example unrelated to litigation. Suppose there are two types of applicants to law school: those who love the law ("Lovers") and those who hate the law ("Haters").[47] Applicants who hate the law nevertheless apply to law school because their parents insist or because they hope to make a lot of money. To keep the example simple, suppose that all applicants are equally qualified based on their applications, except some are Lovers and some are Haters. The Law School must decide whether to accept or reject an applicant without knowing which type he is. If the Law School could differentiate the types, the School would accept only Lovers and reject all Haters, because Lovers contribute to the school and usually have distinguished careers while Haters often end up being miserable and taint the School's reputation.

47. This example is based loosely on the Ph.D. Admissions Game described in Eric Rasmusen, GAMES AND INFORMATION: AN INTRODUCTION TO GAME THEORY 149–52 (2d ed. 1994).

This is a strategic game between the Law School and applicants, and the game has asymmetric information—the applicants know their type but the Law School does not. The Haters will try to pool with the Lovers by lying in their applications and saying that they love the law. The Law School knows this, of course, and will decide whether to accept or reject with the pooling strategy in mind. If the School accepts everyone, then all the Haters will pool and be admitted. But if the School believes there are very few Haters among qualified applicants, then it might do best accepting everyone. This strategy, after all, catches all the Lovers and only a small number of Haters.

However, if the School believes there are lots of Haters interested in applying, it knows that a strategy of accepting all applicants will encourage everyone to apply and result in a class top heavy with law school Haters. What can the Law School do instead? Obviously the Law School cannot reject everyone. But it can reject some applicants randomly (rejection must be random because paper qualifications are identical so there is no verifiable way for the School to determine an applicant's type). Rejection punishes both Lovers and Haters, but if it hurts Haters more than Lovers, then it will discourage more Haters than Lovers from applying. In that case, the applicant pool will have a larger proportion of Lovers and so too will the law school class.

For example, suppose it costs Haters much more than Lovers to apply because Haters have to make up false stories about themselves and are always anxious that their lies might be exposed. Under these circumstances, the extra application cost will make Haters less likely to apply in the face of some likelihood of rejection. Therefore, when the Law School believes that there are lots of Haters who would like to apply, the School's optimal strategy might be to reject some of the qualified applicants randomly in order to discourage pooling.

This example, while hardly rigorous, is meant to anchor the reader's intuitions in what is, hopefully, a more familiar setting than frivolous litigation. Even the rather loose account illustrates the main point—that pooling is often a rational response to asymmetric information and it can set in motion a process of strategic interaction that generates high social costs. In the example, social costs are created when Haters succeed with a pooling strategy (suppose most Haters end up being poor lawyers) and also when the Law School's punishment strategy rejects Lovers (who are denied the opportunity to apply their talents where they would be most productive).

1.2.4 Summary

We have solved the puzzle of frivolous litigation. It turns out that rational plaintiffs do have incentives to file frivolous suits even when they would never take those suits to trial. The reasons are not obvious at first glance, but they can be understood with the help of economic models and game-theoretic reasoning. The formal analysis reveals strategic dynamics that are difficult to discern intuitively but that seem sensible once they are made clear. This is a common pattern—the tools of positive economics function as useful heuristics for uncovering relationships otherwise obscured by the dense network of interactions in complex strategic settings.

1.3 REFINEMENTS: RISK–AVERSION AND REPUTATION

Once the structure of the problem is made clear through a simple model, the tools of positive economics can be used to add more complicated features one by one and analyze their impacts systematically. To illustrate, consider the effects created by adding two additional factors to the frivolous suit models: risk aversion and reputation.

1.3.1 Risk–Aversion

The analysis in Section 1.2 assumed that all parties were risk-neutral. This is a simplifying assumption. In fact, most people are risk-averse.[48] The important difference between a risk-neutral and a risk-averse party is that the risk-averse party incurs higher costs as litigation gets riskier. Roughly speaking, litigation gets riskier as the amount at stake increases and as the probability of success approaches complete randomness (i.e., 50%).

---

48. However, lawyers are likely to be less risk-averse than their clients, which supports the use of contingency fee agreements to reduce risk-bearing costs. This point is discussed more fully in Section 2.4 of Chapter Two.

Risk-aversion makes no difference to the results in the R–S model when a frivolous suit has absolutely no chance of success. For then the trial outcome is certain and there is no trial risk for either party. Moreover, even if a frivolous suit has a small probability of success, the litigation risk will still be tiny as long as the damages are not unusually large.

However, risk-aversion does make a difference for the asymmetric information models. The riskier the litigation, the more serious the frivolous suit problems. When the defendant is risk-averse, he incurs additional risk-bearing costs if he takes a meritorious suit to trial. Therefore, he is more willing to settle and for a larger amount than if he were risk-neutral—all of which gives frivolous plaintiffs even more reason to sue.

1.3.2 Reputation

Reputation plays an important role in many economic models, including models of frivolous litigation. To see how it affects the predictions, consider the R–S model. That model assumes that Diane is concerned only about Paul's suit. But this assumption is unrealistic. As a grocery store owner, Diane can look forward to facing other suits in the future. This means that she can benefit in the long run from building a reputation for fighting frivolous suits. So long as these long-term benefits exceed the short-term cost of litigating rather than settling the first few frivolous suits, Diane's optimal strategy is to file an answer in Paul's suit. By doing so, she establishes a fighting reputation. And if Paul expects this response, he will not sue.

In effect, reputation turns an incredible threat into a credible one. In Section 1.2.3.1, we saw that Diane's threat to file an answer was not credible and would not be believed by Paul. However, the fact that Diane is a repeat litigation player who can reap reputation benefits in future suits turns her threat into a credible one. Once she builds a reputation for fighting frivolous suits, she can credibly threaten to litigate rather than settle, and faced with a credible threat, frivolous plaintiffs will not sue.

Reputation does not always work perfectly. For one thing, it depends on the existence of a mechanism that spreads reputation information widely. But when it does work, it can deter frivolous suits in the R–S model without the need for formal regulation.[49]

1.4   THE LESSONS OF CHAPTER ONE

To recap, we studied a number of different economic tools in the course of searching for solutions

49. Reputation influences the other models in a more complicated way. The reason reputation works so well in the R–S model is that the defendant knows which suits are frivolous and can focus his fighting strategy on frivolous suits exclusively. A reputation strategy is not as effective in the other models because one of the parties is uninformed. For example, when the defendant does not know whether the suit is frivolous, a fighting strategy risks the cost of going to trial in a meritorious suit. The defendant fights sometimes (by refusing to settle) in order to deter the pooling strategy, but fighting all the time is simply too costly.

to the frivolous litigation puzzle. We started with **expected value** and **rational choice**. We used these basic tools to construct a simple **economic model of litigation** and to derive a condition for filing: $\mathbf{pw - c > 0}$. We then examined **PEV** and **NEV** explanations for frivolous litigation and in the process introduced simple **game-theoretic reasoning**, the fundamental idea of an **equilibrium**, and the effect of **asymmetric information** and **pooling**. Finally, we looked at refinements to the models and saw the importance of **risk-aversion** and **reputation effects**.

These concepts and tools are useful for analyzing a wide range of procedure problems. The next chapter applies them to develop a settlement model and explain why PEV suits actually go to trial.

CHAPTER TWO:

THE PUZZLE OF SETTLEMENT, OR WHY DOES ANY LAWSUIT GO TO TRIAL?

CONCEPTS AND TOOLS

- Economic Model of Settlement
  - Settlement Range and Settlement Surplus
- Hard Bargaining
  - Prisoners' Dilemma Game
- Divergent Expectations and Mutual Optimism
- Agency Costs and Fee Arrangements

Almost all cases settle. The best statistics we have indicate that about 70% of the civil cases filed in federal court end in settlement and only six percent actually reach trial (the rest are terminated by pre-trial dismissal, default judgment, summary judgment, and the like).[50] This means that 92% of cases that are not disposed of in some other way settle before trial.[51] Other studies report even lower trial

---

50. For some sources, *see* Judith Resnik, *Trial as Error, Jurisdiction as Injury: Transforming the Meaning of Article III*, 113 HARV. L. REV. 924, 926 nn.10–11 (2000).

51. *See* Russell Korobkin & Chris Guthrie, *Psychology, Economics, and Settlement: A New Look at the Role of the Lawyer*, 76 TEX. L. REV. 77 (1997) (reporting that 90%–95% of cases that are not dismissed before trial end in settlement).

rates, some as low as 2.9%.[52]

In addition, promoting settlement is all the rage in legal circles today. Since the late 1970s, lawyers, judges, and legal academics in increasing numbers have come to view settlement as a desirable, even preferred, outcome of litigation. Indeed, it is quite common today for federal judges to get actively involved in facilitating and encouraging settlements. Even Congress has jumped on the settlement bandwagon by making alternative dispute resolution and settlement national policy goals.[53] As one commentator summed it up when discussing tort litigation: "Settlement is where the action is."[54]

All this enthusiasm for settlement raises two questions. Why do so many lawsuits settle even without active encouragement, and on the flip side, why do any lawsuits go to trial? These two questions might not seem all that difficult at first glance. After all, parties settle because settlement saves litigation costs, and we all know from personal experience that negotiations sometimes fail because of misunderstandings, personality conflicts,

52. *See* Samuel R. Gross & Kent D. Syverud, *Don't Try: Civil Jury Verdicts in a System Geared to Settlement*, 44 UCLA L. Rev. 1, 2 n.2 (1996) (reporting the results of a nationwide study).

53. Congress adopted the Alternative Dispute Resolution Act in 1998 for the express purpose of encouraging alternative dispute resolution and settlement. *See* Pub. L. No. 105–315, 112 Stat. 2993 (1998) (codified at 28 U.S.C. §§ 651–658).

54. Michael J. Saks, *Do We Really Know Anything About the Behavior of the Tort Litigation System–And Why Not?*, 140 U. Pa. L. Rev. 1147, 1212 (1992).

excessive greed, and the like. However, ordinary observations like these, while useful starting points for analysis, cannot explain the complicated features of litigation settlement. This should not be surprising given that settlements are negotiated by lawyers, who have much more negotiating experience and skill than ordinary people.

This then is the puzzle of settlement: Why do cases settle, and more importantly, why do settlement negotiations sometimes fail? It turns out that there are reasons why even perfectly rational and highly skilled lawyers might be unable to reach agreement. These reasons can be explored systematically with the tools of positive economics, and doing so reveals important features of the settlement process and identifies critical parameters that affect settlement success. This deeper level of understanding is a necessary first step in designing an effective regulatory approach to facilitating and encouraging settlement.[55]

2.1 ECONOMIC MODEL OF SETTLEMENT

2.1.1 The Basic Model

Consider the following situation from everyday life. Paul owns a book and Diane wants to buy it.

55. The law-and-economics literature on settlement is voluminous. For a good introduction and a partial bibliography, *see* Bruce L. Hay & Kathryn E. Spier, "Settlement of Litigation" *in* 3 THE NEW PALGRAVE DICTIONARY OF ECONOMICS AND THE LAW 442 (Peter Newman, ed. 1998).

When will Paul and Diane be able to conclude a successful purchase and sale? The answer is when Diane is willing to pay a price that Paul is willing to accept. And for this condition to hold, Diane must value the book more than Paul does. For example, if Diane values the book at $20, she should be willing to pay anything up to $20 to purchase it. If Paul values the book at $10, he should be willing to accept anything more than $10 to sell it. Therefore, a sale is possible at any price between $10 and $20. On the other hand, no sale is possible if Paul values the book at $30, since Diane is only willing to pay up to $20.

The same principles apply to settlement. In a settlement, however, it is not a book that is for sale; it is the plaintiff's right to sue. The plaintiff owns a legal right to sue the defendant, and a settlement involves the plaintiff selling her right to the defendant. By analogy to the sale of a book, settlement is possible only when the defendant (the buyer) values the right more than the plaintiff (the seller).

For the plaintiff, the value of owning the right is just the expected trial value of the claim. For the defendant, the value of owning the right is the expected loss he avoids by preventing the plaintiff from going to trial. Therefore, settlement is possible only when the plaintiff's expected trial value is less than or equal to the defendant's expected trial loss.

To make the analysis more concrete, consider the following hypothetical. Suppose that Pablo Prentice sues his surgeon, Doris Delano, for malpractice, alleging that she was negligent in operating on his knee. Suppose that Doris is considering whether to settle. Assume that Pablo's likelihood of success is 60% and he expects a trial award of $100,000 if he prevails. Moreover, each side expects to spend $20,000 to litigate the case through trial. The following summarizes these facts, where c_P refers to Pablo's litigation costs and c_D to Doris's:

Pablo and Doris Malpractice Example

$$p = 0.6 \quad w = \$100,000$$

$$c_P = c_D = \$20,000$$

Can Pablo and Doris settle their lawsuit, and if so, what is the range of possible settlements? Let's start by determining what Pablo is willing to accept. Pablo will demand a settlement that makes him at least as well off as going to trial. We calculate his expected value of going to trial in the standard way described in Section 1.1.2:

0.6 (probability of winning) × 100,000 (judgment if wins) − 20,000 (litigation cost) = $40,000

Therefore, Pablo should be willing to accept any settlement equal to or greater than $40,000.

As for Doris, she will settle so long as paying the settlement makes her no worse off than going to trial. We calculate Doris's expected trial loss as follows, remembering that Doris must pay not only the trial award but also her litigation costs:

0.6 (probability of losing) × 100,000 (judgment loss if loses) + 20,000 (litigation costs) = $80,000

Therefore, Doris should be willing to settle for any amount equal to or less than $80,000.

With Pablo willing to accept a settlement as low as $40,000 and Doris willing to offer a settlement as high as $80,000, the two should be able to settle. The precise amount will depend on the relative bargaining power of the parties. Pablo will try to get Doris to pay an amount as close to $80,000 as possible, and Doris will try to get Pablo to accept an amount as close to $40,000 as possible. The result will end up somewhere between the two extremes.

Pablo's minimum, i.e., the amount below which he will not go, and Doris's maximum, i.e., the amount above which she will not go, are known as the parties' **reservation prices** (or sometimes "disagreement points"). The range of feasible settlements, which is the range between the parties' reservation prices, is called the **settlement range.** The size of the settlement range is called the **settlement surplus**. In the Pablo–Doris example, Pablo's reservation price is $40,000 and Doris's reservation price is $80,000; the settlement range is the interval from $40,000 to $80,000, and the settlement surplus equals $40,000. In general, settlement is feasible only when a settlement range exists—or equivalently, only when the settlement surplus is greater than or equal to zero.[56]

The best way to understand the settlement surplus is to think of it as the total amount of extra value parties create when they settle rather than go to trial. In our example, settlement saves the parties their litigation costs, so in effect the parties create this amount in value. As we shall see in Section 2.2.2 below, the size of the surplus also depends on the difference, if any, between the parties' respective beliefs about likely success. In this section, however, we assume that the parties share identical beliefs, so the surplus is limited to the litigation costs saved by settling. Since each side saves $20,000 in litigation costs, the total surplus is $20,000 + $20,000 = $40,000.

We can generalize this point. Since litigation costs are always positive, there must always be a positive settlement surplus when parties have identical beliefs, and that surplus is equal to the total litigation costs saved by settling. This implies that the model's result for Pablo and Doris holds generally: parties should always be able to settle a case when they agree on all salient variables, including likelihood of success and trial award.

Each point on the settlement range represents a different division of the surplus. For example, a

56. When the surplus is equal to zero, there is only one point in the settlement range and the parties, though willing to settle, are also willing to go to trial. They are "indifferent" between settlement and trial because each option yields the same expected value.

settlement of $80,000 represents a division in which Pablo gets all of the surplus and Doris gets none of it. When Pablo gets the entire surplus, he ends up with his reservation price of $40,000 *plus* the surplus of $40,000—for a total of $80,000. At the other extreme, a settlement of $40,000 represents a division in which Doris gets all of the surplus and Pablo gets none of it. In that case, Doris in effect pays her reservation price of $80,000 but receives the $40,000 surplus—for a net settlement of $40,000. Of course, one would not usually expect a settlement to lie at the extremes—for that to happen, one of the parties would have to capitulate during the negotiations. For example, if both parties have equal bargaining power, one might expect them to split the surplus equally, in which case each would get $20,000 of the surplus and settle for $60,000.

The following diagram illustrates these points graphically:

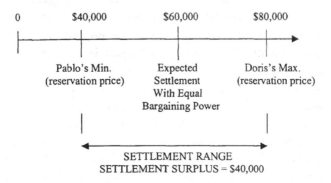

| 0 | $40,000 | $60,000 | $80,000 |
| | Pablo's Min. (reservation price) | Expected Settlement With Equal Bargaining Power | Doris's Max. (reservation price) |

SETTLEMENT RANGE
SETTLEMENT SURPLUS = $40,000

2.1.2 Negotiating Costs

The basic model outlined in the previous section assumed that negotiating a settlement cost nothing. Obviously, this is unrealistic. Parties spend time and money working out settlement terms and drafting documents. These costs narrow the settlement range and reduce the settlement surplus. The reason is easy to see. Without negotiating costs, the settlement surplus just equals the total litigation costs that the parties save by settling. The cost of negotiating the settlement consumes some of these savings and therefore reduces the size of the surplus.

At the same time, it is extremely unlikely for negotiating costs to consume the entire surplus. For that to happen, bargaining would have to be more expensive than litigating a case through trial. Given the high costs of trial, this is virtually impossible.

To illustrate, assume that it would cost Pablo and Diane $5000 each to negotiate a settlement. For settlement to make Pablo at least as well off as trial considering negotiating costs, the settlement must give him his $40,000 expected gain from trial *plus* $5000 additional to cover the cost of negotiating the settlement—for a total of at least $45,000. By the same token, for settlement to make Doris no worse off than trial, the settlement can be at most her $80,000 expected loss from trial less the $5000 she has to pay to negotiate—for a total of $75,000. When she adds in her $5000 negotiation costs, a

$75,000 settlement leaves her out of pocket $80,000, which is just her expected trial loss.

Therefore, the settlement range is narrower with negotiating costs: $45,000 to $75,000, rather than the original $40,000 to $80,000. And the surplus is $10,000 less: $30,000 rather than $40,000. However, for negotiating costs to scuttle settlement entirely, they must consume the entire surplus of $40,000. Bargaining is not likely to be this expensive.

This background frames the next question: If there is always a settlement range even with costly negotiation, then why doesn't every case settle? To answer this question, we need to examine the bargaining process more closely.

2.2 SOLVING THE SETTLEMENT PUZZLE

Everyday experience teaches us that it is not always easy to negotiate a contract. People can be greedy; personalities sometimes conflict, and parties can make errors in valuing assets. For these and other reasons, the fact that a contract is feasible does not necessarily guarantee that the parties will succeed in concluding a deal. This is also true for settlement, but the reasons why require more careful analysis. Most lawyers have experience and skill in negotiating, so it is useful to see if there are reasons why perfectly rational and highly skilled negotiators might fail to reach agreement. It turns out that there are, and because of this, the existence of a settlement range, while necessary to a successful settlement, is by no means sufficient.

Economists use a range of tools to analyze bargaining obstacles in the settlement context. This section describes the tools used to analyze two of the most common obstacles—hard bargaining strategies and mutual optimism—and shows how the settlement model can be modified to include them.

2.2.1 Hard Bargaining

During settlement negotiations, parties try to capture as much of the settlement surplus as possible, and this can lead to hard bargaining strategies even when all the parties are perfectly rational.[57] For example, a plaintiff might start off with an unreasonably high settlement demand and make very few concessions along the way, all in the hope that the defendant will capitulate. But rather than capitulate, the defendant might just adopt a hard bargaining strategy as well.

57. Settlement is an example of what economists call a bilateral monopoly. In perfectly competitive markets, there are lots of identical products and so many buyers and sellers that no single individual can affect the market price by his own actions. In a bilateral monopoly, on the other hand, there is only one seller and one buyer, and as a result, each party has the ability to influence the price by his choice of strategy. Settlement is a bilateral monopoly because there is no competitive market for legal claims. The plaintiff's right to sue is a unique thing, and legal rules such as the rules against champerty and maintenance effectively single out the defendant as the only potential buyer. Therefore, each party can influence the settlement amount (i.e., the price for the plaintiff's legal right) by his choice of bargaining strategy.

Indeed, if the defendant's lawyer expects the plaintiff's lawyer to bargain hard, the defendant's lawyer is likely to bargain hard in response—and vice versa—*even when* the parties would otherwise be inclined to use a more conciliatory approach. The reason is simple: a party who expects his opponent to use hard bargaining fears that he will end up with very little if he signals a willingness to accommodate. Thus, rather than be taken for a "sucker," he responds to hard bargaining by bargaining hard himself.

The problem is that mutual use of hard bargaining strategies makes it extremely difficult for parties to compromise. For one thing, hard bargaining produces a large gap between offer and demand. Both sides dig in and refuse to budge from extreme original positions. Moreover, hard bargaining tends to destroy the good will and mutual trust that are often necessary to a successful outcome.

Economists use game theory to model these intuitions formally, and the model can be used to predict the nature and severity of the adverse effects. The following is a relatively simple example. It illustrates the techniques and also introduces a game theory chestnut that is widely used in law and economics—the **Prisoners' Dilemma Game**.

Recall our earlier hypothetical in which Doris operated on Pablo's knee and Pablo sued Doris for malpractice. Pablo has a 60% likelihood of success and an expected trial award of $100,000, and his and Doris's litigation costs are both $20,000. For simplicity, assume negotiating costs are zero.

Suppose that Pablo and Doris are about to initiate settlement discussions and must choose between a soft and a hard bargaining strategy. A soft strategy involves a willingness to compromise and reach agreement on reasonable terms. A hard strategy is much more aggressive. A party who uses a hard strategy digs in and makes few concessions. Limiting the parties to just two bargaining strategies is unrealistic, of course, but it simplifies the analysis and conveys the essential intuition that underlies more complicated models.

Suppose that if both Pablo and Doris use soft strategies, their mutual desire to compromise always leads to a settlement and their equality of bargaining power results in a settlement that splits the surplus equally. If one party uses a soft strategy and the other a hard strategy, they always reach agreement, but the party using the soft strategy eventually capitulates and agrees to let the other party keep 75% of the surplus. If both parties use hard bargaining strategies, they often end up deadlocked. In particular, suppose they succeed in reaching agreement only 60% of the time, and when they do manage to agree, their equality of bargaining power results in a settlement that splits the surplus equally. The following table summarizes these assumptions (the numbers in parentheses represent the division of the surplus, with the first fraction corresponding to the party who uses the first identified strategy):

Pablo and Doris Bargaining Game

$p=0.6$ $w=100,000$ $c_P = c_D = \$20,000$

soft, soft ◊ always settle; equal split (.5, .5)
hard, soft ◊ always settle (.75, .25)
soft, hard ◊ always settle (.25, .75)
hard, hard ◊ 60% settlement rate (.5, .5)

What bargaining strategies will Pablo and Doris adopt and how often will they reach agreement? If they both use soft strategies, they split the surplus equally and settle for $60,000. If Pablo uses a hard strategy and Doris a soft strategy, Pablo captures 75% of the surplus, and the parties settle for $70,000. If Doris uses a hard strategy and Pablo a soft strategy, Doris captures 75% of the surplus, and the parties settle for $50,000. Finally, if both parties use hard strategies, they settle 60% of the time and when they settle, they split the surplus equally for a settlement of $60,000. The rest of the time settlement fails, and the parties go to trial. Combining the expectations from settlement and trial, we can calculate the parties' total expected gain and loss when they both use hard bargaining strategies. For Pablo, the expected gain is:

0.6 (probability of successful settlement) × $60,000 (amount of settlement if successful) + 0.4 (probability of a trial) × $40,000 (expected value of trial) = $52,000

Using the same approach, we have for Doris, an expected loss equal to:

0.6 × $60,000 + 0.4 × $80,000 = $68,000.

We can summarize these results in what game theorists call a **payoff matrix**. Each cell of a payoff matrix represents a particular combination of strategies, one for each party. In this case, there are four possible combinations: (hard, hard), (hard, soft), (soft, hard), and (soft, soft). Pablo's expected payoff (a gain) is placed in the top left corner of the cell and Doris's expected payoff (a loss and thus a negative number) is placed in the bottom right corner:

DORIS

		Hard	Soft
PABLO	**Hard**	$52,000 − $68,000	$70,000 − $70,000
	Soft	$50,000, − $50,000	$60,000 − $60,000

It is easy to predict what Pablo and Doris will do by inspecting this payoff matrix. They both will choose hard strategies. Pablo is better off using a hard strategy no matter what Doris does, and the same is true for Doris. For example, if Doris uses a hard strategy, Pablo expects $52,000 with a hard strategy compared to only $50,000 with a soft strategy. If Doris uses a soft strategy, Pablo expects $70,000 with a hard strategy compared to only $60,000 with a soft strategy. The same reasoning applies to Doris.

When both parties choose hard strategies in equilibrium (the upper left cell of the matrix), settlement negotiations, by assumption, fail 40% of the time. A game of this sort is known as a **Prisoners' Dilemma Game**.[58] Notice that Pablo and Doris each would be better off if they *both* used soft strategies (the lower right cell).[59] They will not do so, however, because neither can trust the other to stick to a soft strategy when the time comes. Hard strategies are simply too tempting.

To see this point, imagine that Pablo insists he will use a soft strategy hoping that this will get Doris to use a soft strategy as well. If Doris believes Pablo, she will not be able to resist using a hard strategy, because when Pablo uses a soft strategy, she suffers a loss of only $50,000 with a hard strategy compared to $60,000 with a soft strategy. Pablo knows that Doris will give in to this temptation, however, so he expects to be taken for a sucker

58. The name comes from the traditional hypothetical used to illustrate the game, which involves two prisoners being interrogated separately and faced with a choice between confessing or remaining silent. Technically, a Prisoners' Dilemma Game has two critical features: the equilibrium strategies are strictly dominant (i.e., each party chooses the equilibrium strategy no matter what the other party does), and there is another set of strategies that makes *both* parties better off than the equilibrium.

59. If both parties use soft strategies, Pablo expects to gain $8000 more ($60,000 versus $52,000) and Doris expects to lose $8000 less ($52,000 loss versus $60,000 loss).

if he actually uses a soft strategy. Therefore, he will adopt a hard strategy from the outset. The same is true the other way around.

In effect, both parties are driven to use hard strategies by the nature of their strategic interaction and the fact that they cannot commit irrevocably to soft strategies from the outset. This example illustrates the central point: hard bargaining can block an otherwise feasible settlement even when the parties behave perfectly rationally and understand that they are each better off settling than going to trial.[60]

2.2.2 Divergent Expectations and Mutual Optimism

Settlement sometimes fails even when both parties use soft bargaining strategies. Recall that the basic model outlined in Section 2.1.1 assumed that the parties shared identical beliefs about likely success at trial. When those beliefs differ, however, it is not always possible to settle the case. Law-and-economics scholars use the term **divergent expectations** to refer to this situation. Divergent expectations create the most serious problems for settlement when both sides expect to win at trial, a condition known as **mutual optimism**. Since perfectly rational parties with the same information

60. Using a more complicated model with so-called "mixed strategies," we can arrive at a similar prediction employing the more parsimonious assumption that settlement *always* fails when both parties use hard bargaining strategies. With that assumption, the game is no longer a Prisoners' Dilemma and it is much more complicated to analyze.

should arrive at identical estimates of likelihood of success, mutual optimism can exist only when parties have different information or when they are not perfectly rational. In the following discussion, we explore the first possibility: that perfectly rational parties are differently informed.

It is not uncommon for one party to have private information not available to the other. Returning to our Pablo–Doris medical malpractice hypothetical, Doris is likely to have relevant information not available to Pablo if Pablo was under anesthesia at the time of the surgery. Suppose Doris knows that she did nothing wrong, but Pablo believes, on the basis of advice from another doctor, that his symptoms are the result of surgeon error. Under these circumstances, Doris will be optimistic about her success at trial—and so too will Pablo. Of course, Doris will tell Pablo that she did nothing wrong, but Pablo will discount her statements as self-serving. After discovery, Pablo, being rational, will revise his likelihood of success downward, but prior to discovery, it is perfectly rational for him to be optimistic.

When parties are mutually optimistic about success, settlement is difficult achieve. The reason is easy to see. If the plaintiff believes that he has a very good chance of prevailing, he will demand a high settlement. But if the defendant believes that she also has a very good chance of prevailing, she will offer only a low settlement. Under these circumstances, it is extremely unlikely that demand

and offer will ever meet.[61]

Another way to see this point is to consider the effect of divergent expectations on the settlement surplus. In Section 2.1.1, above, we defined the settlement surplus in terms of the total litigation costs saved by settling. However, this definition applies only when the parties share identical beliefs. When beliefs differ, the surplus depends not only on the savings in litigation costs, but also on the difference in belief.

To see this point, it is helpful to consider a simpler example from everyday life. Suppose that Paul owns IBM stock and believes it is overvalued, and Diane wants to acquire IBM stock because she thinks it is undervalued (so the price is likely to go up in the future). Paul and Diane have different beliefs about the true value of IBM stock, and this difference creates an opportunity for trade and a trading surplus.[62]

In a similar way, divergent expectations about trial success in the litigation setting create different beliefs about the value of the legal claim, and this difference affects the size of the surplus from settling. Moreover, this effect can be positive or negative; it can add to the settlement surplus or subtract from it. For example, suppose that both the

61. The opposite result obtains under conditions of mutual pessimism. If the plaintiff is pessimistic about his chance of prevailing at trial, then he should be willing to settle for very little. And if the defendant is also pessimistic, then she should be willing to pay a lot.

62. I am indebted to Chris Sanchirico for suggesting that I use this example to illustrate the effect of beliefs on the settlement surplus.

defendant and the plaintiff are pessimistic about
their own success. The defendant will place a relatively high value on owning the claim because he
believes he is likely to lose at trial, and the plaintiff
will place a relatively low value on owning the claim
because she believes she is likely to lose. Thus, the
situation is similar to the IBM stock example: the
defendant values owning the claim more highly
than the plaintiff does, and the difference between
the two represents an additional gain from trade
that increases the settlement surplus. It works the
other way as well. If both parties are optimistic, the
resulting difference in valuations reduces the surplus.

In general, therefore, the settlement surplus includes two components: litigation costs and differing valuations due to divergent expectations about
trial success. When they settle, the parties share
their saved litigation costs from avoiding a trial of
the case. And they also share the trading surplus
(positive or negative) that results from divergent
expectations about likely success and thus differing
beliefs about the value of the claim.

For a numerical illustration, suppose that both
Pablo and Doris are optimistic: Pablo estimates his
likelihood of success at 70%, and Doris estimates
her likelihood of success at 80% (i.e., estimates
Pablo's chances at 20%). The following summarizes
the hypothetical, where p_π is plaintiff's estimate of
likely success, and p_Δ is defendant's estimate of
plaintiff's likely success:

Pablo and Doris Mutual Optimism Example

$p_\pi = 0.7$ $p_\Delta = 0.2$ $w = \$100,000$

$c_P = c_D = \$20,000$

We calculate the settlement range and surplus in the same way we did in Section 2.1.1. Pablo's expected gain from going to trial is $0.7 \times 100,000 - 20,000 = \$50,000$. Therefore, he will demand at least \$50,000 to settle. Doris's expected trial loss is $0.2 \times 100,000 + 20,000 = \$40,000$. So she will never pay more than \$40,000 to settle. Therefore, settlement is not possible no matter what bargaining strategies the parties adopt: Pablo will insist on at least \$50,000, but Doris will pay no more than \$40,000.[63]

63. One can generalize this result with some simple algebra. The reader whose algebra is a bit rusty can skip this footnote and all other footnotes with algebraic expressions without any problem. Plaintiff's reservation price is his expected gain from trial, which is $p_\pi w - c_P$. Defendant's reservation price is her expected loss from trial, which is $p_\Delta w + c_D$. Therefore, settlement is feasible if and only if $p_\Delta w + c_D \geq p_\pi w - c_P$. Rearranging this inequality, we get the settlement feasibility condition:

$$p_\pi - p_\Delta \leq (c_P + c_D)/w.$$

When the parties agree on likelihood of success, $p_\pi = p_\Delta$ and the settlement feasibility condition reduces to $(c_P + c_D)/w = 0$, which is always true. Therefore, a feasible settlement always exists, a result we derived intuitively in Section 2.1.1. Moreover, the settlement feasibility condition is unlikely to hold when the parties are mutually optimistic because then p_π is large and p_Δ is small, so $p_\pi - p_\Delta$ is very large—and thus likely to be greater than

The settlement surplus is negative in this hypothetical (actually it is –$10,000). We can decompose this surplus into its litigation-cost and divergent-expectations components. The parties save $40,000 in litigation costs by settling. This means that the settlement surplus would be $40,000 if the parties shared identical beliefs about likely success. However, the parties are mutually optimistic, and this has a negative effect on the settlement surplus. In particular, Pablo values the legal claim (ignoring litigation costs) at $70,000 (i.e., $0.7 \times 100,000$) and Doris values it at $20,000 (i.e., $0.2 \times 100,000$). The difference of $50,000 reduces the $40,000 settlement surplus associated with litigation cost savings. Therefore, the net surplus is negative: $40,000 − $50,000 =–$10,000.

As the lawsuit progresses and Pablo learns through discovery that Doris is telling the truth about the surgery, Pablo's estimate will drop from a

$(c_P + c_D)/w$. By contrast, the condition should always hold when parties are mutually pessimistic. For then p_π is small and p_Δ is large, so the difference $p_\pi - p_\Delta$ is less than zero and thus less than $(c_P + c_D)/w$.

We can calculate an expression for the settlement surplus in the following way. The surplus is just the difference between the defendant's and the plaintiff's reservation prices: $p_\Delta w + c_D − (p_\pi w − c_P)$. Rearranging, this becomes:

$$\text{Settlement Surplus} = (c_P + c_D) + (p_\Delta − p_\pi)w$$

This expression shows the two components of the surplus clearly. The term $(c_P + c_D)$ is the contribution from litigation cost savings, and the term $(p_\Delta - p_\pi)w$ is the contribution from differing valuations due to divergent expectations. When $p_\Delta < p_\pi$, as in our Pablo and Doris example, this second term is negative and reduces the surplus.

high of 0.7 to something much closer to 0.2 (the informed estimate). At some point along the way, the parties estimates are likely to converge sufficiently to create a settlement range and a positive settlement surplus (although, as the next section shows, this depends on how fast the parties sink their litigation costs). But until that point is reached, the parties will not be able to settle, even though settlement is in their mutual best interests from an objective point of view.

To sum up, hard bargaining and divergent expectations due to mutual optimism are two reasons that settlement bargaining can fail even when settlement is in fact superior to trial for both sides. Economists model hard bargaining by using game theory to analyze the strategic obstacles, and they model divergent expectations by modifying the basic settlement model to permit different estimates of likelihood of success.[64]

2.2.3 The Effect of Sunk Costs

As we saw in the previous section, the expectations of the parties are likely to come closer together as the litigation progresses and each side learns more about the case through discovery and independent investigation. Thus, a case that cannot be settled early because of mutual optimism might be able to settle later after expectations converge sufficiently.

64. Expectations can diverge for reasons other than different estimates of success. For example, the parties might disagree about the expected trial award or about litigation costs.

However, we saw in Section 1.1.3 of Chapter One that the expected value of trial increases as the litigation progresses and the plaintiff sinks more of his litigation costs. This sunk-cost effect also has an impact on settlement. As the parties sink more of their costs, going to trial becomes less expensive and therefore more attractive. Accordingly, each side demands more favorable terms to settle and the settlement range gets smaller. Thus, while convergent expectations make settlement more likely, sunk costs make it less likely. Whether and when settlement becomes feasible depends on how these two countervailing effects interact.

To illustrate, consider the Pablo and Doris example from the previous section. At the beginning of the suit, Pablo estimates his chance of success at 70% and Doris, who knows what happened, estimates Pablo's chance at 20%. The parties are mutually optimistic and unable to settle. Now suppose that each side's expected litigation costs are spread over three stages: pre-discovery ($3000 each), discovery ($8000 each), and trial ($9000 each). Also, suppose that Pablo revises his estimate downward as the litigation progresses, from 70% to 60% to 40%. The following diagram depicts these assumptions:

PABLO AND DORIS EXAMPLE IN THREE STAGES

PRE-DISCOVERY	DISCOVERY	TRIAL
$3,000	$8,000	$9,000
70% (Pablo) 20% (Doris)	60% (Pablo) 20% (Doris)	40% (Pablo) 20% (Doris)

First, note that if Pablo's estimate of trial success was 40% at the beginning of the suit, the same as it is at the completion of discovery, the parties would be able to settle. Pablo's minimum demand would be $20,000 (i.e., 0.4 × 100,000 − 20,000). And Doris's maximum offer would be $40,000. Therefore, the settlement range would extend from $20,000 to $40,000, and the settlement surplus would equal $20,000.

However, the fact that Pablo's estimate falls to 40% only late in the litigation, after each side has sunk $11,000, makes a big difference to the feasibility of settlement. With only $9000 left to spend on the litigation, Pablo's minimum settlement demand at the close of discovery is $31,000.[65] Moreover, Doris also looks forward to spending only $9000 on the rest of the suit, so her maximum offer falls to $29,000.[66] As a result, there still is no settlement range.[67]

65. 0.4 × 100,000 − 9,000 = $31,000.

66. 0.2 × 100,000 + 9000 = $29,000.

67. The same is true at the end of the pre-discovery stage. Pablo's estimate drops to 60%, but with only $17,000 left to

The general point is a simple but important one. We can rely on procedures like discovery to try to correct divergent expectations and encourage settlement, but if we do so, we must remember that parties sink litigation costs by using those procedures and this can make settlement more difficult. Roughly speaking, the reason Pablo and Doris cannot settle even though Pablo's estimate of trial success drops from 70% to 40% and converges on Doris's is that the parties sink litigation costs too quickly compared to the rate at which Pablo's estimate falls. The general point is simply an application to settlement of the observation made in Section 1.1.3: that sunk-cost and information effects pull against one another and create countervailing litigation incentives. This is a point to which we shall return later in the book.

2.3 PREDICTING THE SETTLEMENT AMOUNT

The basic settlement model predicts the range of possible settlements, but it does not predict the precise settlement amount. The settlement amount depends on the relative bargaining power of the parties, as well as other factors. Relative bargaining power is correlated with the fraction of the surplus the plaintiff is able to capture. The larger that spend on the litigation, his minimum demand is $43,000 (i.e., 0.6 × 100,000 − 17,000), and Doris's maximum is $37,000 (i.e., 0.2 × 100,000 + 17,000). So once again, there is no settlement range.

fraction, the more bargaining power the plaintiff has relative to the defendant.

This relationship gives us a way to model relative bargaining power. Let α be the fraction of the surplus that the plaintiff expects to capture. The closer α is to 1, the stronger the plaintiff's relative bargaining power, and the closer α is to 0, the stronger the defendant's relative bargaining power. When $\alpha = 0.5$, the parties have identical bargaining power and split the surplus equally. With α defined in this way, the predicted settlement equals the plaintiff's reservation price *plus* α *times* the surplus. For the Pablo–Doris example (assuming that both parties estimate Pablo's likelihood of success at 60%), we have:

SETTLEMENT = \$40,000 (Pablo's reservation price) + $\alpha \times$ \$40,000 (the surplus)

However, this method is not terribly useful. It simply substitutes one uncertainty (finding α) for another (predicting the settlement amount), and the substitution does not make the problem any easier.

Economists use a number of more sophisticated techniques to predict bargaining outcomes. One approach constructs a game-theoretic model of the bargaining process and then solves the model for an equilibrium outcome.[68] A second approach, called the "axiomatic method," posits certain conditions

68. For example, the simple alternating offer game structures the bargaining process as a series of alternating offers with each party able to accept or reject the other party's offer at each stage and with the asset diminishing in value over time. The diminish-

that a bargaining outcome should satisfy and then derives an outcome that satisfies those conditions.[69] These methods are mathematically complex and beyond the scope of this book.

The fact is that law-and-economics scholars have paid much more attention to the frequency of settlement than to its quality. This is understandable because predicting bargaining outcomes is an extremely difficult task, one that economists have yet to tackle in a convincing way. At the same time, this gap is unfortunate, since from a normative perspective settlement quality is at least as important as settlement quantity. There is, after all, little social benefit in encouraging bad settlements.

2.4 A REFINEMENT: AGENCY COSTS AND FEE ARRANGEMENTS

The analysis so far has assumed that the parties are the ones who control the settlement decision. In the real world, however, it is the lawyers who negotiate settlement terms. To be sure, a lawyer is required by the rules of professional ethics to get his client's approval before agreeing to a settlement. But the lawyer is in a good position to persuade his client to accept a settlement, especially when the

ing value of the asset puts pressure on the parties to reach agreement.

69. The most famous application of this approach is the "Nash Bargaining Solution," named after the same John Nash who is associated with the "Nash Equilibrium."

client lacks the information and expertise necessary to make an independent evaluation. This gives the lawyer substantial power over the settlement decision and creates a risk that lawyers will serve their own interests at the expense of their clients.

This risk is an example of a more general problem known in economics as the **agency problem**. The agency problem arises when an agent's self-interest diverges from the interest of his principal. For example, an employee on salary might wish to spend more time on the golf course than in the office, and a contractor hired for a fixed project fee might use cheap materials and cut corners in order to minimize costs and maximize profit. In these and many other situations, the agent has an incentive to shirk or otherwise act in a way that maximizes his own private benefit at the expense of his principal.

There are strategies that a principal can use to reduce agency problems. For example, he can monitor the agent or build incentives into the principal-agent contract. But each such strategy is imperfect, and all are costly to implement. Economists use the term **agency costs** to refer to all the costs of agent disloyalty, including the cost of controlling deviance and the cost of bad results that cannot be prevented.

Agency problems arise in the principal-agent relationship that exists between a lawyer and a client. To be sure, many—perhaps most—lawyers represent their clients faithfully and try to behave ethically, or at least respond to the threat of bar discipline and malpractice liability. Still, it would be naive to assume that all lawyers are loyal agents all the time. The fact is that the lawyer-client relationship has special features that invite agency problems. The market for lawyers is imperfect and ordinary clients have difficulty accessing reliable information about attorney reputation or negotiating contract terms to discourage attorney dereliction.

Settlement is a particularly fertile environment for lawyer opportunism. Settlements are usually negotiated in private and out of sight of clients and the public. Moreover, lawyers have considerable power to sell settlement offers to skeptical clients. By stressing the weakness of a case or the cost of going to trial, the lawyer can make a wide range of offers seem attractive.

With broad power over settlement, lawyers can serve their own interests, and those interests often differ from client interests at the settlement stage. The most common source of conflict has to do with fees.[70] Many plaintiffs, especially those suing in tort to recover for personal injury or property damage, retain lawyers on a **contingency fee** basis. The client agrees to pay the lawyer a fraction of the recovery—often one-third—if he wins but nothing if he loses.[71] On the other hand, corporate defendants

70. However, this is not the only source of potential conflict. For example, a lawyer in a high profile case might prefer to litigate rather than settle, even when settlement would be in the best interests of his client, if he expects substantial publicity and reputation benefit from the litigation.

71. Technically, the client is supposed to pay the overhead expenses, such as copying charges, filing fees, and the like, but this seldom happens in practice.

or insurance companies usually hire lawyers on a **fee-for-services** basis. In this arrangement, the client agrees to pay his lawyer for the hours worked whether or not he wins the case.

The effect of attorney-client agency problems on settlement depends on the nature of the fee arrangement.[72] A complete analysis of these effects is beyond the scope of this book. However, it is easy to understand the dynamics intuitively. To see what happens, suppose agency problems are so severe that the attorney has complete control over settlement—in other words, he can get his client to accept any terms. Suppose as well that the attorney relentlessly pursues his own self-interest in maximizing his fee. These are extreme assumptions, of course, but they make it possible to focus on the agency problems in a clear and simple way.

First, consider what happens with a fee-for-services arrangement. The conventional wisdom holds that attorneys paid on a fee-for-services basis will reject or delay settlement in order to run up billable hours. After all, the more the attorney works on a case, the more he gets paid. This prediction assumes, however, that the attorney cannot easily find another client willing to pay his hourly rate. If settlement simply frees the attorney to take a new client and that client pays the same rate, there is no incentive for the attorney to prolong the litigation. Still, finding a new client is often a risky proposi-

72. Professor Geoffrey Miller was one of the first to provide a systematic analysis. *See* Geoffrey P. Miller, *Some Agency Problems in Settlement*, 16 J. LEGAL STUD. 189 (1987).

tion and always involves transaction costs, so the view that agency problems impede settlement has some force. The opposite result is also possible in some special cases. If demand for the attorney's services suddenly skyrockets and he is able to charge more (perhaps because of the positive publicity of a high profile case), he would accept any settlement without regard to his client's interest so he can take on a new client at the higher hourly rate.

Now consider what happens under a contingency fee arrangement. The conventional wisdom is that an attorney on contingency will settle for less than the full settlement value of the claim. The reason is that the attorney pays the full cost of the litigation but receives only a fraction of the benefit. When someone gets only part of the benefit, he is willing to pay only part of the cost. In the case of an attorney investing in a legal claim, this ends up shortchanging the value of the claim because that value depends on how much the attorney is willing to invest. If the claim ends up being valued at less than the optimal amount, the settlement also will be less than optimal. Let's look at this point a bit more closely.

From an economic perspective, the optimal investment is the investment a person would make if he received the full benefit and paid the full cost. Such a person would invest at the level that maximized aggregate benefit net of cost. More precisely, the person would keep investing in the litigation as long as an additional dollar produces more than a dollar gain in the expected trial award—and he would stop just at the point where an additional dollar produces only a dollar's worth of gain. This stopping point is the optimal level of investment.[73]

Because an attorney paid on contingency receives less than the full benefit of anything he invests, he will invest less than the optimal amount. Suppose, for example, that spending $2000 to take another deposition increases the expected trial award by $3000. Clearly, the additional expenditure is desirable since it nets a $1000 increase in the trial value of the claim. However, if the attorney receives only one-third of any recovery, he will not take the deposition because he gains only $1000 (1/3 of the $3000) but must pay the full cost of $2000.

Moreover, the defendant knows this about the attorney, so the defendant calculates his expected loss—and thus his reservation price—based on the value of the claim without the additional deposition. And the attorney, of course, calculates his expected gain using the same trial benchmark. The impact on settlement is obvious: the settlement will be less than it would be if there were no agency problems.[74]

73. Obviously, anything less than this amount shortchanges the claim's value because at any point short of the optimal amount the claim's value can be increased by spending more. This is an example of what economists call "marginal analysis." The idea is that the optimal investment is achieved where marginal benefit equals marginal cost.

74. The defendant is willing to offer less and the attorney is willing to accept less, so the settlement range shifts downward and the expected settlement gets smaller.

2.5   THE LESSONS OF CHAPTER TWO

To recap, we studied a number of different economic tools for predicting settlement behavior. We used the idea of expected value and the simple model of litigation to construct a **basic model of settlement**. We introduced the concepts of **settlement range** and **settlement surplus** and used them to define conditions for a feasible settlement. These conditions generated the settlement puzzle: Why don't all cases settle? We examined two different solutions to this puzzle: **hard bargaining strategies** and **divergent expectations based on mutual optimism**. In the course of discussing hard bargaining, we introduced the **Prisoners' Dilemma Game**, and in the course of discussing mutual optimism, we saw how private access to information and sunk costs affect settlement behavior, two factors that we also explored in Chapter One.

Finally, we examined a refinement to the settlement model that takes account of the fact that lawyers are not always loyal to their clients. The discussion introduced the idea of **agency costs** and explained the effect of different **fee arrangements** on settlement.

Chapter Three:
The Limits of Rational Choice

CONCEPTS AND TOOLS

- Bounded Rationality Heuristics
  - Self-Serving Bias
- Cognitive Limits
  - Endowment Effect
  - Framing Effect

There is considerable empirical evidence to suggest that people do not always behave as rational choice models predict. This is true of litigation even though the litigation environment fits rational choice assumptions rather well. As human beings, parties and lawyers are susceptible to the same cognitive limitations and "irrational" heuristics and rules of thumb (i.e., ways of solving problems) that affect human decisionmaking more generally. This chapter briefly surveys some (but not all) of the empirical literature and describes attempts to adjust the economic models to take account of its findings.[75]

75. For a good overview, *see* Russell Korobkin and Thomas S. Ulen, *Law and Behavioral Science: Removing the Rationality*

3.1 OVERVIEW

That people deviate at times from rational choice predictions is hardly surprising. If these deviations were randomly and symmetrically distributed, there would be little reason for concern. Symmetrically distributed deviations are likely to cancel out over a sufficiently large population, leaving the rational choice prediction as the best account of *average* behavior. However, the experimental evidence suggests that deviations are neither random nor symmetric.

One broad category of deviation, usually referred to by the term "bounded rationality," involves the use of decisionmaking heuristics or "rules of thumb," either consciously or subconsciously, to simplify complex decisions. Some scholars believe that these heuristics are rational strategies to cope with human limitation, strategies that have evolved over time to confer an adaptive advantage. If this view is correct, then these heuristics present no challenge to the ideal of rationality itself, although they still require adjustments to rational choice predictions.

However, there is another type of deviation, one I shall call "cognitive limits," which does seem to present a challenge to the rationality ideal. Cognitive limits include the endowment effect and the

Assumption from Law and Economics, 88 Cal. L. Rev. 1051 (2000). The following summary borrows heavily from this article, although it does not cover all the topics (such as reliance on fairness intuitions).

framing effect, neither of which appear to be simply adaptive responses to complexity.

3.2 BOUNDED RATIONALITY

3.2.1 In General

The empirical literature identifies several different bounded rationality heuristics and biases, all of which are easily recognizable as familiar patterns of human behavior. Each somehow involves discounting or ignoring reliable information in favor of less reliable but more easily applied decisionmaking strategies. The following are important examples:

> *Representativeness heuristic*—Individuals rely excessively on stereotypical attributes at the expense of more reliable statistical information.[76]

> *Availability heuristic*—Individuals tend to make predictions by extrapolating from specific incidents that are highly salient and memorable even when those incidents are statistically aberrational.[77]

76. For example, jurors in a criminal case might be excessively inclined to find that a defendant committed murder if those jurors are told that the defendant has a prior felony conviction. The reason, according to the representativeness heuristic, is that jurors tend to rely on the stereotypical view that felons commit murders even though the statistical correlation is weak. *See id.* at 1087 (discussing this example).

77. For example, people tend to overestimate the probability that toxic chemical exposure causes disease when there is a great deal of publicity and a few high profile incidents.

Overconfidence bias—Individuals tend to overestimate the likelihood that good things will happen *to them* and underestimate the likelihood that bad things will happen *to them*—even when their estimates conflict with reliable statistical information.

Self-serving bias—Individuals tend to interpret information so as to confirm their preconceptions.

Hindsight bias—Individuals tend to adjust probabilities to fit a known result when they estimate the chance of the result happening in advance.

Anchoring and adjustment bias—Individuals tend to use numerical or verbal information to anchor probability estimates and make adjustments using the anchor as a starting point. This creates problems when the anchoring information is flawed.

3.2.2 The Heuristics Applied to Litigation

Empirical studies indicate that at least some of these heuristics affect litigation behavior in predictable ways. Among those studied are the self-serving bias, hindsight bias, and anchoring and adjustment bias. To illustrate, consider the self-serving bias. It appears that litigating parties sometimes interpret information in ways that confirm or reinforce their own preconceived notions about likelihood of success.[78] For example, if they start off optimistic—which would not be surprising given the overconfi-

---

78. *See, e.g.,* George Lowenstein et al., *Self-Serving Assessments of Fairness and Pretrial Bargaining*, 22 J. LEGAL STUD. 135

dence bias—then additional information might end up reinforcing their initial optimism.

This finding has implications for settlement. The analysis in Chapter Two identified two obstacles to settlement: hard bargaining strategies and differential access to information. The self-serving bias suggests a third possibility. Even when parties have the same information, they might still interpret that information to support their own litigation positions. If each side adopts a self-serving interpretation, mutual optimism is a likely result, and this tends to scuttle settlement.

The self-serving bias also has implications for the relationship between discovery and settlement. The economic model predicts that discovery will reduce the gap between divergent probability estimates by equalizing information across the party line, thereby improving prospects for settlement. The self-serving bias identifies a possible counter-effect. If parties have a strong tendency to interpret additional information in a favorable light (even when the interpretation is forced), discovery might simply reinforce divergent views—or at least have a reduced impact in narrowing the probability gap.

None of these results, however, destroys the value of the settlement model. Quite the contrary. As we learn more precisely how the self-serving bias works in litigation, our models can be altered to take account of its effects. The result will be more accurate and precise predictions. The same is true for all

(1993); Linda Babcock et al., *Biased Judgments of Fairness in Bargaining*, 85 AM. ECON. REV. 1337 (1995).

the bounded rationality heuristics.[79] If empirical evidence shows substantial enough effects, models can be modified and predictions adjusted to take them into account.

3.3 COGNITIVE LIMITS

Two well-known examples of cognitive limits are the so-called "endowment effect" and "framing effect." The endowment effect refers to the tendency of people to place a higher monetary value on something when they own it. The effect is also known as "loss aversion" because one consequence is that people value losses more highly than gains of equivalent value.[80] The framing effect refers to the

79. For example, anchoring and adjustment bias can also affect settlement. In Chapter 2, we discussed hard bargaining as one possible reason for settlement failure. It turns out that the anchoring and adjustment bias can interact with hard bargaining to increase the likelihood of settlement. Because initial offers tend to anchor the expectations of the opposing party, a hard bargaining strategy with a low initial settlement offer might make a larger final offer seem more generous than it would otherwise appear without the anchoring effect. If so, this would increase the likelihood of acceptance. For a discussion of the effect of the anchoring and adjustment bias on settlement, *see* Russell Korobkin & Chris Guthrie, *Opening Offers and Out of Court Settlement: A Little Moderation Might Not Go a Long Way*, 10 OHIO ST. J. ON DIS. RES. 1 (1994); Russell Korobkin & Chris Guthrie, *Psychological Barriers to Litigation Settlement: An Experimental Approach*, 93 MICH. L. REV. 107 (1994). For a general discussion of judging and hindsight bias, *see* Chris Guthrie et al., *Inside the Judicial Mind*, 86 CORNELL L. REV. 777 (2001).

80. It is also known as the "offer/asking problem" because one of its implications is that people ask a higher price to sell

way decisions are influenced by the manner in which a choice is framed. In one important manifestation, subjects tend to exhibit risk-averse behavior when a choice is framed as a gain and risk-seeking behavior when the same choice is framed as a loss. [81]

Rational choice theory has difficulty accounting for endowment and framing effects. A person's preference for a particular item should not vary depending on whether he owns it, at least if there is no possibility of emotional attachment or other source of additional utility. [82] Nor should the way a choice

something they own than they offer to buy the same thing owned by someone else.

81. For example, experimental results show that a person given $1000 is very likely to choose a certain payment of an additional $500 over a 50% chance at $1000, but the same person given $2000 is very likely to choose a 50% chance of losing $1000 rather than a certain loss of $500. From the perspective of rational choice theory, these two choice situations are identical— both are equivalent to a choice between $1500 for sure and a gamble with a 50% chance of winning $2000 and a 50% chance of winning $1000. Rational choice theory predicts that individuals will make the same choice no matter how the problem is framed. But the experimental results show otherwise—people tend to choose the certain option of $1500 when the problem is framed as a gain over a baseline but choose the gamble when the problem is framed as a loss. *See* Korobkin & Ulen, *supra* note 75, at 1105 (noting that 84% of experimental subjects chose the certain gain, and 70% chose to gamble on the loss).

82. Ownership sometimes produces emotional attachment, which can increase the value of the item to the owner, but the endowment effect obtains even when there is no possibility of emotional attachment. It appears that ownership alone is sufficient to create the difference in valuation. In fact, the endowment effect seems to be one example of a more general "status quo bias." People tend to place a higher value on the status quo

is framed affect an individual's rational decision when the choice is exactly the same in all its various frames.

Endowment and framing effects have consequences for settlement. If a plaintiff perceives settlement as the sale of something she owns (a legal claim) and the defendant perceives it as the purchase of something owned by another, then the endowment effect might be triggered. Under these circumstances, the plaintiff will place a higher value on the claim than the defendant even when both parties have identical information. This valuation gap is likely to increase plaintiff's minimum demand and thus reduce the settlement range. This might make settlement impossible if plaintiff's minimum demand ends up above defendant's maximum offer and the settlement range disappears.[83]

However, the parties are unlikely to think about settlement in this way. They are more likely to view settlement and trial as opportunities for gains and losses relative to a status quo baseline. According to this view, plaintiffs perceive the choice between settlement and trial as a choice between possible gains, while defendants perceive it as a choice between possible losses. If this is an accurate descrip-

just because it is the status quo, and endowment effects result when people include what they own in the status quo. *See* Korobkin & Ulen, *supra* note 75, at 1111.

83. As long as this does not happen, the effect might be to make settlement more likely if the reduction in the settlement surplus reduces incentives to engage in hard bargaining. *See* the discussion of hard bargaining in Section 2.2.1, *supra*.

tion, then the framing effect might be triggered. One manifestation of the framing effect is that individuals tend to be risk-averse when they choose between gains and risk-seeking when they choose between losses. In the settlement context, this result implies that the plaintiff, who chooses between gains, will favor the less risky alternative of settlement, whereas the defendant, who chooses between losses, will favor the more risky alternative of trial. Some scholars hypothesize that this difference might explain some of the difficulty parties have reaching settlement even when access to information is identical.[84]

Litigation research exploring the implications of cognitive limits for party and attorney behavior is still at an early stage. If further studies show that endowment and framing effects have only a slight impact, it might not be worthwhile including them, especially given the fact that the models already abstract from numerous contextual factors. Moreover, it might not be worth the costs to intervene to correct a problem that is not substantial. More empirical studies of actual lawyers and parties in real litigation settings are needed before strong conclusions can be made with confidence.

84. *See, e.g.,* Jeffrey J. Rachlinski, *Gains, Losses, and the Psychology of Litigation*, 70 S. CAL. L. REV. 113 (1996) (proposing that in order to encourage settlement the legal system should focus on defendant's incentives). Professor Chris Guthrie has also used the framing effect, or more precisely, something called "prospect theory," to explain frivolous litigation. Chris Guthrie, *Framing Frivolous Litigation: A Psychological Theory*, 67 U. CHI. L. REV. 163 (2000).

Nevertheless, if framing and endowment effects do turn out to be significant in litigation, the proper response is not to reject rational choice. Like bounded rationality heuristics, endowment and framing effects can be incorporated into the models by adding or modifying variables or by adjusting predictions. Indeed, at this point, we do not have any overarching behavioral theory that can explain the assortment of ways people deviate from rational choice. So far, bounded rationality heuristics and cognitive limits are mostly just a collection of ad hoc factors. Until there is a coherent theory that explains all the different phenomena and generates predictions in all cases, the best (some would say the only) approach is to use rational choice as the starting point and modify the models and the results to take account of potential deviations.[85]

85. This is not to say that there are no theoretical problems with this strategy. Insofar as particular patterns of deviation conflict with the axioms of rational choice, it might be logically inconsistent to combine the two. After all, any conclusion can be derived from logically inconsistent premises. This might be true as an abstract matter, but experience tells us that the two approaches can be usefully combined in practice.

Part Two:

THE TOOLS OF NORMATIVE ECONOMICS

Part One explained the basic tools of positive economics. Part Two describes the tools of normative economics. These consist of the evaluative standards and analytic methods economists use to translate predictions into prescriptive judgments.

The usual way law-and-economics defines the normative goal is in terms of a cost-benefit analysis. Individual gains and losses from adopting a legal rule are measured in terms of what individuals are willing to pay to obtain the gain or avoid the loss. The sum of individual gains is the social benefit of the rule, and the sum of individual losses is the social cost. The goal is to maximize social benefit net of social cost. Because benefits usually involve costs that are avoided by a particular choice of rule, this goal can also be expressed in terms of minimizing total social costs.

For example, it is commonplace in first year Torts courses to interpret the famous "Hand Formula" for negligence in cost-minimization terms. The Hand Formula is named after Judge Learned Hand, who formulated it in *United States v. Carroll Tow-*

ing Co.[1] According to the formula, stated in economic terms, a defendant has a duty of reasonable care when the burden of taking care (B) is less than the expected loss from failing to take care (P, the probability of injury, multiplied by L, the loss from injury)—or when $B < P \times L$. The basic idea is that accidents are costly, but so are precautions taken to prevent accidents.[2] The economic objective is to choose the negligence rule that minimizes the sum of accident and precaution costs. This means that a party should invest in precautions up to the point where an additional dollar invested produces only one dollar in accident cost savings, and "reasonable care" is defined as this optimal level of investment.

The same approach applies to procedure. Procedures are analogous to precautions, except that procedures reduce the risk of error rather than the risk of accident. Errors, like accidents, are costly and so too are procedures taken to prevent them. The economic objective is to choose the procedural rule that minimizes the sum of error and process costs.[3]

1.   159 F.2d 169 (2d Cir.1947).

2.   This relationship can also be expressed in terms of benefits and costs. Precautions are costly but they create social benefits by reducing accident costs. The goal is to find the level of investment in precaution that maximizes these benefits net of precaution costs. This is equivalent to the goal of minimizing total accident and precaution costs because the benefit is equivalent to the accident costs that are avoided through investment in precaution.

3.   For a useful discussion of accuracy in adjudication from an error and process cost perspective, *see* Louis Kaplow, *The Value*

It is important to recognize that error reduction is not an end in itself. Accuracy has social value because it furthers the goals of the substantive law, which in economic terms are to create incentives for socially desirable behavior. The substantive law affects incentives by attaching sanctions (i.e., damages, penalties, etc.) to behavior that violates a substantive norm (and sometimes rewards to behavior that complies with it). For sanctions to have the desired impact, however, individuals must expect to incur the sanction when they misbehave and avoid the sanction when they behave, and these expectations depend on the accuracy with which the procedural system sorts the two situations. To take an extreme example, suppose a procedural system found everyone liable whether or not they actually violated the law. Under these circumstances, there would be no incentive to comply with the substantive law because compliance would have no effect on the likelihood of sanction.

For this reason, it is sometimes important, in conjunction with a conventional error and process cost analysis, to give explicit attention to the more direct effects procedure might have on incentives to comply with the substantive law.[4] This can be rath-

of Accuracy in Adjudication: An Economic Analysis, 23 J. LEGAL STUD. 307 (1994).

4. This is a particularly strong theme in the work of Professor Chris Sanchirico, especially his work on evidence law. *See, e.g.,* Chris William Sanchirico, *Character Evidence and the Object of Trial*, 101 COLUM. L. REV. 1227 (2001). But the idea is also important to other law-and-economics writing in the procedure field. *See id.* at 1235 n. 17 (collecting sources).

er complicated, and we shall examine some of the complexity in Chapter Five, in the course of analyzing the American and British Rules on attorney's fees.

The general class of economic approaches to problems of social choice, of which cost-minimization is one example, is known as "welfare economics." Before studying the application of cost-minimization to procedure, it might be useful to say a few words about this broader theoretical framework (although the reader can skip this discussion and proceed directly to Chapter Four without missing anything essential). The reader should keep two caveats in mind, however. First, the following account greatly simplifies what is in fact a very complex area and one with a rich scholarly literature. Second, the discussion focuses exclusively on the analytic structure of welfare economics and does not address broad questions of normative justification.

WELFARE ECONOMICS AND THE IDEA OF A SOCIAL WELFARE FUNCTION

An economic approach, no matter what form it takes, seeks to maximize social welfare. For the economist, social welfare is an aggregate of the welfare of individuals within the society. It follows that an economic approach requires two things: (1) a definition of individual welfare, and (2) a method for aggregating the welfare of different individuals into a measure of social welfare.

The first requirement is not easy to satisfy. Classical utilitarians, such as Jeremy Bentham, defined individual welfare in terms of how much pleasure or happiness a person experienced, psychological states that at least in theory could be quantified and compared between individuals. Most economists today take a different approach. They define individual welfare in terms of preference satisfaction. The idea is simple: people have subjective preferences and their welfare or "well being" is enhanced whenever their preferences are satisfied.[5]

Economists use the concept of "utility" to represent preferences in numerical form. In Part One, we avoided using the utility concept and we will continue to do so for the rest of this book. However, it cannot be avoided in this introductory discussion. Here the reader should think of utilities as numbers that represent an individual's relative preferences

5. Economists tend to equate preference satisfaction with well-being and preferences with what an individual would choose. For example, if John *prefers* strawberry to chocolate ice cream, John would *choose* strawberry over chocolate and his *well-being* would improve as a result. However, it turns out that there are problems with equating these different ideas, problems illuminated by questions like the following: Isn't it possible that a drug addict's "well being" could be impaired by satisfying his preference for drugs? Isn't it possible for someone to make a mistake so that his choices do not reflect his actual preferences? Does it ever make sense to say that a person has sacrificed the sort of life she would have liked to have lived—and thus her "well being" as she understands it—in order to serve a moral obligation to help others? If the answer to any of these questions is yes, it is possible that a person's preferences might be different than her choices and her choices different than what advances her well being.

for different outcomes or states of affairs. For example, John has a higher utility for outcome A than for outcome B if and only if he prefers A to B.[6]

The second requirement—a method for aggregating the welfare of individuals—is also tricky. As a purely mathematical matter, there are infinitely many ways to aggregate. One might, for example, simply add up everyone's utility, or, alternatively, weight the utilities of some more heavily than the utilities of others before adding. As it turns out, however, not every method qualifies as an attractive way to decide social policy questions. Economists use the term **social welfare function** to refer to those that satisfy minimum conditions of efficacy and rationality.[7]

One very simple and straightforward social welfare function is the "utilitarian social welfare function," which simply adds up everyone's utility. For example, suppose in a two-person society, John has a utility gain of 10,000 with policy A and Mary has a utility loss of 8000. The utilitarian social welfare function adds these utilities together to yield a

6. It is still necessary to defend preference satisfaction, understood in this way, as a normatively desirable goal in order to justify the economic approach on normative grounds. That is an extremely complicated matter and well beyond the scope of this book.

7. For example, a social welfare function must be comprehensive in the sense that it is capable of choosing between any possible pairs of policy options. In addition, it must be transitive: if it chooses A over B and B over C in pairwise comparisons, it must also choose A over C. There are other requirements as well. For a more rigorous and thorough account, *see* David M. Kreps, A Course in Microeconomic Theory 156–164 (1990).

social welfare gain of 2000 if policy A is implemented.[8]

The cost-benefit approach of law-and-economics shares a great deal in common with a utilitarian social welfare function. Costs and benefits for a given individual are measured in terms of that individual's willingness to pay. For example, consider a proposal to build a new school on what is now a forested public park. John, who has school-age children, prefers the school to the park. Mary, who is childless and enjoys hiking, prefers the park to the school. John should be willing to pay an amount to see that the school is built, and Mary should be willing to pay an amount to see that it is not built. The amount each would pay measures the utility gain or loss each would experience if the proposal were adopted.

In the usual case, we do not actually measure each person's willingness to pay. Instead, we rely on market prices. For example, suppose the administrative cost of enforcing a particular rule is $100,000. This means that the resources needed to administer the rule will cost $100,000 at market prices. But this cost, at least in a rough way, represents an aggregate of individual utility losses.

8. It should be obvious that there is no universally correct social welfare function. The choice of a particular function depends in part on the values that the analyst wishes to promote. For example, an economist concerned about social inequality might give more weight to the utility of the poorest individuals in the society, or someone who cares a lot about environmental protection might weigh utilities for environmental quality much more strongly than utilities for other goods.

The $100,000 payment must come from somewhere, and it comes from individual members of the society through taxes, private expenditures, and the like. These payments are monetary losses to those who make them, and the monetary losses are reflected as utility losses for each of those individuals.

The correspondence between costs and benefits based on market prices, on the one hand, and utility losses and gains, on the other, is more complicated and more problematic than this brief description suggests.[9] The important point for our purposes is that the cost-benefit (or cost-minimization) approach has enough practical advantages that those working in the field of law-and-economics are willing to rely on it despite its shortcomings.[10]

THE IDEA OF ECONOMIC EFFICIENCY

It is quite common to describe a rule or policy that minimizes social costs as "efficient." Efficiency, however, is an imprecise concept. There are two different versions of the idea in common use. The version most closely aligned with the cost-minimization approach of law-and-economics is known as **Kaldor-Hicks efficiency**, and the other version is

9. For a useful theoretical overview of cost-benefit analysis, *see* Mathew D. Adler & Eric A. Posner, *Rethinking Cost–Benefit Analysis*, 109 YALE L. J. 165 (1999).

10. One reason to rely on willingness-to-pay at market prices is that it is more difficult for people to misrepresent their subjective preferences when those preferences are based on market choices. On the other hand, market choices are constrained by individual budgets, so preference revelation through the market can be distorted by unequal distribution of wealth.

known as **Pareto efficiency**.[11]

First, consider the concept of Pareto efficiency. The basic idea is that there are some social choices that make at least one person better off (in utility terms) without making anyone else worse off. For example, suppose John and Mary are the only two people in the society and that John's utility would increase by 100 if a particular proposal were implemented while Mary's utility would remain the same. We say that the proposal is **Pareto-superior** to the status quo because it makes John better off without making Mary any worse off. A state of affairs is **Pareto-efficient** if all Pareto-superior changes have been made; in other words, if there is no way to make a Pareto-superior improvement.[12]

Pareto efficiency is a particularly attractive social welfare function for at least two reasons. First, it has strong intuitive appeal. At first blush, it is difficult to see how one could legitimately object to a policy choice that makes some individuals better off without harming anyone. In fact, there are some legitimate objections, but they are quite limited.[13] Second, the Pareto criterion does not require com-

11. For a discussion of Kaldor–Hicks efficiency, *see* Allan M. Feldman, "Kaldor–Hicks compensation" *in* 2 THE NEW PALGRAVE DICTIONARY OF ECONOMICS AND THE LAW 417 (Peter Newman, ed. 1998), and for a discussion of Pareto efficiency, *see* Allan M. Feldman, "Pareto optimality" *in* 3 *ibid* 5.

12. More precisely, an option is Pareto-optimal (and thus Pareto-efficient) among the available alternatives if it is Pareto-superior to the status quo and no other alternative is Pareto-superior to it.

13. For example, one might object on the ground of distributive equality if the benefits were concentrated in the hands of a

parisons of utility gains and losses between individuals. One need only ask whether an individual is better or worse off *by his own reckoning*. This is an advantage because the concept of utility is not well designed to compare preference orderings between *different individuals*; it is designed instead to measure a *single* individual's relative preferences over different outcomes. In other words, it is designed to make *intra*-personal rather than *inter*-personal comparisons.[14]

However, Pareto efficiency suffers from a serious disadvantage as a social welfare function. It is hardly ever capable of deciding policy issues. In a society as large and diverse as ours with such complex social institutions, it is seldom, if ever, the case that a proposal does not make at least one person worse off. Given this, we need some way to compare the losses of some with the gains of others.

The second efficiency criterion, Kaldor–Hicks efficiency, addresses this problem. The intuition is rela-

few wealthy individuals. For another kind of objection, known as the "Paradox of the Paretian Liberal," *see* Amartya Sen, *The Impossibility of a Paretian Liberal*, 78 J. POL. ECON. 152 (1970).

14. For example, if John gets a utility of 5 from chocolate ice cream and a utility of 10 from strawberry ice cream, we can say that John likes strawberry ice cream more than chocolate. However, if Mary gets a utility of 10 from chocolate ice cream, it does not follow that Mary likes chocolate ice cream more than John does. To draw that conclusion, John's and Mary's utilities would have to be measured on a common scale, but there is no common scale that is free of conceptual problems. Law-and-economics uses money as a common scale and measures preference in terms of willingness to pay at competitive prices. This is a workable approach, but it has analytic flaws.

tively simple, although the supporting theory is quite complex. A rule or policy is **Kaldor-Hicks efficient** if those who are better off under it *could* compensate those who are worse off, so that no one would be worse off and at least one person would be better off. In other words, a rule or policy is Kaldor–Hicks efficient if there is a set of compensatory transfers that would make it Pareto superior to the status quo if those transfers could be made in a costless way. The Kaldor–Hicks criterion does not require that the transfers actually take place; only that they exist.

One way to implement the Kaldor–Hicks criterion is to add up all utility losses and gains—or when utility is measured by willingness-to-pay, to add up all costs and benefits. If the total is positive, gains must exceed losses and therefore those who gain theoretically should be able to compensate those who lose. The fact that compensation does not necessarily take place, however, makes the Kaldor–Hicks criterion much more controversial than the Pareto criterion. Furthermore, this way of implementing Kaldor–Hicks runs headlong into the problem of interpersonal utility comparisons. There is a vast literature discussing this problem and much disagreement about how serious it actually is.

In sum, most law-and-economics scholars use some form of cost-benefit (or cost-minimization) analysis. This approach shares with all social welfare functions a commitment to making social choices on the basis of aggregating individual welfare (understood as preference satisfaction). Indeed, cost-benefit analysis relies on a kind of utilitarian social welfare function, in which utilities are measured in terms of willingness to pay at market prices, and on a Kaldor–Hicks efficiency criterion. The Kaldor–Hicks criterion is needed because it is too difficult to satisfy the strict conditions of Pareto efficiency in the real world.[15]

15. There is a popular misconception that law-and-economics scholars care only about efficiency and pay no attention to distributional equity, that is, to the equity implications of how total welfare is distributed among individuals in the society. This view is incorrect. To be sure, the dominant law-and-economics approach to the analysis of legal rules focuses on efficiency, but this does not mean that all, or even most, economists believe equity is irrelevant to social policy. For a useful discussion of attitudes and approaches to equity among law-and-economics scholars, *see* Chris William Sanchirico, *Deconstructing the New Efficiency Rationale*, 86 CORNELL L. REV. 1003 (2001).

CHAPTER FOUR:

WHICH PLEADING RULE IS OPTIMAL?

CONCEPTS AND TOOLS

- Expected Error Cost
  - False Negatives and False Positives
  - Error Probability and Error Cost
  - Cost-Ratios and Cut-Off Points
  - Secondary Effects
- Expected Process Cost
- Combining Error and Process Costs

In recent years, a great deal of attention has focused on pleading rules as a solution to frivolous litigation. During the 1980s and early 1990s, for example, a number of federal courts required plaintiffs in civil rights, antitrust, securities fraud and other cases to plead detailed factual allegations.[16] Moreover, in 1995, Congress made detailed pleading a statutory requirement for securities fraud class

---

16. *See, e.g.*, Richard L. Marcus, *The Revival of Fact Pleading Under the Federal Rules of Civil Procedure*, 86 COLUM. L. REV. 433 (1986).

actions.[17] And detailed factual pleading has been proposed for other types of litigation as well.[18]

One advantage of using detailed pleading requirements to screen frivolous suits is that pleading operates as a gatekeeper. If detailed pleading screens effectively, frivolous suits can be deterred or eliminated at the outset. On the other hand, detailed pleading can generate high costs.

In this chapter, we use the problem of choosing an optimal pleading rule as a concrete example of how to do an error and process cost analysis of procedure. The goal of any such analysis is to minimize the sum of error and process costs, and these costs are estimated with the help of the positive theories of frivolous litigation developed in Chapter One.

4.1   PLEADING RULES IN GENERAL

The party with the responsibility to raise an issue and thus make it part of the case is said to have the pleading burden on that issue. For example, a plaintiff alleging negligence has the burden to plead duty, breach, causation, and harm, while the defendant has the burden to plead contributory negli-

17.   *See* Private Securities Litigation Reform Act, Pub. L. No. 104–67, 109 Stat. 737 (1995).

18.   For example, the Class Action Fairness Act of 2001, H.R. 2341, 107th Cong. (2001) would, if enacted, have required specificity for class action allegations.

gence. If the plaintiff does not plead properly, he risks dismissal for failure to state a claim.

Every pleading burden has an assignment and a quantum. The assignment identifies which party—plaintiff or defendant—has the burden, and the quantum specifies how onerous that burden is, that is, how much the party must plead. We shall examine two pleading rules that differ in how heavy a burden they impose: **notice pleading** and **strict pleading**.

Notice pleading requires very little by way of allegation. In federal court, for instance, the plaintiff need only allege enough so that the defendant has notice of what the dispute is generally about.[19] Strict pleading imposes a much heavier burden. To satisfy strict pleading, the plaintiff must allege a substantial amount of factual detail, although the precise amount varies with the particular version of strict pleading in force.[20]

Notice pleading has essentially one purpose: to give defendants notice of the dispute. Strict plead-

19. *See* Conley v. Gibson, 355 U.S. 41, 47–48 (1957).

20. For example, the strict pleading rule that applies to securities fraud class actions in federal court requires that the complaint "specify each statement alleged to have been misleading [and] the reason or reasons why the statement is misleading" and also, when liability depends on defendant's state of mind (such as intent or reckless disregard), "state with particularity the facts giving rise to a strong inference that the defendant acted with the required state of mind." 15 U.S.C. § 78u–4(b)(2).

ing has two purposes: to give the defendant notice *and* to screen frivolous suits.[21] The idea is that plaintiffs will not be able to plead facts with specificity if there are no facts to support their claims.

4.2 BASIC ERROR COST ANALYSIS

4.2.1 False Positives, False Negatives, and Expected Error Cost

The difference between notice pleading and strict pleading turns on the relative screening effects of the two rules. In an ideal world, a pleading rule would screen all frivolous suits and let in all meritorious suits. But ours is not an ideal world. Notice pleading makes it easy for plaintiffs to file frivolous suits, and strict pleading makes it hard for plaintiffs to file meritorious suits. Neither rule functions as an ideal lawsuit screen.

Departures from the ideal are errors of the pleading system. These errors include frivolous suits that slip by the pleading stage and meritorious suits that are dismissed or never filed because of an onerous pleading burden. All errors are costly in one way or another, and the goal of an error cost analysis is to minimize the expected cost.

Sometimes the choice is easy. Suppose, for example, that a strict pleading rule reduces the number of frivolous suits compared to notice pleading without affecting meritorious suits in any way. Focusing

---

21. The traditional common law pleading system focused on narrowing the issues in dispute, but modern pleading has largely abandoned this objective—although there is some support for reviving it as a way to reduce litigation costs and strategic abuse.

exclusively on error costs (and ignoring process costs), strict pleading is the obvious choice.

The fact is, however, that policy choices are seldom so simple. Usually a rule increases one type of error at the same time as it reduces another. To analyze these more complex decisions, economists distinguish between two types of error: **false positive** (or "Type I") errors and **false negative** (or "Type II") errors. Most people are familiar with this terminology from the medical field, where a false positive is a test result that indicates disease in a patient who is actually healthy and a false negative is a test result that indicates health in a patient who is actually ill. The same distinction is relevant to pleading rules.

In the pleading context, a false negative is a frivolous suit that is not dismissed at the pleading stage. A false positive is a meritorious suit that is dismissed at the pleading stage or not filed because of the fear of dismissal. This assignment of labels is analogous to the assignment in the medical field.[22] Imagine that a judge applies a test to detect frivolous suits. When the test yields a negative result but the suit is really frivolous, the error is a false negative, and when the test yields a positive result but the suit is really meritorious, the error is a false positive. The following summarizes these definitions:

22. Any assignment is essentially arbitrary. It works just as well to switch the labels so long as one is careful to be consistent.

> False Negative — A frivolous suit that is filed and not dismissed at the pleading stage.
>
> False Positive — A meritorious suit that is filed and dismissed at the pleading stage, or that is not filed because of the dismissal risk.

Strict pleading reduces false negatives but increases false positives. Notice pleading reduces false positives but increases false negatives. The choice between the two pleading rules depends on the relative costs of the two kinds of error and their relative frequency.

To see this point more clearly, consider a familiar example unrelated to pleading: the choice between a preponderance-of-the-evidence and a beyond-a-reasonable-doubt rule for the burden of persuasion in a criminal case. Neither rule is an easy choice on the basis of error rate alone. Compared to the preponderance standard, the beyond-a-reasonable-doubt standard reduces the number of erroneous convictions, but it also increases the number of erroneous acquittals. The choice between the two rules depends on the relative magnitude of these effects, but it also depends—and more importantly in this case—on how one assesses the social cost of erroneous convictions relative to erroneous acquittals. The selection of a beyond-a-reasonable-doubt standard for criminal cases reflects a judgment that the cost of erroneous convictions—the potential deprivation of liberty—is much greater than the cost of erroneous acquittals. As the familiar saying goes, it is better to acquit ten guilty men than convict an innocent one.

Returning to our pleading example, each type of error produces its own social costs. False negatives (failure to dismiss frivolous suits) undermine the deterrent effect of the substantive law, waste litigation costs, lead to inefficient and unjustified settlements, and chill socially useful activity. False positives (screening of meritorious suits) undermine the deterrent effect of the substantive law, distort other socially valuable incentives, and if frequent enough, might even impair the law's long-term growth by eliminating opportunities for the creation of new precedent.

[margin handwriting: costs of plead, false neg/pos]

When the costs of the two types of error differ, it is necessary to compare both costs and probabilities. The way to do this is to use an expected value, which in this context is an **expected error cost**. Expected error cost equals the probability of an error *multiplied by* the social cost of the error if it materializes.

For example, suppose that a notice-pleading rule lets 80% of the frivolous suits and all the meritorious suits past the pleading stage. The error probability depends on how many frivolous and meritorious suits there are. If 20% of filed suits are frivolous, then 80% of this 20% get by the pleading stage, so the probability of a false negative is 16% (i.e., $0.8 \times 0.2 = 0.16$). On the other hand, since no meritorious suits are dismissed, the probability of a false positive is 0%. Therefore, if a false negative costs $5000 on average and a false positive $1000, the expected error costs are:

Expected Cost of a False Negative:

0.16 (probability) × 5000 (cost) = $800

Expected Cost of a False Positive:

0.0 (probability) × 1000 (cost) = $ 0

TOTAL EXPECTED ERROR COST $800

The following is a summary of the general method:

EXPECTED ERROR COST ANALYSIS

1. For each rule, standard, or policy:
   a. Estimate the probability of a false positive error and the probability of a false negative error.
   b. Estimate the cost of a false positive and the cost of a false negative.
   c. Multiply the cost by the probability to get the expected cost of each type of error.
2. Add the expected costs to obtain a total expected error cost and compare total expected error costs for the different options.

4.2.2 A Concrete Example

Suppose that notice pleading dismisses only 20% of the frivolous suits and none of the meritorious suits, and suppose that strict pleading dismisses 75% of the frivolous suits and 40% of the meritorious suits. Assume 20% of all lawsuits are frivolous and that pleading rules affect only dismissal rates and have no impact on filing incentives (we relax this assumption in Section 4.2.4, below). The following summarizes these assumptions:

PLEADING EXAMPLE #1
(No effect on filing)

Probability that suit is frivolous – 20%

Notice Pleading	Strict Pleading
Prob. friv. suit not dismissed – 80%	Prob. friv. suit not dismissed – 25%
Prob. merit. suit dismissed – 0%	Prob. merit. suit dismissed – 40%

4.2.2.1 Calculating Error Probabilities

In order to compare the two rules, we must calculate expected error costs, and to do that, we must first determine error probabilities. Consider notice pleading first and then strict pleading.

For a false negative to occur, two things must happen at once: a suit must be frivolous *and* it must not be dismissed. We know the probability of each of these things happening separately. The probability that a suit is frivolous is 20%, and the probability that a frivolous suit is not dismissed under a notice pleading rule is 80%.[23] How does one calculate the probability that these two things will happen concurrently? The answer from probability theory is to multiply the separate probabilities together. This is

23. The latter probability is the probability that a suit is not dismissed *given that it is frivolous*. In probability theory, this is known as a "conditional probability." It is a conditional probability because the probability is conditioned on the suit being frivolous. The probability of a false negative is just this conditional probability without the condition; in other words, when the condition is satisfied too.

intuitively sensible, since the 80% probability acts on suits that are frivolous and 20% of the lawsuits are frivolous. Therefore, the probability of a false negative under notice pleading is 0.16: [24]

0.2 (probability suit is frivolous) × 0.8 (probability a frivolous suit is not dismissed) = 0.16.

We can calculate the probability of a false positive in exactly the same way. A false positive requires that two things happen concurrently: a suit must be meritorious *and* it must be dismissed. The probability that a suit is meritorious is 80%, and the probability that a meritorious suit is dismissed under notice pleading is 0%. Therefore, the probability that both things happen together is zero:

0.8 (probability suit is meritorious) × 0.0 (probability meritorious suit is dismissed) = 0.0

Generalizing, we obtain the following two formulae for calculating error probabilities ("Prob [ ]" means "probability of" whatever is in the brackets):

---

24. One can confirm this result by using numbers rather than probabilities. Suppose there is a total of 100 lawsuits. With a 20% probability of a frivolous suit, 20 suits should be frivolous and 80 meritorious. Notice pleading results in 80% of the 20 frivolous suits getting through the pleading stage for a total of 16 false negative errors. Since there are 100 suits, the probability of a false negative error is $16 \div 100 = 0.16$, the same result derived in the text.

> Prob [False Negative] = Prob [suit is frivolous] x
> Prob [frivolous suit is not dismissed]
>
> Prob [False Positive] = Prob [suit is meritorious] x
> Prob [meritorious suit is dismissed]

These two formulae are also useful for calculating error probabilities under strict pleading. The probability of a false negative is $0.2 \times 0.25 = 0.05$,[25] and the probability of a false positive is $0.8 \times 0.4 = 0.32$.[26] The following error probability table summarizes the results for both rules:

TABLE I—ERROR PROBABILITY TABLE FOR
PLEADING EXAMPLE #1

	Notice Pleading	Strict Pleading
False neg. prob. (friv. suit not dismissed)	$0.8 \times 0.2 =$ 0.16	$0.25 \times 0.2 =$ 0.05
False pos. prob. (merit. suit dismissed)	$0.0 \times 0.8 =$ 0.0	$0.4 \times 0.8 =$ 0.32
TOTAL ERROR PROBABILITY	0.16	0.37

From Table I alone, we can see that notice pleading is superior when error costs are equal: it generates a 16% total error rate versus a 37% total error rate for strict pleading. However, when error costs are not equal, the analysis must combine costs and

25. 0.2 (prob. suit is frivolous) $\times$ 0.25 (prob. frivolous suit is not dismissed) = 0.05.

26. 0.8 (prob. suit is meritorious) $\times$ 0.4 (prob. meritorious suit is dismissed) = 0.32.

probabilities into an expected error cost estimate, as discussed in the following section.

4.2.2.2 Incorporating Error Costs

Suppose that false negatives are four times more costly than false positives. In particular, assume a false negative costs $400 on average and a false positive $100. The following table summarizes the expected error cost calculations (based on the error probabilities in Table I):

TABLE II—EXPECTED ERROR COSTS
FOR EXAMPLE #1

	Notice Pleading	Strict Pleading
False neg. exp. error cost (friv. suit not dismissed)	0.16 × 400 = 64	0.05 × 400 = 20
False pos. exp. error cost (merit. suit dismissed)	0.00 × 100 = 0	0.32 × 100 = 32
TOTAL EXP. ERROR COST	$64	$52

Table II indicates that strict pleading is the better choice on error cost grounds. Strict pleading produces an expected cost of $52 compared to $64 for notice pleading. Roughly speaking, strict pleading is superior because it does a better job of controlling the more costly kind of error (i.e., false negatives).

The result depends, of course, on the relative costs of the two errors. Suppose, for example, that false negatives are only twice as costly as false positives: $200 for false negatives versus $100 for false positives. The new expected error cost table looks like this:

TABLE III—NEW EXPECTED ERROR COST TABLE

	Notice Pleading	Strict Pleading
False neg. exp. error cost (friv. suit not dismissed)	$0.16 \times 200 =$ 32	$0.05 \times 200 =$ 10
False pos. exp. error cost (merit. suit dismissed)	$0.00 \times 100 =$ 0	$0.32 \times 100 =$ 32
TOTAL EXP. ERROR COST	\$32	\$42

Notice pleading is now the better choice. This illustrates a simple but important point. It matters not only *whether* one type of error is more costly than the other; it matters *how much more* costly it is. In our example, when the cost of a false negative is four times the cost of a false positive, strict pleading is the better choice, but when the cost of a false negative is only two times the cost of a false positive, notice pleading is the better choice.

4.2.3 Estimating the Variables: Cost–Ratios and Cut-off Points

Estimating error probabilities and costs can be a difficult task. To estimate probabilities, for example, one must know how well courts are likely to perform under each rule and what parties are likely to do in response. To estimate costs, one must be able to quantify the adverse impact of frivolous suits and the costs of screening meritorious suits.

Nevertheless, rough estimates are possible. For example, experienced lawyers are likely to have some sense of how accurately judges handle dismissal motions and how parties and their attorneys behave. Moreover, as we shall see in Section 4.4, below, positive models of the litigation process help predict strategic responses to different rules. As for costs, one should be able to approximate the wasted litigation cost of a frivolous filing on average once one has some idea of the kind of case and the likely delay before settlement.

In any event, there is no way to avoid estimating these variables, no matter how one approaches the issues. Any policy analysis must compare the frequency and cost of error. There is simply no other way to tell whether a rule's benefits in vindicating meritorious suits are worth the cost of tolerating frivolous suits.

Fortunately, error cost analysis has a special property that simplifies the estimation process. What matters is the ratio of costs, not the absolute numbers. For example, the ratio of false negative to false positive cost in Table II above is 400:100 or 4:1, and as we saw, strict pleading turned out to be the superior rule. In fact, for the specified probabilities, any combination of error costs that has the same 4:1 **cost-ratio** supports the same strict pleading recommendation. It doesn't matter whether false negatives cost $4000 and false positives $1000, or false negatives cost $6 billion and false positives $1.5 billion.

Moreover, it is not even necessary to know the actual cost-ratio. What is important is the relationship between the ratio and a **cut-off point** that depends only on the error probabilities. Any cost-ratio above the cut-off favors one rule, and any cost-ratio below the cut-off favors the other rule. The cut-off point is calculated from the error probabilities.[27] For example, the error probabilities in Tables II and III generate a cut-off point of 2.91. This means that strict pleading is superior whenever the cost-ratio is greater than 2.91:1 (as it was for the 4:1 ratio in Table II), and notice pleading is superior whenever the cost-ratio is less than 2.91:1 (as it was for the 2:1 ratio in Table III). It does not matter what the actual cost-ratio is; it only matters whether the ratio is greater or less than the cut-off point. For example, strict pleading is still the better choice whether false negatives are three times, one hundred times, ten million times, or ten billion times as costly as false positives.

4.2.4 Secondary Effects on Filing Incentives

The previous sections describe the core elements of an error cost analysis: false negative versus false positive error, expected error cost (error probability

27. One can prove these properties with some simple algebra. When the cost-ratio is expressed as the ratio of false negative to false positive costs, the cut-off point turns out to be the difference between false positive probabilities under the two rules divided by the difference between false negative probabilities (always making the result a positive number). Formally, if $P_{fn}{}^A$ and $P_{fp}{}^A$ and $P_{fn}{}^B$ and $P_{fp}{}^B$ are false positive and false negative probabilities for Rule A and Rule B, respectively, then the cut-off point (corresponding to a false negative to false positive cost-ratio) is:

$$\text{Cut–Off Point} = (P_{fp}{}^A - P_{fp}{}^B)/ (P_{fn}{}^B - P_{fn}{}^A)$$

times error cost), and the cost-ratio and cut-off point. However, the discussion in those sections made an assumption that simplified the analysis. It assumed that the choice of rule affected only dismissal rates and had absolutely no impact on filing incentives. This assumption is unrealistic. Strict pleading is virtually certain to deter frivolous filings and very likely to deter meritorious filings as well.

The following discussion explains how to incorporate secondary filing effects into the error cost analysis. Section 4.2.4.1 deals with the easiest cases, those in which the rule affects only frivolous filings. Section 4.2.4.2 deals with the harder cases, those in which both frivolous and meritorious filings are affected.

4.2.4.1   Effects on Frivolous Filings

If strict pleading deters frivolous filings, then a strict pleading rule reduces false negatives in two different ways: it dismisses frivolous suits after they are filed *and* it deters them before they are filed. Although both effects lead to the same result— fewer frivolous suits make it past the pleading stage—the two effects contribute to this result in different ways so it is important to treat them separately.

Adding filing effects to the analysis involves no new principles. Recall that a false negative requires two things: suit must be frivolous, and it must not be dismissed. The resulting formula for calculating false negative probability works fine so long as all potential suits are filed, as the analysis in Section 4.2.2.1 assumed, because in that case there is no need to distinguish between potential and filed suits. But the formula must be modified when some potential suits might not be filed. In that case, the first condition for a false negative—that a pending suit be frivolous—needs to be changed.

In order for a suit to be frivolous when some potential frivolous suits are not filed, two things must happen concurrently: (1) a potential suit must be frivolous *and* (2) the potential frivolous suit must be filed. The probability of these two things happening concurrently is the product of the probabilities they will happen separately.[28] Therefore, we have the following formula:

Prob [filed suit is frivolous] = Prob [potential suit is frivolous] × Prob [frivolous suit is filed]

Incorporating this expression into the original formula, we have the following expanded formula that applies when filing suit is not a sure thing:[29]

28. The reasoning is the same as that described in footnote 23, *supra*. The probability that a frivolous potential suit is filed is, in fact, a conditional probability; that is, it is the probability that a suit is filed *conditional on the suit being frivolous*. Therefore, the probability that a filed suit is frivolous equals the probability that a potential suit is filed *given that* the potential suit is frivolous *multiplied by* the probability that the potential suit is frivolous.

29. This formula includes the formula in Section 4.2.2.1, *supra*, as a special case that obtains when all potential frivolous suits are filed.

Prob [False Negative] =

Prob [potential suit is frivolous] x
Prob [frivolous suit is filed] x
Prob [filed frivolous suit is not dismissed]

To illustrate, modify Pleading Example #1 (in Section 4.2.2, above) so that strict pleading deters 60% of frivolous filings. Also assume that 20% of all *potential* suits are frivolous. Keep all other assumptions the same. The probability of a false negative with strict pleading is 0.02:[30]

0.2 (prob. potential suit is frivolous) × 0.4 (prob. frivolous suit is filed) × 0.25 (prob. filed frivolous suit is not dismissed) = 0.02

4.2.4.2 Effects on Frivolous and Meritorious Filings

Effects on meritorious filings are analyzed in the same way as effects on frivolous filings. A false positive can occur in two ways: when a meritorious

30. A reader who still has trouble understanding the formula might think about it in terms of numbers rather than probabilities. Suppose we start with a total of 100 potential suits. According to our assumptions, 20% of those suits are frivolous. Therefore 20 are frivolous and 80 are meritorious. Under strict pleading, 40% of the frivolous suits are filed. This means that there are 8 filed frivolous suits. Finally, 25% of those filed frivolous suits make it past the pleading stage—for a total of two frivolous suits that are not dismissed. These two suits are out of 100 potential suits, which is 2%—or 0.02 probability of a false negative.

suit is dismissed and also when a potential meritorious suit is not filed. For a meritorious suit to be dismissed (when filing is not guaranteed), three things must happen concurrently: a potential suit must be meritorious, it must be filed, *and* it must dismissed. Therefore, the probability of a meritorious suit dismissal is:

Prob [Merit. Suit Dismissed] = Prob [potential suit is meritorious] × Prob [meritorious suit filed] × Prob [filed meritorious suit dismissed]

For a meritorious filing to be deterred, two things must happen concurrently: a potential suit must be meritorious *and* it must not be filed. Therefore, the probability of this event is:

Prob [Merit. Suit Deterred] = Prob [potential suit is meritorious] × Prob [meritorious suit is not filed]

The total false positive probability is just the sum of the probabilities associated with these two components. This can be summarized as follows:

Prob [False Positive] =

Prob [potential suit is meritorious] x
Prob [meritorious suit is filed] x
Prob [filed meritorious suit is dismissed]
+
Prob [potential suit is meritorious] x
Prob [meritorious suit is not filed]

The rest of this section illustrates these tools with a modified version of Pleading Example #1.

PLEADING EXAMPLE #2
(Strict pleading affects frivolous and meritorious filings)

Prob. that potential suit is frivolous – 20%

Notice Pleading		Strict Pleading	
Prob. friv. suit is filed	– 100%	Prob. friv. suit is filed	– 40%
Prob. merit. suit is filed	– 100%	Prob. merit. suit is filed	– 80%
Prob. friv. suit not dismissed	– 80%	Prob. friv. suit not dismissed	– 25%
Prob. merit. suit dismissed	– 0%	Prob. merit. suit dismissed	– 40%

Since notice pleading has no effect on filing incentives, its error probabilities are the same as in Table I above. However, strict pleading deters both frivolous and meritorious filings, so filing effects must be included in its analysis. First, consider false negatives. The probability of a false negative, as we saw above, is 0.02:

0.2 (prob. a potential suit is frivolous) × 0.4 (prob. frivolous suit is filed) × 0.25 (prob. filed frivolous suit is not dismissed) = 0.02

The probability of a false positive with strict pleading breaks into two components. The first component is the probability that a meritorious suit is filed and then dismissed, which is 0.256.[31] The second component is the probability that a suit is meritorious and not filed, which is 0.16.[32] Therefore, the total false negative probability under strict pleading equals 0.256 + 0.16 = 0.416.

Recall that without filing effects, false negative and false positive probabilities with strict pleading were 0.05 and 0.32, respectively. Adding filing effects reduces the first figure to 0.02 and increases the second figure to 0.416. This result makes intuitive sense. Strict pleading deters frivolous filings, which reduces the frequency of false negatives, and it also deters meritorious filings, which increases the frequency of false positives. The cut-off point also changes slightly from 2.91 to 2.97. However, none of these changes are terribly significant. This result is not uncommon. In many situations, plausi-

31. 0.8 (prob. potential suit is meritorious) × 0.8 (prob. meritorious suit is filed) × 0.4 (prob. filed meritorious suit is dismissed) = 0.256.

32. 0.8 (prob. potential suit is meritorious) × 0.2 (prob. meritorious suit is not filed) = 0.16.

ble filing effects make only a slight difference to error probabilities and cut-off points.

4.3 PROCESS COSTS

Error costs are only half the story. Economists also worry about process costs. A rule that reaps large benefits in error cost reduction might still be undesirable if its implementation adds substantially to process costs. Process costs include the administrative and litigation costs of complying with and enforcing the rule. In the case of pleading rules, compliance costs include the cost of preparing the pleading and investigating the facts that support the allegations, and enforcement costs include the costs of filing, litigating, and processing motions to dismiss.

The analysis of process effects, like the analysis of error effects, depends on expectations rather than absolute costs. For the choice between pleading rules, **expected process cost** equals the average cost of filing suit multiplied by the probability that a suit will be filed *plus* the average cost of litigating a motion to dismiss multiplied by the probability that a motion will be filed. Breaking the analysis down in this way highlights an important aspect of a strict pleading rule. While strict pleading increases average costs, it reduces the probability of suit and might also reduce the probability of a dismissal motion. As a result, it does not necessarily increase expected process costs.

There is no question that strict pleading increases the average cost of filing suit and litigating a dismissal motion. Investigating and preparing a complaint should be more costly because of the need to allege greater factual detail. Moreover, the cost of litigating and processing a motion to dismiss should be greater because the parties have more to argue about and the judge more to deliberate upon.

The effect on probabilities is less certain. Insofar as strict pleading deters frivolous and meritorious filings, it reduces the probability of suit. In this regard, strict pleading's adverse impact on meritorious litigation reduces process costs even as it increases error costs. Ironically, what is harmful from the point of view of error cost is beneficial from the point of view of process cost.

However, it is not clear whether strict pleading reduces or increases the probability of a dismissal motion. A strict pleading rule makes motions more attractive by making it more likely that defendants will succeed. But the rule also makes motions less attractive by reducing the number of worthwhile targets for dismissal. With fewer frivolous filings and more careful attention to pleading, there will be fewer opportunities to succeed in obtaining dismissal.[33] The net result is unclear: the probability of a

33. After all, for a rational plaintiff to be confident enough to incur the costs of filing, she must have a good reason to believe that her complaint will survive dismissal, and that reason should also convince at least some defendants that seeking dismissal is not worthwhile. Moreover, meritorious plaintiffs might be able to amend their complaints in response to a dismissal motion and this option reduces defendant's prospects of obtaining dismissal.

motion might be less or greater with strict pleading than with notice pleading.

There is another factor that must be considered when evaluating process costs: the impact of a rule on process costs at other points in the litigation. If strict pleading does a good job of screening frivolous suits, then procedures like summary judgment and directed verdict, which aim to screen frivolous suits at later stages, would presumably be employed less often. The reduction in litigation costs is a benefit that should be included in the process cost analysis.

To sum up, strict pleading increases the average cost of a filing and a motion to dismiss, but it reduces the probability of filing and might also reduce the probability of a motion. Moreover, it reduces process costs at later stages of the litigation. The result might be a net reduction in expected process cost, but it also might be a net increase. It is impossible to tell without more empirical information.

The important point to understand is that a process cost analysis is complicated because rules have multiple effects. In particular, expected process cost depends not just on the average cost of applying the rule to a given case, but also on the number of cases that invite application of the rule and the effects of the rule on other stages of the litigation. A rule that generates higher costs per case might generate lower expected process costs overall if it reduces the frequency of cases that require its application.

4.4 PULLING IT ALL TOGETHER

We now have all the main elements of error and process cost analysis in place. The final step is to apply this framework to the normative problem of choosing an optimal rule. The discussion in this section focuses on the choice of an optimal pleading rule in the setting of actual litigation. However, the general approach is relevant to many policy choices in procedure. In all such cases, positive models are used to predict effects on error and process costs and the results are compared across the different policy alternatives.

Recall that the positive analysis in Chapter One identified different categories of frivolous litigation, summarized in the following chart. The remainder of the discussion in this section follows the same organizational scheme.

	Defendant Knows Suit is Frivolous	**Defendant Does Not Know Suit is Frivolous**
Plaintiff Knows Suit is Frivolous	1 No Serious Problem	2 Potentially Serious - Frivolous filings - Bad settlements - Wasted litig. costs
Plaintiff Does Not Know Suit is Frivolous	3 Potentially serious - Frivolous filings - Bad settlements - Wasted litig. costs	4 [Not Discussed][34]

4.4.1 Category 1 (Plaintiff and defendant both know suit is frivolous)

Recall from Section 1.2.3.1 of Chapter One that a frivolous plaintiff in the Rosenberg–Shavell model files suit only when he expects a settlement in excess of his filing cost, and the defendant settles only when the settlement amount is less than the cost of answering. Since answering is seldom more costly than filing, the model predicts that few frivolous plaintiffs will find it worthwhile to sue.

The only way a strict pleading rule deters frivo-

34. I did not discuss this fourth box, where both parties are ignorant of the merits, in Chapter One; nor do I do so here. It involves special complications that might tax the reader's patience without adding anything important of pedagogical value. In fact, if we did the analysis, we would see that mutual ignorance also invites frivolous filings that can produce high costs in equilibrium.

lous litigation in this model is by increasing plaintiff's filing cost. This makes it less likely that the gain from settlement will cover the expense of suit. Still, there is so little incentive to file frivolous suits even with notice pleading that the marginal benefit is likely to be quite small. Therefore, given that strict pleading deters meritorious suits and might increase process costs, the cost-benefit balance almost certainly favors notice pleading in Category 1.

4.4.2 Category 2 (Plaintiff knows suit is frivolous but defendant does not)

In Category 2, frivolous plaintiffs masquerade as meritorious and sometimes obtain substantial settlements. As we saw in Section 1.2.3.2.1 of Chapter One, the model predicts potentially serious frivolous suit problems.

Strict pleading is not likely to deter frivolous suits in this model. When plaintiff knows that suit is frivolous and files anyway, he (and his lawyer) must be willing to lie, and a lying plaintiff will have little trouble with a strict pleading rule. He will simply fabricate the necessary allegations. Fabricating might require a bit more effort but not enough to discourage suit. Some dishonest plaintiffs might think twice before lying about factual details, but there is little reason to believe that the additional burden will deter many, especially given the prospect of a large settlement. Moreover, any small benefit in this regard must be balanced against strict pleading's adverse impact on meritorious filings. Thus, notice pleading is probably the better choice for Category 2.

There is one possible exception. With a strict pleading rule, the defendant might be able to identify a lying plaintiff by verifying the truth of the factual allegations. The defendant then would know that suit is frivolous, and the case would shift to Category 1, in which frivolous suit problems are not serious. However, this strategy requires an investigation and investigations can be extremely costly. This is especially true for those cases, like the trip-and-fall example discussed in Section 1.2.3.2.1, in which the plaintiff has sole access to the critical information. Indeed, frivolous plaintiffs are likely to choose allegations that are difficult to verify.

4.4.3 Category 3 (Defendant knows suit is frivolous but plaintiff does not)

In Category 3 cases, plaintiffs can discover whether their suits have merit by investigating before filing, but not all plaintiffs choose to investigate. The formal model, discussed briefly in Section 1.2.3.2.2 of Chapter One, predicts a potentially serious frivolous suit problem. In equilibrium, plaintiffs file frivolous suits and take some of those suits all the way through discovery before dropping. Moreover, some plaintiffs with meritorious suits drop early, mistakenly believing that their suits are frivolous. And some meritorious suits go to trial when they would have been settled but for the presence of frivolous suits.

Analyzing the effect of pleading rules is a bit complicated. Unlike Category 2, not all cases in Category 3 should be labeled "frivolous" (in the sense of being objectionable). For example, a suit that lacks merit should not be considered frivolous if a pre-filing investigation would have been prohibitively expensive. A meritless lawsuit is "frivolous" only when the plaintiff *should* have investigated before filing; that is, only when a pre-filing investigation is a "reasonable" option.

Whether an investigation is "reasonable" depends on its costs and benefits, or more precisely, on whether the expected costs are lower with it than without it. If investigation costs are so high that plaintiffs would not sue if they had to investigate, then requiring a pre-filing investigation would scuttle a great deal of socially beneficial litigation and generate costs far in excess of benefits. On the other hand, if investigation is only moderately costly, social benefits are likely to exceed social costs and pre-filing investigation should be a reasonable option.[35]

The benefit of a strict pleading rule is that it encourages more pre-filing investigation than notice pleading. While plaintiffs might simply lie about their allegations, as we thought they would do in Category 2, there are two factors that discourage lying. First, it is much less clear in Category 3 that plaintiffs and their lawyers would be willing to lie.

35. The formal model generates a somewhat more precise definition. *See* Robert G. Bone, *Modeling Frivolous Suits*, 145 U. PA. L. REV. 519, 564–66 (1997). Roughly speaking, a pre-filing investigation is reasonable if it is the kind of investigation that a plaintiff would conduct if he knew that the only other alternative for verifying the merits was to litigate all the way through discovery.

That they would file without investigating when notice pleading lets them get away with minimal but truthful allegations does not mean that they would also lie when more detailed allegations are required. One can easily imagine a basically honest lawyer in a small firm who has lots of cases and is pressed for time choosing not to investigate when he can easily meet the liberal standards of notice pleading, but refusing to lie when strict pleading requires more. Second, it is much more difficult to get away with a lie when the defendant knows the truth than when he does not. A plaintiff runs the risk of being revealed as uninformed and thus losing his strategic advantage if his fabricated allegations do not fit the defendant's understanding of the case.

Thus, strict pleading encourages more pre-filing investigations. And when a frivolous plaintiff investigates, he discovers his suit lacks merit. As a result, both parties are informed, and the case shifts to Category 1, in which frivolous suit problems are not serious. It follows that a strict pleading rule reduces the expected cost of false negatives in Category 3.

But what about the rule's impact on false positives and expected process costs? If a strict pleading rule applies across the board, including to those cases in which investigation is too costly for plaintiffs to obtain the necessary information before filing, it would deter lots of meritorious suits. Because of this, one might confine the rule's application only to cases where investigation is reasonable. But identifying those cases is bound to be administratively costly. Moreover, if strict pleading invites more motions to dismiss, the additional motions will also add to process costs. As a result, a strict pleading rule is virtually certain to increase false positives, expected process costs, or both.

Although it is not possible to choose between the two rules without more information, it is clear from this brief analysis that Category 3 is the only serious candidate for adoption of a strict pleading rule. That it is possible to derive such a significant conclusion from relatively limited information is a testament to the usefulness of the economic approach. Moreover, the analysis points to other tentative recommendations. Strict pleading should be applied selectively, only to lawsuits where plaintiffs are likely to be uninformed about the merits and the cost of investigating is likely to be moderate. [36] Also, courts should be cautious about requiring too much specificity, especially for those issues that are difficult to investigate before filing. A heavy burden runs too great a risk of deterring meritorious suits and thus generating high false positive error costs.[37]

36. For example, the Private Securities Litigation Reform Act adopts a targeted approach. It applies a strict pleading rule to securities fraud class actions, a category of suits that are likely to be filed quickly and without a pre-filing investigation. However, some circuits, such as the Ninth Circuit, interpret the statute to require a great deal of specificity. *See* Elliott J. Weiss, *Pleading Securities Fraud*, 64 Law & Contemp. Prob. 5, 17–27 (Spring/Summer 2001). It is not clear that this is a good idea, given the false positive error costs that are likely to be produced.

37. The error and process cost framework can be used to evaluate other regulatory approaches as well. For example, con-

4.5   THE LESSONS OF CHAPTER FOUR

To recap, we saw how to do a normative analysis of procedural rules using pleading as a concrete example. We saw the essential elements of an **expected error cost** analysis, including the importance of distinguishing between false negative and sider a system of penalties, like the sanctions imposed on frivolous suits by Rule 11 of the Federal Rules of Civil Procedure. Because penalties target only frivolous suits, they hold out the hope of generating fewer false positives than strict pleading. On the other hand, identifying which suits are frivolous requires hearings and judicial deliberation, all of which adds to expected process costs. Furthermore, courts are bound to make mistakes and occasionally classify meritorious suits as frivolous, so penalties will deter some meritorious filings. As the penalty increases, the chilling effect will spread to stronger and stronger cases, especially when plaintiffs are risk-averse. Penalties also have another problem. Since most suits settle without the actual imposition of penalties, deterrence depends on the penalty threat reducing the settlement amount. It turns out that the penalty must be set so high in Category 2 cases that lots of meritorious suits are likely to be chilled as well. *See* Avery Katz, *The Effect of Frivolous Suits on the Settlement of Litigation*, 10 INT'L REV. L. & ECON. 3, 20 (1990). By contrast, even a modest penalty can have substantial deterrence benefits in Category 3 cases, a result that points to Category 3 as the appropriate focus of a penalty system.

As for the relative merits of penalties versus strict pleading in Category 3 cases, penalties have the advantage of working even when plaintiff's attorney is inclined to fabricate allegations. Moreover, a modest penalty might not have too serious an impact on meritorious suits or on process costs, at least when the court is relatively accurate at the penalty stage. This means that modest penalties might be superior to strict pleading, although more information is needed. The point here is not to defend any particular choice. The point is to demonstrate the analysis and

false positive error and considering the probability and cost of each type of error separately. We also saw how to simplify the analysis by using **cost-ratios** and **cut-off points**. And we saw how to include secondary effects on filing incentives.

We also studied the main components of an **expected process cost analysis**, including the importance of considering a rule's effects on probability as well as cost. And we saw how the multiple effects of a procedural rule can complicate the process cost analysis. Finally, we saw how to apply the error and process cost framework to the choice between strict pleading and notice pleading.

show what it is capable of doing. *See generally*, Bone, *supra* note 35, at 589–93 (discussing the pros and cons of a penalty system).

CHAPTER FIVE:

SHOULD THE UNITED STATES ADOPT THE BRITISH RULE?

CONCEPTS AND TOOLS

- Analyzing Multiple Incentives
  - Filing Incentives
  - Settlement Incentives
  - Investment Incentives
  - Compliance Incentives
- Analyzing Interaction Effects

There is a great deal of interest today in the "British Rule" as a cure for the maladies of the court system. The British Rule—so-called because it applies in the United Kingdom—is also known as the "loser pays rule" because it requires the losing party to pay the winning party's attorney's fees (and other costs). The current rule in effect in the United States—the "American Rule"—requires each side to pay its own fees, win or lose.[38]

38. Neither rule is applied in pure form; exceptions are recognized in the United Kingdom and in the United States. In the United States, for example, the main exceptions to the American Rule are statutory. For some types of cases, such as civil rights, copyright, and antitrust suits, Congress has authorized "prevailing parties" to obtain fees from the losing side.

Supporters of the British Rule contend that it discourages the filing of weak cases and encourages settlement. They argue that the risk of having to pay an opponent's fees if one loses at trial makes filing less attractive for losing cases and also makes settlement more attractive than gambling on a trial loss.

The following discussion takes a close look at these and other arguments for the British Rule. I focus on this policy debate because the analysis enlists all the economic tools we have developed so far. Moreover, it nicely illustrates the importance of considering a range of incentives, as well as patterns of interaction among them. In the end, we shall see that the case for the British Rule is much more complex and uncertain than the simple argument suggests.

5.1 FILING INCENTIVES

5.1.1 The Simple Argument

The British Rule increases expected trial value by adding plaintiff's own fees to the payoff if plaintiff wins, but also reduces expected trial value by adding defendant's fees to the loss if plaintiff loses. Which of these two effects dominates depends on the strength of the case. In strong cases, plaintiff is much more likely to win than lose, so the first effect dominates, expected value increases under the British Rule, and filing becomes more attractive. In weak cases, plaintiff is much more likely to lose than win, so the second effect dominates, expected value declines under the British Rule, and filing becomes less attractive.[39]

To illustrate, suppose that the plaintiff has a weak case with only a 25% probability of success at trial and that he expects a trial award of $100,000 if he prevails. Also suppose that both sides expect to pay $20,000 to litigate the case through trial (assume all these costs are attorney's fees). Under the American Rule, plaintiff's expected trial value is $0.25 \times 100,000 - 20,000 = \$5000$. Therefore, a rational plaintiff will sue.

Under the British Rule, the expected trial value is calculated as follows. If plaintiff wins (a 25% probability), he gets $100,000 *plus* his litigation costs paid by the defendant for a net gain of $100,000 free and clear. If he loses (a 75% probability), he pays his own litigation costs *plus* the defendant's for a total loss of $40,000. Therefore, the expected trial value is $0.25 \times 100,000 - 0.75 \times 40,000 =$

39. There is a value p^* such that for cases stronger than p^* ($p > p^*$) expected value increases and for cases weaker than p^* ($p < p^*$) expected value falls. To derive an expression for p^*, note that the British Rule increases expected value when $pw - (1-p)(c_P + c_D) > pw - c_P$. Solving for p gives $p^* = c_D/(c_P + c_D)$. If $c_P = c_D$, for example, $p^* = \frac{1}{2}$. For a thorough discussion of these points, *see* Steven Shavell, *Suit, Settlement, and Trial: A Theoretical Analysis Under Alternative Methods for the Allocation of Legal Costs*, 11 J. LEGAL STUD. 55 (1982) (discussing the effect of fee allocation rules on filing and settlement and noting risk-aversion and other problems).

–$5000. Since the result is negative, a rational plaintiff will not sue.

At the other extreme, the British Rule might encourage some strong suits that would not be cost-justified under the American Rule because of unusually low stakes or unusually high litigation costs. Examples with high litigation costs include some complex product liability cases and some cases involving injuries from toxic chemicals or other toxic materials that require extensive scientific investigation and lots of expensive expert testimony. For instance, suppose that the plaintiff's products liability case has a probability of success of 70% and an expected trial award of $500,000. Suppose that the plaintiff and the defendant each expect to spend $400,000 litigating the case through trial due to the presence of complicated scientific issues. In this situation, plaintiff's suit is NEV under the American Rule (i.e., 0.7 × 500,000 − 400,000 = –$50,000). But it is PEV under the British Rule (i.e., 0.7 × 500,000 − 0.3 × 800,000 = $110,000).[40]

Thus, switching from the American to the British Rule changes the composition of filed cases, but does not necessarily change the total number. The

40. For an example with unusually low stakes, suppose a plaintiff sues to recover for property damage to his car from an automobile collision. Suppose that the damage and thus the expected trial award is $5000, and he has a 90% probability of success. Also, suppose that the plaintiff and the defendant each expect to spend $5000 litigating the case through trial. Plaintiff's suit is NEV under the American Rule: his expected value is 0.9 × 5000 − 5000 = –$500. However, his suit is PEV under the British Rule: his expected value is 0.9 × 5000 − 0.1 × (5000 + 5000) = $3500.

British Rule discourages the filing of some low-probability/high-stakes suits that would be filed under the American Rule, but it also encourages the filing of some high-probability suits with low stakes or high costs that would not be filed under the American Rule.

5.1.2 A Closer Look: Effects on Meritorious Filings

Even though the British Rule discourages weak suits and encourages strong ones, its effect on filing incentives is not unambiguously positive. Some of the weak cases that the Rule discourages might be meritorious forms of litigation from a social point of view. For example, a civil rights case that is weak on the merits because it tests a new legal theory might nevertheless be important to the development of civil rights law and thus a desirable candidate for trial.

Moreover, the British Rule can have even more serious consequences for risk-averse plaintiffs, depending on their level of risk aversion. If a plaintiff loses under the American Rule, he pays only his own litigation costs. But if he loses under the British Rule, he pays his own *plus the defendant's* costs. This larger downside risk makes litigation less attractive for risk-averse plaintiffs, especially those of moderate wealth for whom a large liability for litigation costs is a major burden.[41]

41.   More precisely, the British Rule increases the risk of the litigation gamble in two ways: by increasing the downside loss *and* by increasing the upside gain. These two effects make the

Furthermore, defendants have strategic incentives to exploit plaintiff risk-aversion by inflating their own litigation costs. The fact that defendants must pay those inflated costs themselves if they lose at trial acts as a brake on this strategy. But defendants still come out ahead as long as plaintiff's probability of success is less than 50%.[42]

Plaintiffs might be able to reduce the effects of risk aversion by using contingency fee arrangements. A contingency fee shifts some of the litigation risk to the lawyer, who can manage it better by maintaining a diversified portfolio of cases. But there are limits to this strategy. For one thing, it is not easy to implement with the British Rule, where the attorney is at risk not only of absorbing his own fees but also paying the defendant's. Furthermore, some areas of practice—civil rights litigation might be a good example—are too specialized to permit effective diversification.

5.1.3 A Closer Look: Effects on Frivolous Filings

For the simple argument to work and weak cases to be deterred, a case must be strong enough to be cost-justified under the American Rule, yet weak

"distance" between the two outcomes larger, which increases the variance of the gamble and thus the risk.

42. More precisely, plaintiff's expected value under the British Rule is $pw - (1-p)(c_P + c_D)$, and defendant's expected loss is $p(w + c_P + c_D) = pw + p(c_P + c_D)$. Therefore, when the defendant increases c_D, it reduces plaintiff's expected value by a factor of $(1-p)$ and increases defendant's expected loss by a factor of p. Therefore, when $p < 0.5$, the plaintiff suffers more than the defendant.

enough to be non-cost-justified under the British Rule. It is only in these marginal cases that switching to the British Rule makes a difference to filing incentives. This means that the simple argument has very little to say about truly frivolous litigation, as defined in Section 1.2.1 of Chapter One (that is, lawsuits in which there is a virtual certainty that the defendant is not in fact liable under the legal theories alleged). The argument predicts some deterrence benefits for frivolous suits that are positive expected value under the American Rule, but as we saw in Section 1.2.2, these suits should be quite rare because trial error must be unusually high to generate a positive expected value in a frivolous suit. Most frivolous suits have negative expected value under the American Rule, and the simple argument does not apply to NEV suits.

To evaluate the impact of the British Rule on frivolous suits, therefore, it is necessary to examine the NEV models of frivolous litigation described in Chapter One. These models distinguish different types of cases according to whether one or both parties know suit is frivolous. The following discussion is organized around these categories (see Section 4.4 of Chapter Four for a summary chart).

5.1.3.1   Category 1: Plaintiff and defendant both know suit is frivolous

The British Rule deters frivolous filings in Category 1 cases. When the defendant knows he can get his fees and any other costs paid by a losing plaintiff, the defendant can make a credible threat to litigate a frivolous suit all the way through trial. Therefore, a frivolous plaintiff will not file because he knows he cannot obtain a settlement. This benefit is not terribly significant, however, since frivolous litigation is not a serious problem for Category 1 anyway. And the fact that the British Rule also chills meritorious suits argues against its adoption when the benefits are not large.

5.1.3.2   Category 2: Plaintiff knows suit is frivolous but defendant does not

In Chapter One, we saw that the model for Category 2 cases predicts two different equilibria. In the first equilibrium, the fraction of potential frivolous suits is small enough that the defendant finds it worthwhile to settle all cases, frivolous and meritorious alike. In the second equilibrium, the fraction of potential frivolous suits is large enough that the defendant finds it worthwhile to deter frivolous filings by refusing to settle some of the time.

The effect of switching to the British Rule depends on the average strength of meritorious suits. Suppose meritorious suits are strong enough so that the British Rule increases their expected trial value. Then a meritorious plaintiff's minimum settlement demand increases and the defendant must pay more to settle. The effect of an increase in the settlement amount differs between the two equilibria. In the first equilibrium, all lawsuits settle for the value of a meritorious suit, so frivolous plaintiffs receive a larger windfall.

The effect in the second equilibrium is more complicated. With settlement more expensive, the defendant settles fewer cases, so frivolous plaintiffs file less frequently. However, a lower settlement rate also forces more meritorious suits to trial, which increases the private and public costs of litigation. In the formal model, the second effect can dominate the first when public as well as private costs are counted, and total costs can increase as a result.[43]

Even this brief discussion shows that switching to the British Rule can increase the social costs of frivolous litigation, at least when the meritorious suits are strong on the merits. Defendants suffer unjustified losses because they pay more to frivolous plaintiffs in the first equilibrium. And more litigation costs are wasted because of the presence of frivolous suits in the second equilibrium.

5.1.3.3 Category 3: Defendant knows suit is frivolous but plaintiff does not

In Category 3 cases, the defendant knows that the suit is frivolous but the plaintiff does not unless she investigates. As we saw in Chapter One, defendants in meritorious suits have an incentive to pretend their suits are frivolous because an uninformed plaintiff might drop, and this pooling strategy causes most of the problems. Switching to the British Rule can have a beneficial impact by reducing the incentive to pool. The analysis is quite complicated, but the intuition is relatively easy to grasp.

43. *See* Katz, *supra* note 37, at 17–19 (analyzing impact on private costs).

Suppose meritorious suits are strong enough on average so that switching to the British Rule increases expected trial value. With more to gain from meritorious litigation, plaintiffs benefit more from knowing whether their suits are meritorious, so they investigate more often. When plaintiffs investigate more often, fewer plaintiffs are uninformed so defendants in meritorious suits have less to gain from pretending their suits are frivolous—and as a result they pool less often and settle more often. This combination of more investigation and more settlement leads to fewer frivolous filings and fewer trials—and therefore lower litigation costs.

Still, these benefits are limited. Switching to the British Rule does not eliminate frivolous filings or induce reasonable pre-filing investigations in all cases. This is important because the British Rule also generates additional costs by chilling some meritorious suits, and possibly also by increasing expected process costs, as described in the following section.

5.1.4 Effects on Expected Process Costs

Under the American Rule, there is no need for a court to get involved in awarding fees unless the client refuses to pay his lawyer. By contrast, any reasonable implementation of the British Rule will involve someone—most likely the judge—checking the veracity and reasonableness of a winning party's claim for litigation costs. Without such a check, a winning party might pad his claim to increase his recovery.

Verification requires hearings and judicial determinations of reasonableness. These additional procedures are likely to be quite costly, especially if experience with fee-shifting exceptions to the American Rule is a reliable guide. The actual impact on *expected process costs*, however, depends not only on the cost of processing fee applications, but also on the number of cases in which fee applications are filed (or more precisely, on the probability that a fee application will be filed). If the British Rule applies universally, the additional process costs will be incurred in *all* cases that do not settle. On the other hand, the more settlements there are, the fewer fee applications there will be that need processing. Therefore, the magnitude of any impact on expected process costs depends on settlement incentives.

5.2   SETTLEMENT INCENTIVES

5.2.1   The Simple Argument

The simple argument that the British Rule encourages more settlements than the American Rule assumes that the British Rule makes trial less attractive by adding fees to the expected loss. The problem with this argument is that it applies only to parties who believe they are going to lose. The British Rule actually makes trial more attractive for parties who believe they are going to win, and when trial is more attractive, parties are less likely to settle.

Therefore, settlement incentives under the British Rule depend not only on trial losses but also on trial wins and party beliefs about the probability of winning versus losing. In fact, switching to the British Rule can hurt rather than help settlement incentives. To see this point, we shall focus on the two causes of settlement failure described in Chapter Two: divergent expectations and hard bargaining.

5.2.2 A Closer Look: Divergent Expectations

The divergent expectations model identifies mutual optimism as the main source of settlement failure under the American Rule. When the plaintiff believes her case is very strong, she will demand a large settlement, but when the defendant believes his case is very strong, he will offer only a small settlement. Therefore, a settlement range is unlikely to exist.

It is easy to see why switching to the British Rule cannot help parties settle in these cases. The British Rule drives them even further apart by adding fees and costs to the trial payoff and thus making trial more attractive when each side believes he is going to win. To illustrate, consider the Pablo and Doris mutual optimism example from Chapter Two:[44]

44. *See* Section 2.2.2, *supra*.

Pablo and Doris Mutual Optimism Example

$$p_\pi = 0.7 \quad p_\Delta = 0.2 \quad w = 100,000$$

$$c_P = c_D = \$20,000$$

We saw that under the American Rule the least Pablo will accept is \$50,000 and the most Doris will offer is \$40,000, so settlement is not feasible. The British Rule only makes matters worse. Pablo's minimum demand increases to \$58,000, and Doris's maximum offer falls to \$28,000.[45] Indeed, with some simple algebra, it is possible to prove that the British Rule can *never* create a settlement range when there is none under the American Rule.[46]

This analysis assumes risk-neutrality. If one or both parties are risk-averse, switching to the British Rule can make a difference in some cases. Because the British Rule increases the risk-bearing costs of going to trial, it makes trial less attractive and

45. Pablo's expected trial value is $0.7 \times 100,000 - 0.3 \times 40,000 = \$58,000$. Doris's expected trial loss is $0.2 \times (100,000 + 20,000 + 20,000) = \$28,000$. (Remember that Doris loses nothing if she wins because Pablo pays her litigation costs.)

46. The proposition is easily proved by showing that the following two conditions can never hold simultaneously: $p_\pi w - c_P > p_\Delta w + c_D$ and $p_\pi w - (1 - p_\Delta)(c_P + c_D) < p_\Delta(w + c_P + c_D)$. The first is the condition for settlement to be impossible under the American Rule and the second is the condition for settlement to be possible under the British Rule.

settlement more attractive for risk-averse parties. Put differently, the additional risk-bearing costs reduce plaintiff's minimum demand and increase defendant's maximum offer. This brings the parties closer together and increases the likelihood of settlement.

Therefore, mutual optimism and risk-aversion have opposite effects under the British Rule: mutual optimism drives the parties further apart by adding to the trial payoff and risk-aversion brings them closer together by burdening trial with risk-bearing costs. When the parties are sufficiently risk-averse and not too optimistic, the latter effect can dominate the former and make settlement feasible when it would not be under the American Rule.

5.2.3   A Closer Look: Hard Bargaining

As we saw in Chapter Two, parties use hard bargaining strategies if they think they can capture more of the settlement surplus by negotiating aggressively. However, when both parties negotiate aggressively, they reduce the chance of reaching agreement.

The British Rule makes a difference by affecting the size of the settlement surplus. Parties should negotiate more aggressively as the surplus gets larger and there is more to gain from hard bargaining. If so, then procedures that increase the surplus should increase the probability and intensity of hard bargaining and thus reduce the likelihood of settlement—and vice versa.

If the parties are risk-neutral and agree on likely success, switching to the British Rule has no effect on the settlement surplus.[47] Under both the American and British Rules, the surplus is the same: it equals the total litigation costs saved by settling rather than going to trial. This means that for the surplus to change, one or both parties must be risk-averse or the two must have divergent expectations.

First consider risk-aversion. If either party is risk-averse, the British Rule increases the surplus and, with it, incentives to engage in hard bargaining. Recall that the risk of trial is higher under the British Rule because the downside loss is greater. When trial is riskier, risk-averse parties save their additional risk-bearing costs by settling, which adds to the settlement surplus.[48]

Next, suppose that the parties are risk-neutral, but their expectations diverge because they have different estimates of the plaintiff's likelihood of success. When plaintiff's estimate exceeds defendant's, switching to the British Rule reduces the size of the surplus. Intuitively, the British Rule makes trial look rosier to both parties, which nar-

---

47. This assumes that the British Rule has no effect on litigation costs. However, as explained in the following section, switching to the British Rule is likely to increase litigation costs. If this happens, the surplus will be larger and the chance of settlement smaller, even when both parties are risk-neutral and agree on likelihood of success.

48. There is another way to see this point. By making trial more costly, the British Rule reduces a risk-averse plaintiff's minimum demand and increases a risk-averse defendant's maximum offer. So the difference between the two—which is the settlement surplus—gets larger.

rows the settlement range. The problem, however, is that the British Rule can easily reduce the settlement surplus so much that settlement becomes infeasible. It turns out that the two estimates have to be quite close together to avoid scuttling settlement completely. This means that there is only a small set of cases for which switching to the British Rule has a salutary effect on bargaining strategy while still preserving the possibility of settlement.[49] In all other cases, switching renders settlement impossible, or it increases the settlement surplus and, with it, the temptation to engage in hard bargaining.[50]

49. With some simple algebra, one can show that the general condition for the British Rule to reduce the settlement surplus without scuttling settlement altogether is:

$$0 < p_\pi - p_\Delta \leq (c_P + c_D)/(w + c_P + c_D)$$

Therefore, the two estimates cannot deviate by more than $(c_P + c_D)/(w + c_P + c_D)$, which is likely to be quite small. Moreover, when this condition is satisfied, the British Rule reduces the surplus by an amount equal to $(p_\pi - p_\Delta)(c_P + c_D)$.

50. In particular, switching to the British Rule increases the surplus in cases of mutual pessimism. Mutual pessimism is the opposite of mutual optimism. In cases of mutual pessimism, both parties are pessimistic about their respective chances of winning. These cases are the most likely to settle under the American Rule because the plaintiff is willing to accept a relatively low amount and the defendant is willing to make a relatively high offer (so a settlement range is very likely to exist). Switching to the British Rule increases the surplus because it makes the defendant willing to offer even more and the plaintiff willing to accept even less. It does this because each side, being pessimistic, puts a high probability on losing and thus having to pay his opponent's fees as well as his own. If a larger surplus encourages hard bargaining and as a result reduces the likelihood of settlement, then switching to the British Rule could produce a nega-

This analysis assumes that a larger surplus makes settlement more difficult. However, some theorists believe that a larger surplus increases the likelihood of settlement by creating a broader range of possible agreement points. In fact, the truth probably lies somewhere in between. A larger surplus makes hard bargaining more attractive *and* also creates a larger target that might be easier for parties to hit. Which effect dominates depends on the nature of the case. Even so, it is probably safe to assume that large increases in the surplus will have substantial negative effects on bargaining strategy.

5.3   INVESTMENT INCENTIVES

The British Rule increases the amount at stake for both sides by adding fees to potential gains and losses. Rational parties tend to invest more when the stakes are higher because additional investment enhances the likelihood of success, which reaps a larger expected return when there is a larger amount at stake. It follows then that switching to the British Rule should increase the parties' investment incentives and thus increase litigation costs.

This result could be socially beneficial if the additional expenditures produced a more thoroughly argued case and thus a more accurate outcome. However, it is also possible that the additional

tive effect in precisely those cases that are most likely to settle under the American Rule.

investments will cancel one another out and end up as a waste for society and the litigating parties. For example, if larger stakes lead the plaintiff to hire an expert witness, and the defendant does the same, a jury might end up confused by the dueling testimony and ignore both experts. Even if each party expects the additional testimony to be worthless, neither would be willing to do without it for fear that his opponent's expert testimony would go unchallenged. In other words, each party hires an expert to avoid being taken for a "sucker" even though neither benefits from the investment.

This strategic bind can be modeled as a Prisoners' Dilemma. As we saw in Section 2.2.1 of Chapter Two, the Prisoners' Dilemma Game yields a perverse equilibrium in which both parties end up worse off than they would be if they could cooperate. In this case, both parties are better off not hiring an expert *only if each can trust the other to stick with that decision.* The problem is that each party has a strong temptation to deviate, and this temptation destroys any hope of cooperation and drives the parties toward the wasteful equilibrium.

To illustrate, let's modify the Pablo and Doris example in Section 2.2.1 of Chapter Two. Pablo Prentice, a patient, sues Doris Delano, his surgeon, for medical malpractice. Pablo expects a trial award of $100,000 if he wins. Suppose that Pablo and Doris each must decide whether to hire an expensive medical expert. Expected litigation costs without the expert are $20,000 and expected litigation costs with the expert are $45,000. Suppose that if neither party hires an expert, the chance of success is 50%. If both hire experts, the experts cancel one another out, so the likelihood of success remains at 50%. But if one party hires an expert and the other does not, the party with the expert gets a substantial advantage and his chance of winning improves to 70%. The following summarizes these assumptions:

PABLO AND DORIS LITIGATION INVESTMENT EXAMPLE

w = \$100,000 c^H (with an expert) = \$45,000
c^L (without an expert) = \$20,000

―――

	0.5	If neither Pablo nor Doris hires an expert
$p\pi$ =	0.7	If Pablo hires an expert and Doris does not
	0.3	If Pablo does not hire an expert and Doris does
	0.5	If Pablo and Doris both hire experts

―――

The following are the payoff matrices[51] for the American and British Rules (assuming the loser pays all the expert-related fees and costs under the British Rule). Pablo's expected value is in the upper left corner of each cell and Doris's expected value is

51. Recall from Section 2.2.1, *supra*, that a payoff matrix is a way of representing each party's expected value from each combination of possible strategies. Here there are two strategies—hire an expert or don't hire an expert—and therefore each payoff matrix shows the expected trial value for each side corresponding to each of the four possible combinations of the two strategies.

in the lower right corner (negative numbers indicate losses):

AMERICAN RULE

DORIS

		Expert	No Expert
PABLO	Expert	$5,000 − $95,000	$25,000 − $90,000
	No Expert	$10,000 − $75,000	$30,000 − $70,000

BRITISH RULE

DORIS

		Expert	No Expert
PABLO	Expert	$5,000 − $95,000	$50,500 − $115,500
	No Expert	− $15,500, − $49,500	$30,000 − $70,000

By inspecting each matrix, it is easy to see what the parties will do. Under the American Rule, each side is better off not hiring an expert, no matter what the other side does. For example, if Doris hires an expert, Pablo gets $10,000 when he does not hire an expert versus only $5000 when he does. And if Doris does not hire an expert, Pablo gets $30,000 when he also does not hire an expert versus only $25,000 when he does. The same situation holds for Doris. Therefore, neither party hires an expert.

However, switching to the British Rule creates the opposite result. Each side is better off hiring an expert, no matter what the other side does. For example, if Doris hires an expert, Pablo gets $5000 when he also hires an expert, versus losing $15,500 when he does not. And if Doris does not hire an expert, Pablo gets $50,500 when he hires an expert, versus only $30,000 when he does not. The same situation holds for Doris. Therefore, both parties hire experts even though the experts are expensive and cancel one another out.

The reason for the different results is quite simple. An expert does not make enough of a difference to likely success to justify the cost if, as under the American Rule, the hiring party must bear the full expense, win or lose. However, an expert does make enough of a difference to justify the cost if, as under the British Rule, the hiring party can force the other side to pay if he wins. This makes it tempting to deviate from the cooperative outcome, which drives the parties to the perverse equilibrium.

This simple example illustrates the point. Switching to the British Rule can encourage parties to spend more on litigation even when the extra expense produces no private or public benefit. This possibility must be considered along with the other possibility that additional investment will improve outcome accuracy.

5.4 INTERACTION EFFECTS AND COMPLIANCE INCENTIVES

So far, the discussion has examined the effect that switching to the British Rule might have on three different types of litigation incentives. To recap, the British Rule is likely to increase the fraction of relatively strong cases in the population of meritorious suits actually filed—a result that has benefits as well as potential costs. The British Rule creates mixed results for frivolous litigation. It can make the situation worse when the plaintiff knows suit is frivolous and the defendant does not, but it can improve matters when the defendant knows and the plaintiff can find out by investigating before filing. As for settlement, the British Rule tends to reduce the likelihood of settlement by increasing the stakes for both sides and making trial more attractive. And the increase in stakes is likely to increase party investment in litigation and thus increase litigation costs for those cases that do not settle—an undesirable result unless greater expenditures translate into substantial gains in outcome accuracy.

However, this analysis is incomplete. For one thing, it ignores interaction effects among the different incentives. For example, if switching to the

British Rule increases litigation investment and thus litigation costs, the parties have more to save by settling, which creates a larger settlement surplus. In some cases, this effect will create a settlement range where none exists under the American Rule and thus make settlement possible. In other cases, it will simply enlarge the surplus and invite hard bargaining that reduces the likelihood of settlement.

Furthermore, our analysis has yet to consider the effect of the British Rule on incentives to comply with the substantive law. Compliance incentives are important in their own right and also important for their contribution to interaction effects. Indeed, compliance incentives are intimately wrapped up with filing and settlement incentives. A comprehensive analysis of the British Rule must treat these incentives in a single model that allows each to interact with the others. Any such model is far too complex to discuss here, but it is possible to describe what happens intuitively.[52]

The first step is to recognize that the background rate of compliance affects the estimate of likely success when the plaintiff does not know for sure

52. The following discussion is based on the work of Professor Keith Hylton, who has constructed a model of competing attorney's fee rules that allows for interaction among different incentives. *See* Keith N. Hylton, *Litigation Cost Allocation Rules and Compliance with the Negligence Standard*, 22 J. LEG. STUD. 457 (1993); Keith N. Hylton, *Fee Shifting and Incentives to Comply with the Law*, 46 VAND. L. REV. 1069 (1993); Keith N. Hylton, *An Asymmetric Information Model of Litigation*, 22 INT'L. REV. L. & ECON. 153 (2002).

whether the particular defendant in his case has complied with the substantive law. For example, if most injuries are the result of noncompliance, then an injured plaintiff can be reasonably sure that the particular defendant who caused his injury did not comply and is therefore liable. As a result, the plaintiff will estimate a high probability of success. More generally, the higher the rate of noncompliance in the background population, the more likely it is that a particular defendant has not complied and the higher will be plaintiff's estimate of likely success at trial.

Suppose that the rate of noncompliance in the background population is high under the American Rule. Plaintiffs will estimate a high probability of success and conclude that their cases are strong. Since the British Rule encourages the filing of strong cases, switching to the British Rule should result in more suits being filed. When more suits are filed, more wrongdoers pay for the injuries they cause, so parties should have stronger incentives to comply with the substantive law. Thus, the compliance rate should increase. But a higher compliance rate reduces plaintiff's estimate of likely success and thus reduces the filing rate. Compliance rate and filing rate should adjust back and forth in response to one another until an equilibrium is reached. In the resulting equilibrium, both compliance and filing rates should be higher under the British Rule than they were under the American Rule.

The final step is to see how an increase in compliance rate affects the settlement rate. This is the most complicated part of the analysis. A higher compliance rate means more defendants are innocent. But with more innocent defendants in the lawsuit mix, guilty defendants have a better chance of hiding among the innocent and thus a stronger incentive to pool, that is, to pretend they are innocent in order to trick an uninformed plaintiff. (For a description of pooling, see Section 1.2.3.2.3 of Chapter One.) Plaintiffs know this, so they refuse to settle some of the time in order to penalize guilty defendants and discourage the pooling strategy. But refusing to settle forces guilty defendants to trial and reduces the settlement rate. Thus, switching to the British Rule is likely to reduce the settlement rate in this model by increasing the stakes for both sides (as we saw in previous sections) *and* also by increasing the fraction of defendants who are innocent and exacerbating the perverse results of pooling.

The following box sketches this sequence of logical steps, which is triggered by switching from the American Rule to the British Rule, assuming an initially high rate of noncompliance under the American Rule ("A.R." is American Rule and "B.R." is British Rule):

High rate of noncompliance under A.R. ⇒
High estimate of probability of success ⇒
More suits filed when switch to B.R. ⇒
More compliance ⇒ More innocent defendants
⇒ Fewer settlements and higher costs

Thus, the British Rule has the advantage of increasing the compliance rate but the disadvantage of increasing litigation costs by increasing the filing rate and reducing the settlement rate. Whether the net result is an improvement over the American Rule depends on the magnitude of the positive compliance effect, the benefits of greater compliance compared to the litigation costs, and the amount of the increase in process costs under the British Rule when more suits reach trial.[53]

53. In fact, Professor Hylton has argued in published writing that a one-way fee shifting rule that shifts fees in favor of a winning plaintiff but not a winning defendant is superior to both the American and the British Rules. And in another article that uses a slightly different model, Professor Hylton suggests that the British Rule might be the best option in the end. However, none of these analyses considers process costs or effects on frivolous litigation.

Different results obtain when the noncompliance rate starts out low under the American Rule and also when the informational asymmetry is different. For example, when the noncompliance rate starts out low, plaintiffs tend to perceive their cases as weak and therefore are less inclined to file under the British Rule. This reduces the compliance rate, reduces the number of suits that are filed, and increases the fraction of guilty defendants in the lawsuit mix.

5.5 THE LESSONS OF CHAPTER FIVE

To recap, we saw how to pull together the different strands of positive and normative analysis to evaluate a complex procedural issue; in this case, the choice between the American and British rules on attorney's fees. We saw how to use the positive models to predict the impact on four incentives: **filing, settlement, investment,** and **compliance.** We also saw how to plug the positive results into the error and process cost framework. Finally, we saw the importance of considering **interactions** among the different incentives. These interactions can alter the normative results in significant ways.

As for an assessment of the British Rule, the rule has positive and negative effects. On the positive side, it might reduce the cost of frivolous suits when the defendant has private information about the merits, encourage the filing of relatively strong meritorious suits, and sometimes improve compliance incentives. At the same time, it is likely to exacerbate frivolous suit problems when the plaintiff has private information, deter the filing of meritorious suits (and, with risk-aversion, even strong suits), reduce the frequency of settlement, and increase process costs by requiring fee-request hearings in all cases that do not settle.

This is typical of the results usually obtained with an economic analysis. Any proposal is likely to have costs and benefits and those costs and benefits are likely to vary with the type of case. As a result, it usually requires more precise empirical information to say with confidence whether a proposal should be implemented. This is certainly true for the British Rule.

Still, the analysis is useful for a number of reasons. First, it reinforces the importance of taking a skeptical view of any simple argument for a procedural reform; litigation is too complex a strategic environment for simple arguments to carry much weight. Second, the analysis provides a framework for thinking about procedural problems, a framework that can process empirical information as it becomes available and generate more refined predictions and better recommendations. Third, the analysis helps to identify variables and causal relationships that are difficult to discover in other ways. Finally, the analysis supports a concrete recommendation similar to the one for pleading rules. The case for the British Rule varies so much with the particular features of different types of cases that it should be implemented, if at all, only in a substance-specific way.[54] This conclusion challenges the

54. For example, medical malpractice litigation might be a good candidate for the British Rule if frivolous suit problems are as rampant as some believe and settlement is not too seriously impaired. These cases have some of the structural features, such as privately informed defendants and a plaintiff's bar with the ability to spread risks through diversification, that suggest gains from switching to the British Rule. On the other hand, civil rights cases would not be good candidates if the civil rights bar tends to be risk-averse. So long as the costs of sorting individual cases to determine the applicability of the British Rule are not too high, targeting is likely to be superior to a uniform approach.

traditional preference for trans-substantive procedural rules; that is, rules that apply to all cases
regardless of substantive differences.

CHAPTER SIX:

THE LIMITS OF NORMATIVE ECONOMICS

CONCEPTS AND TOOLS

- Fairness versus Economic Efficiency
- Process-Based Fairness
  - Psychological Theories
  - Dignitary Theory
- Outcome-Based Fairness

Normative economics focuses on maximizing social welfare. This is not necessarily the only goal that should count in designing a procedural system. Many people argue that fairness values should have weight independent of economic efficiency, citing the long tradition in American civil adjudication of valuing procedural rights. This chapter describes the main features of fairness theories in the procedure literature. The discussion is brief, consistent with the book's focus on law-and-economics. Still, it is important to have at least a general understanding of how economics fits into the broader normative landscape.

6.1 FAIRNESS VERSUS EFFICIENCY

It is customary in the legal and philosophical literature to contrast fairness and rights theories with efficiency and utilitarianism. The general idea is that society must be concerned not only with how everyone fares in the aggregate—the focus of economic efficiency, welfare economics, and utilitarianism more generally. Society must also be concerned with how each person fares individually, such as whether his rights are respected or whether he is treated equally in the distribution of social goods.

For example, an egalitarian might invoke fairness to object to an unequal distribution on the ground that the distribution is unjust even if it increases total social wealth in the long run by allocating larger shares to more productive individuals. So too, a libertarian might object to a government policy of wiretapping on the ground that it violates a right of privacy even if the wiretapping also clearly increases aggregate utility by deterring crime at little cost.

As these examples indicate, the distinctive feature of a fairness theory is that it limits, constrains, or trumps social decisions aimed at maximizing aggregate welfare. One important type of fairness theory has to do with protecting individual rights. To recognize a "right" is to guarantee its holder certain benefits or treatment even when doing so produces a net reduction in aggregate welfare. For instance, the First Amendment's right to freedom of speech guarantees an opportunity to speak even when the content of the speech is so distasteful to others that it creates high social costs and reduces aggregate utility. In such a case, a political majority voting its own self-interest could easily pass legislation that bars the speaker from speaking, but the First Amendment right trumps majority will.

6.2 THEORIES OF PROCEDURAL FAIRNESS

Theories of procedural fairness and procedural rights fall into two broad categories: process-based and outcome-based. Process-based theories evaluate fairness by the way procedure treats litigants within the litigation process itself, independent of outcome quality. Outcome-based theories evaluate fairness by the quality of the outcomes a procedural system generates.

For example, most people condemn the use of torture to extract evidence not only on the ground that the evidence might be unreliable (outcome-based), but also—and more importantly—on the ground that torture is offensive to human dignity even when it produces perfectly good results (process-based). For a less dramatic example, consider the debate over limiting the scope of discovery. One might argue that narrow discovery rules impede a litigant's ability to obtain a fair outcome (outcome-based), or one might argue that they violate a litigant's right to a day in court by constraining his ability to participate fully in the litigation (process-based).

6.2.1 Process–Based Theories

6.2.1.1 Psychological

One rather popular version of process-based theory relies on a body of work in empirical psychology known as "procedural justice."[55] Most of this literature involves experiments that show that litigants are more likely to be satisfied with an adverse outcome and think the process fair if they have a chance to participate personally and "tell their story" to the decisionmaker. Extrapolating from these empirical results, some procedure scholars defend broad litigant rights to participate in and control litigation on the ground that these rights are necessary to assure feelings of just treatment.[56]

There are several problems with this psychological theory. Perhaps the most serious is that it seems unable to ward off utilitarianism.[57] If feelings are

55. *See, e.g.,* E. Allan Lind & Tom R. Tyler, THE SOCIAL PSYCHOLOGY OF PROCEDURAL JUSTICE 26–40, 61–83, 93–127 (1988) (collecting these studies).

56. Even the United States Supreme Court has endorsed this view. *See* Carey v. Piphus, 435 U.S. 247, 260–61 (1978) (describing process-based value in terms of avoiding feelings of unjust treatment).

57. Another problem is that in real lawsuits, unlike the procedural justice experiments, parties do not actually control the litigation; their lawyers do. Indeed, the client seldom keeps track of what is going on except when an important substantive decision must be made, such as whether to accept a proposed settlement. Because of this, it is questionable how much psychological value parties actually glean from the litigation process

what matters, then we must consider the feelings people have about schools, roads, public utilities, and all other social goods. But when we count *everyone's* feelings about *everything* on an equal basis, it is not clear how we can justify insulating procedural policy from ordinary utilitarian trade-offs. In other words, for a theory to be about procedural fairness, it must offer a reason to assign procedure special weight in the social calculus capable of trumping other social goods. It is not clear that a psychological theory can supply such a reason.

6.2.1.2 Normative

There is, however, a normative version of process-based theory: the dignitary theory of participation based on a Kantian ideal of respect for persons.[58] According to this theory, certain elements of civil process, such as individual participation and rational decisionmaking, are implicit in what it means to respect human dignity. For example, binding a party to an adverse judgment without giving him a

itself. *See, e.g.,* David Rosenberg, *Of End Games and Openings in Mass Tort Cases: Lessons from a Special Master,* 69 B.U. L. Rev. 695, 701–03 (1989).

58. *See* Jerry L. Mashaw, Due Process in the Administrative State 158–253 (1985); Laurence H. Tribe, American Constitutional Law §§ 10–6, 10–7 (2d ed. 1988); *see generally* Robert G. Bone, *Rethinking the "Day in Court" Ideal and Nonparty Preclusion,* 67 N.Y.U. L. Rev. 193, 264–79 (1992). For a somewhat different approach that links adjudicative participation rights to intrinsic and instrumental theories of democratic legitimacy, *see* Christopher J. Peters, *Adjudication as Representation,* 97 Colum. L Rev. 312 (1997).

chance to participate is wrong on this view because it fails to accord the party the respect he is due as an autonomous person. And it is wrong even if it means that the party can relitigate issues that have already been vigorously litigated by others and even if, as in a mass tort, relitigation creates huge social costs without equally large social benefits.

There are objections to the dignitary theory. One objection has to do with its broad potential reach. Society does not value litigant control so highly that it is willing to tolerate enormous costs to guarantee it. Yet it is not clear how to extract limits from the concept of human dignity, or how to take social costs into account when the theory is supposed to trump aggregate cost concerns.

In addition, some critics object that honoring participation rights on dignitary grounds can create perverse results by making everyone worse off.[59] For example, there are cases in which all parties would be better off (in terms of utility) if they could agree in advance to limit discovery because limits reduce the expected cost of future litigation and free up resources that can then be used to improve party welfare. However, parties often have difficulty agreeing in advance because of high transaction costs. Under these circumstances, a procedural rule that limits discovery can substitute for an agreement. Therefore, insisting on a strong dignitary

59. For an argument and examples of how procedural fairness theories not based on party welfare, like the dignitary theory, can end up reducing the welfare of all litigants, *see* Louis Kaplow & Steven Shavell, *Fairness versus Welfare*, 114 Harv. L. Rev. 961, 1188–1225 (2001).

right to broad discovery ends up making all parties worse off in the name of respecting their dignity, a result that is hard to justify on fairness grounds.

Finally, some critics wonder whether process-based theories are even coherent. The problem has to do with the fact that adjudication is primarily about producing good outcomes, not about giving people a chance to participate or another opportunity in their lives to exercise autonomous choice. Given this, the question is why adjudication should value individual participation for its own sake. The standard answer is that participation is necessary to institutional legitimacy. But this answer simply invites more questions. Why is outcome quality itself not sufficient for legitimacy? Why does it not respect persons sufficiently to satisfy the Kantian ideal that each is given an opportunity to obtain a fair outcome? A right to participate and control litigation choices might be justified as instrumental to fair outcomes, but this would be an outcome-based, not a process-based theory.

6.2.2   Outcome–Based Theories

Outcome-based theories evaluate the fairness of procedure by the quality of the outcomes it produces. Any theory of this sort needs a definition of the relevant outcome and a metric for evaluating outcome quality. It is customary to define the relevant outcome as the final decision or settlement and to measure its quality by its accuracy, that is, the extent to which it reflects an accurate application of relevant law to the facts of the case. This does not mean that there must be a uniquely correct outcome; accuracy can be defined as any result that falls within a range of equally acceptable outcomes.[60] If outcome accuracy is the measure, however, then outcome-based fairness must be a function of the risk of error that a given set of procedures creates. The challenge for an outcome-based theory is to explain how procedural fairness is related to error risk.

It is worth noting at the outset that it is not enough to condemn a procedure as unfair just because a party receives less or has to pay more with it than without it. Being made worse off is *unfair* only when a party has a right or other moral claim to be treated better. For example, an argument that contrasts a litigant's prospects under limited procedure with his prospects in an individual suit assumes that the individual suit is the normatively appropriate baseline for evaluating fairness. But it is the appropriate baseline only if the procedural treatment it affords is the kind of treatment that a litigant is entitled to receive.

Nor does it make sense to condemn a procedural system as unfair simply because it produces errone-

60.   For example, the accuracy metric fits at least one view of common law decisionmaking. In a common law system, the quality of outcomes is not simply a matter of how well they fit precedent. Quality is also judged by how well the decision advances the policies of the law. Nevertheless, so long as it is possible to criticize a decision as wrong, the set of acceptable outcomes must be bounded and those boundaries can be used to define accuracy. However, if there is radical disagreement about what constitutes an acceptable decision, then it might be impossible to settle on boundaries and impossible to define accuracy.

ous outcomes. Such a position is tantamount to giving each party a right to a perfectly accurate outcome. But then no procedural system could ever be fair because perfect accuracy is impossible to achieve. It simply makes no sense to evaluate the fairness of a human institution by a standard that the institution can *never* satisfy.

A more realistic possibility is to define fairness in terms of maximum feasible accuracy where feasibility depends on what human beings are capable of doing, given cognitive and other natural human limitations. Procedures that create error would be fair in this view, but only if it was not possible to reduce the error by any known means. Although this standard is more realistic, it is still too demanding and does not fit conventional understandings of procedural fairness. The fact is that it is always possible to reduce the risk of error by adding more procedure.[61] Therefore, defining fairness as maximum feasible accuracy would demand, in the name of fairness, an unlimited investment in procedure, with potentially devastating consequences for other worthwhile social programs.[62]

Thus, any sensible theory of procedural fairness must incorporate cost-based limits and allow trade-

61. For example, the more times a case is relitigated, the smaller the risk of error if one takes the average (i.e., the mean of the distribution) or the most commonly occurring result (i.e., the mode of the distribution). Therefore, a right to maximum feasible accuracy would in theory give parties a right to relitigate indefinitely despite the high social costs.

62. Recall that satisfying the demands of fairness is supposed to take priority over promoting social welfare in the aggregate.

offs between outcome accuracy and other social goods. As it turns out, this is difficult to do without compromising the theory's utility-trumping character. One approach, due to Professor Ronald Dworkin, defines procedural rights in terms of distributive fairness.[63] His idea is to recognize a right not to a particular level of error risk, but rather to procedures that distribute the risk of error fairly among different cases and litigants. For Professor Dworkin, a fair distribution is one that reflects the relative moral importance of the underlying substantive interests at stake.

For example, suppose that the legal system places a much higher value on protecting freedom of speech than on compensating for minor property damage. An error risk as high as 40% in free speech cases might be fair if property damage cases had an error risk of 70%, but it would be unfair if property damage cases had an error risk of only 2%. The 40%/70% comparison roughly corresponds to the relative degree of moral harm from erroneous decisions (much higher for free speech claims than for property damage claims), but the 40%/2% comparison does not.

Professor Dworkin's theory, like all the others, is vulnerable to a number of criticisms. But this is not the place to discuss these issues in detail. The important point is that there are normative theories of procedure that sound in fairness and that seek to avoid the aggregative metric of welfare economics.

63. *See* Ronald Dworkin, *Principle, Policy, Procedure, in* A MATTER OF PRINCIPLE 72 (1985).

Any proper evaluation of a procedural system must take these alternative views into account.

*

Part Three:

ADDITIONAL APPLICATIONS

Parts One and Two outlined the general framework of positive and normative economics as it applies to the procedure field. The discussion introduced the basic tools and concepts and showed how to use them to solve two empirical puzzles—the puzzle of frivolous litigation and the puzzle of settlement—and to analyze two normative questions—whether to switch from notice to strict pleading and whether to adopt the British Rule on attorney's fees.

In Part Three, we take a look at some other areas of procedural law. The analysis applies the concepts and tools that have already been developed and introduces some new ideas along the way. The purpose is not to furnish a comprehensive analysis; each topic would require a book of its own. The purpose is to show the way economists think about a range of different issues. The interested reader can use the sources cited to read in greater depth.

CHAPTER SEVEN:

DISCOVERY

CONCEPTS AND TOOLS

- Voluntary Disclosure Incentives and Unraveling Effects
- Excessive Discovery and External Costs
- Abusive Discovery and the Prisoner's Dilemma
- Mandatory Disclosure

Since the mid–1970s, critics of the litigation system have focused on discovery abuse as a major cause of the system's woes.[1] They complain about lawyers engaging in excessive discovery and serving burdensome document requests and noticing large numbers of depositions just to wear down opponents and pressure favorable settlements. Anecdotal and survey evidence provides some support for these complaints.[2] When asked, many lawyers can

1. For an historical account of the efforts to contain discovery since the mid–1970s, *see* Richard L. Marcus, *Discovery Containment Redux*, 39 B.C. L. Rev. 747 (1998).

2. *See* Linda S. Mullenix, *Discovery in Disarray: The Pervasive Myth of Pervasive Discovery Abuse and the Consequences for Unfounded Rulemaking*, 46 Stan. L. Rev. 1393, 1432–42 (1994).

cite examples of extreme abuse (always perpetrated by others, of course), and judges express concern that discovery is out of control.[3] However, the results of more rigorous empirical studies are less alarming.[4] They suggest that parties engage in relatively low or only moderate levels of discovery in most cases.[5] The most serious problems appear to be confined to large and complex cases with high stakes and numerous opportunities for strategic maneuvering.

The broad discovery that is commonplace today is in fact a relatively recent procedural innovation, first introduced on a national scale for the federal courts by the Federal Rules of Civil Procedure in

3. *See, e.g.,* Frank H. Easterbrook, *Discovery as Abuse*, 69 B.U. L. REV. 635, 636 (1989) (noting that discovery abuse is common).

4. One must be careful about inferring conclusions from empirical studies because discovery problems can affect the data in ways that hide the existence of a problem. For example, suppose that discovery was out of control in a certain set of cases. Each side could credibly threaten to impose high discovery costs on his opponent and as a result both sides would have an interest in settling prior to discovery to avoid these costs. If settlement were common enough, then a sample of cases might reflect very little actual discovery, but only because of the discovery problem (which would be manifest in socially undesirable settlements distorted by the discovery threat).

5. *See, e.g.,* James S. Kakalik et al, DISCOVERY MANAGEMENT: FURTHER ANALYSIS OF THE CIVIL JUSTICE REFORM ACT EVALUATION DATA, xx (RAND Institute for Civil Justice 1998); Mullenix, *supra* note 2, at 1432–42; Thomas E. Willging et al, *An Empirical Study of Discovery and Disclosure Practice Under the 1993 Federal Rule Amendments*, 39 B.C. L. REV. 525 (1998).

1938.[6] During most of the nineteenth and early twentieth centuries, discovery opportunities were limited.[7] In addition, many countries of the world offer much less in the way of discovery than the United States.[8]

All of this has led many to question whether broad discovery is really such a good idea after all and whether a more limited regime might achieve a reasonable level of information disclosure and exchange at lower cost. The following discussion examines what an economic analysis can offer to a better understanding of these questions.

6. *See generally* Stephen Subrin, *Fishing Expeditions Allowed: The Historical Background of the 1938 Federal Discovery Rules*, 39 B.C. L. REV. 691 (1998). Even after the Federal Rules of Civil Procedure went into effect, not all states were willing to follow the federal lead and adopt a broad discovery regime for their state courts. *See* Robert G. Bone, *Procedural Reform in a Local Context: The Massachusetts Supreme Judicial Court and the Federal Rule Model*, in THE HISTORY OF THE LAW IN MASSACHUSETTS: THE SUPREME JUDICIAL COURT 1692–1992, at 393 (1992) (describing resistance to the federal rule model in Massachusetts and the intense opposition to oral depositions).

7. For a brief summary of the history of discovery, *see* Jack H. Friedenthal, Mary Kay Kane & Arthur R. Miller, Civil Procedure § 7.1 (3rd ed. 1999). In most actions at law, for example, parties could obtain almost nothing by way of discovery directly from the law court aside from what was in the pleadings. Instead, they had to file a bill of discovery in equity, and the discovery opportunities available to them were much more limited than they are today. *See id.* at 386.

8. *See e.g.* Vincent Mercier & Drake D. McKenney, *Obtaining Evidence in France for Use in United States Litigation*, 2 TUL. J. INT'L & COMP. L. 91, 94–96 (1994) (noting that discovery in France is severely limited in comparison to the United States).

7.1 OVERVIEW

The purpose of formal discovery is to force reluctant opponents to disclose information and evidence relevant to a case. The standard rationale assumes that the parties, the judicial system, and the society at large all benefit from disclosure. The parties benefit because discovery makes it possible to litigate cases more fully and obtain more accurate results and because it reduces informational asymmetry and makes settlement easier to reach. The judicial system benefits by producing more accurate decisions and better settlements with a more complete factual record, and by saving litigation costs with a higher settlement rate. And society benefits by realizing deterrence gains from greater outcome accuracy and reduced process costs with a higher settlement rate.

At the same time, discovery generates costs of its own; not only the costs of promulgating and responding to discovery requests, but also the administrative costs of judicially resolving discovery disputes and the strategic costs associated with parties using discovery for purposes other than legitimate fact-finding. From an economic perspective, the case for formal discovery depends on whether the benefits exceed the costs.

7.2 THE BENEFITS OF FORMAL DISCOVERY

Let us begin by taking a closer look at the benefit side of this balance. The crucial question for the economist is not how much social benefit a litigation system with formal discovery creates, but how much *more* social benefit it adds compared to a system without discovery. The answer to this question requires an analysis of information-sharing incentives in the absence of discovery, and that analysis draws on the tools of positive economics.

At first glance, one might think that parties would have no reason to share information with their adversaries if they were not forced to do so. If this were true, hardly any information would be exchanged; cases would be decided on impoverished factual records, and settlements would be difficult to reach. In fact, however, there are many reasons for parties to share information voluntarily.

7.2.1 Disclosure of Favorable Evidence

Law-and-economics scholars have studied disclosure incentives rather extensively.[9] One result is obvious. Parties tend to disclose information that is favorable to their side. In litigation, this disclosure is likely to happen early because of the advantages for settlement. When the defendant discloses favorable information, a rational plaintiff should revise

---

9. *See, e.g.,* Steven Shavell, *Sharing of Information Prior to Settlement or Litigation*, 20 RAND J. Econ. 183 (1989).

her estimate of likely success downward and reduce her demand. Similarly, when the plaintiff discloses favorable information, a rational defendant should revise his estimate of *plaintiff's* likely success upward and increase his offer.

There are exceptions. Sometimes parties are better off not disclosing early, such as when they perceive a large benefit from limiting their opponent's time to respond. Also, the beneficial effects of voluntary disclosure depend on the disclosure being truthful. But disclosing parties have incentives to misrepresent that they have favorable evidence when they do not. The receiving party might be able to catch some of these misrepresentations by reviewing documentary or other tangible evidence and interviewing witnesses identified by the disclosing party. Yet verification is not always possible. Given this, the recipient will to some extent discount the truth of the information disclosed, which should dampen disclosure incentives.

In addition, the argument for voluntary disclosure turns on the recipient processing the information and altering his probability estimates in a rational and accurate way. However, we saw in Chapter Three that the self-serving bias leads parties to interpret new information in ways that reinforce preconceived notions. This means that the recipient of a disclosure might interpret it more favorably than is perfectly rational, in which case disclosures will have a weaker impact and the incentives to make them will be reduced.

Nevertheless, these factors do not have equal force in all circumstances, and settlement benefits are likely to be strong in many cases. Therefore, one would expect a good deal of voluntary disclosure of evidence favorable to the disclosing party's case.

7.2.2 Disclosure of Unfavorable Evidence

It also turns out that there are incentives to disclose unfavorable evidence. This follows from a well-known result in game theory, called the **unraveling effect**.[10] The intuition is simple. A party will reveal unfavorable information when he benefits from showing that he is not as bad as others might think he is. For example, if two people are arrested for a robbery and killing, the driver of the get-away car might confess to the robbery in order to persuade the police that he was not directly involved in the killing.

To see how this result applies to litigation, suppose that Pablo sues his doctor, Doris Delano, for malpractice. Doris has most of the evidence bearing on liability, so Pablo is uncertain about the strength of his case. Suppose that, in general, medical malpractice cases fall into five different categories, depending on their strength. Category 1 includes cases in which the evidence for liability is so weak that the plaintiff has only a 10% chance of success. Category 2 includes cases where the evidence is slightly stronger and plaintiff has a 30% chance of

10. For an application of the unraveling effect to information disclosure in litigation, *see* Bruce L. Hay, *Civil Discovery: Its Effects and Optimal Scope*, 23 J. LEGAL STUD. 481, 484–94 (1994).

success. Category 3 includes cases with a 50% chance; Category 4 a 70% chance, and Category 5 a 90% chance. Suppose that the number of cases in each category is the same. Given these assumptions, Pablo, if he knows nothing about what Doris did, will calculate an average over all the possible categories and estimate a 50% likelihood of success.[11]

Doris knows that Pablo will do this. So if Doris has evidence showing that Pablo's case is in fact weaker than 50%—in other words, that it belongs to Category 1 or Category 2—she should reveal that evidence in order to correct Pablo's misperception and obtain a more favorable settlement. Pablo knows that Doris will do this, however, so if he hears nothing, he will conclude that his case is not a Category 1 or 2 case and must therefore belong to Category 3, 4, or 5. Knowing this, he will recalculate his likelihood of success by taking an average over these three categories and arrive at an estimate of 70%.[12]

But then the same chain of reasoning applies again. Doris knows that Pablo will recalculate, so she has an incentive to disclose any information that shows Pablo's case really belongs to Category 3 (i.e., 50%). Therefore, if Pablo hears nothing, he will conclude that his is not a Category 3 case and so belongs to Category 4 or 5. He then will recalculate his estimate by taking an average over those two categories and arrive at 80%. But then Doris will reveal information that puts the case in Catego-

11. $(0.1 + 0.3 + 0.5 + 0.7 + 0.9) \div 5 = 0.50$.
12. $(0.5 + 0.7 + 0.9) \div 3 = 0.70$.

ry 4 (i.e., 70%). So if Pablo hears nothing, he will conclude he has a Category 5 case. Thus, all the categories unravel and Pablo learns the strength of Doris's case.

The same incentives work the other way around—to induce disclosure of private information by plaintiffs. Thus, when the unraveling effect works perfectly, all parties reveal unfavorable as well as favorable evidence in order to avoid being treated as if their cases were worse than they actually are. However, the unraveling effect does not work perfectly in practice. For one thing, its efficacy depends on the truthfulness of disclosures, yet disclosing parties have incentives to misrepresent the strength of their case. The recipient should be able to catch these misrepresentations sometimes but not always. Furthermore, the unraveling effect is limited by high litigation costs, interpretive difficulties, and other factors. Still, these limitations are not likely to undermine the unraveling effect completely, so it is reasonable to suppose that at least some damaging evidence will be disclosed in a wide range of cases.

One qualification is critical, however. The unraveling effect works only if the uninformed party—Pablo in our example—at least knows enough about the existence of the information and its value to be able to make a credible threat to subpoena it at trial. Otherwise, there is no reason for parties like Doris to disclose, because there is no way for the information to affect the trial result. This observation supports an important conclusion. Given that parties have incentives to disclose both favorable evidence and unfavorable evidence that they believe will come out at trial anyway, then formal discovery might be most useful as a tool for eliciting *unfavorable* evidence that would *never* come out at trial.[13] This additional evidence has social value insofar as it improves the accuracy of trial outcomes and the quality of settlements negotiated in light of those outcomes.

7.2.3 Settlement Effects

7.2.3.1 Settlement Frequency

Voluntary disclosure of evidence *favorable* to the discloser should improve settlement prospects in cases of mutual optimism, which are the most difficult to settle under the American Rule, because favorable evidence makes opponents more pessimistic.[14] However, voluntary disclosure of evidence *unfavorable* to the discloser has the opposite effect: it makes each side more optimistic, which makes settlement less likely. Therefore, the net effect of relying on voluntary disclosure depends on the mix of favorable and unfavorable evidence that is actually disclosed. At the extreme, if *all* information is

13. Evidence might not come out at trial because one side does not know enough to be aware of its existence and therefore does not request it and the other side has no interest in disclosing it.

14. In Chapter Two, we saw that mutual optimism often eliminates a settlement range: plaintiff demands a high settlement, but defendant is willing to offer only a low amount. Bilateral disclosure of favorable information reduces each side's optimism and thus makes it more likely that a settlement range will exist.

disclosed voluntarily, then rational parties should arrive at the same estimates and be able to settle the case.

How does formal discovery affect these results? The answer is that discovery can increase or reduce the settlement rate, depending on the mix of information that would be disclosed voluntarily in its absence. Suppose, for example, that there is no unraveling in a case, so parties voluntarily disclose only information favorable to their own side. These voluntary disclosures make the opposing party more pessimistic about its success and therefore reduce mutual optimism and make settlement more likely. Adding formal discovery to this picture gives the parties a tool to elicit unfavorable information as well, which might reduce the chance of settlement by increasing both parties' optimism about their own success.[15]

7.2.3.2 Settlement Quality

At least theoretically, formal discovery has a clear benefit for the quality of settlements. Settlements based on a full factual record are more likely to reflect accurate trial outcomes and correspond more closely to the substantive law. This conclusion assumes, however, that discovery actually takes place and settlements are negotiated in light of the information it reveals. But this is not necessarily so. In fact, offering formal discovery increases the costs of

15. *See* Robert D. Cooter & Daniel L. Rubinfeld, *An Economic Model of Legal Discovery*, 23 J. LEGAL STUD. 435 (1994).

litigation and makes early settlement even more attractive to the parties.[16]

To evaluate formal discovery's impact on settlement quality, therefore, we must consider two countervailing factors: discovery facilitates information exchange, which benefits settlement, but it also increases incentives to settle before the discovery takes place.[17] The second effect undermines the benefits of the first. The net result is likely to be some improvement in settlement quality, but not nearly as much as one might expect.

Let us examine this point more closely. The first thing to note is that the availability of formal discovery can improve settlement quality even if it is never actually used. This is so because parties settle in light of expectations about possible discovery results. The second thing to note is that when settlements occur before discovery takes place, the beneficial effect is muted significantly because parties can only guess at what discovery would reveal. These two points together predict some, but still limited, benefits for settlement quality.

To illustrate, suppose the defendant has unfavorable information that will not come out at trial unless discovery is available. In the absence of discovery, neither party has any reason to consider that information when estimating probabilities since there is no way it can affect the trial outcome.

16. These costs can get very large if parties anticipate excessive or abusive discovery.

17. Professor Bruce Hay considers this effect in his discovery article. *See* Hay, *supra* note 10.

Formal discovery changes this picture significantly. When the defendant knows that the plaintiff will learn the information through discovery, the defendant will consider the effect of that information at trial and increase her maximum offer to reflect the higher probability of a trial loss. The plaintiff too will consider the evidence, though in a different way. Unlike the defendant, he does not know what, if anything, actually exists. But he does know in general the range of damaging evidence discovery reveals in similar cases. So he can calculate an expectation for his case. As a result, he will raise his minimum demand to reflect the average value of the kind of evidence discovery typically reveals in the average case.

Therefore, both plaintiff's minimum demand and defendant's maximum offer will increase as compared to the situation without formal discovery. This means that the settlement range should shift upward and the resulting settlement should be closer to the substantive ideal of an expected trial award based on full information.[18]

18. The defendant is likely to increase his maximum offer more than the plaintiff increases his minimum demand, a result that will increase the settlement range and thus the likelihood of settlement absent aggressive bargaining. To see why, consider the defendant's incentives if her evidence is less damaging than the plaintiff's average probability estimate. In that case, the defendant will make a point of revealing her evidence before or during settlement discussions in order to get the plaintiff to revise his estimate downward. Therefore, whatever evidence remains concealed must be evidence that is more damaging than the average estimate used by the plaintiff.

Even so, the positive effect on settlement is limited. Because the plaintiff does not know the damaging evidence that exists in his case, he does not know that the defendant's reservation price is as high as it actually is. Therefore, he will be reluctant to push for a settlement amount any higher than what he believes to be the defendant's maximum offer without the information. Of course, if the plaintiff happens to insist on a settlement above this point but below defendant's true maximum, the defendant might eventually capitulate (perhaps to plaintiff's surprise). But the defendant has a strong incentive to pretend that any such settlement is way out of the settlement range.[19] Furthermore, the plaintiff's minimum demand with discovery will reflect only an average over all similar cases. Therefore, depending on how strong the concealed evidence actually is in plaintiff's case compared to the average case, plaintiff's adjustment might be smaller (or larger) than it would be if plaintiff actually conducted the discovery and obtained the information.[20]

19. This discussion ignores the possibility that the defendant will tip the plaintiff off to the existence of the damaging evidence during settlement negotiations.

20. For a concrete example, consider the Pablo and Doris hypothetical. First suppose there is no discovery. Pablo and Doris believe that Pablo has a 60% chance of success at trial; the expected trial award is $100,000, and expected litigation costs are $20,000 for each side. Pablo's expected value of going to trial is $0.6 \times 100,000 - 20,000 = \$40,000$, and Doris's expected loss is $0.6 \times 100,000 + 20,000 = \$80,000$. If the parties settle and they have equal bargaining, the probable settlement is $60,000. Now suppose that there is formal discovery and the parties negotiate a settlement before discovery takes place. Suppose that for an additional cost of $4000 to each side, Pablo could learn damaging

The basic point is simple. When parties settle before discovery, they settle in light of expectations about possible discovery results. If one of the parties does not know for sure what discovery will reveal, that party will be at a disadvantage in settlement negotiations, and that disadvantage will be reflected in the settlement. Thus, the availability of discovery improves pre-discovery settlements, but the prospect of settlement still reduces the information-revealing benefits of discovery.[21]

evidence in Doris's possession that would increase Pablo's chance of success to 80%. Doris knows this because she knows exactly how valuable the information is, but Pablo does not know that there is any damaging evidence at all. Nevertheless, Pablo estimates, based on his experience with similar cases, that defendants in malpractice cases conceal damaging evidence that, when revealed, improves the probability of success, on average, by an increment of 5%. As a result, Pablo estimates his likelihood of success at 60% + 5% = 65%. Since Pablo can credibly threaten to do the discovery if the parties do not settle, both parties will negotiate on the assumption that if they do not settle, discovery will actually take place. This means that Pablo will calculate his minimum demand to be $0.65 \times 100,000 - 24,000 = \$41,000$, and Doris will calculate her maximum offer to be $0.8 \times 100,000 + 24,000 = \$104,000$. With equal bargaining power, they will now settle for $72,500, which is $12,500 more than they would settle for without the availability of discovery and closer to but still short of the ideal expected trial outcome of $80,000.

21. The literature includes a number of more sophisticated game-theoretic models of discovery, some of which examine the interaction with settlement. *See, e.g.,* Joel Sobel, *An Analysis of Discovery Rules*, 52 LAW & CONTEMP. PROBS. 133 (1989); Joel L. Schrag, *Managerial Judges: An Economic Analysis of the Judicial Management of Legal Discovery*, 30 RAND J. ECON. 305 (1999).

7.2.4 Summary

In sum, it is not clear how much benefit a system of formal discovery adds to litigation. Even without discovery, parties have incentives to exchange some information voluntarily. Discovery reveals more information, especially information that otherwise would not come out at trial. This improves the accuracy of trial outcomes, but its impact on settlement is more uncertain. Discovery might increase or reduce the frequency of settlements, depending on the voluntary-disclosure baseline. Its availability should enhance settlement quality, but by how much depends on how often cases settle and how much additional pressure discovery creates.

7.3 THE COSTS OF FORMAL DISCOVERY

Discovery is costly even when it is used properly, and much more costly when it is used excessively or abused.[22] Still, these costs must be evaluated in perspective, and two general points are worth mentioning in this regard.

First, discovery costs must be viewed from the perspective of settlement as well as trial. As we saw above, parties have substantial incentives to settle before discovery or at least before a lot of costly

---

22. In one empirical study based on lawyer surveys, attorneys reported that discovery costs consume approximately 50% of total litigation costs. *See* Thomas E. Willging et al., DISCOVERY AND DISCLOSURE PRACTICE, PROBLEMS, AND PROPOSALS FOR CHANGE 15 (Federal Judicial Center 1997).

discovery takes place. Pre-discovery settlement avoids the process costs of discovery and focuses more attention on the error costs created by strategic discovery threats. Moreover, even when parties routinely use discovery, the additional discovery costs have to be compared to the savings in trial costs if discovery corrects for divergent expectations and increases the likelihood of settlement.

Second, whatever litigation costs a discovery system creates must be compared to the additional costs of party investigation in the absence of discovery. This is particularly important because, without formal discovery, parties might resort to sophisticated methods to gain access to secrets. Anticipating this, the potential targets would invest in precautions to prevent disclosure, which might then elicit a counter-response in the form of even more sophisticated measures to circumvent the precautions—and so on, as one side escalates and the other responds in kind. Discovery offers an alternative to this wasteful "arms race" and thus helps reduce its costs.[23]

With these considerations in mind, let us consider the two major complaints about discovery costs: that parties use discovery excessively, and that they use it abusively as a strategic weapon to force settlements.

23. At the same time discovery creates a different sort of "arms race" of its own. Parties often withhold information under claims of privilege, which can elicit tit-for-tat responses and an escalating litigation battle over motions to compel and motions for contempt.

7.3.1 Excessive Discovery

In economic terms, an additional investment in discovery is "excessive" whenever the social costs of the investment exceed the social benefits. It is easy to see why parties engage in excessive discovery (defined in this way). The reason is that the party promulgating the discovery request does not bear the full costs and, in particular, does not have to pay an opponent's response costs. Thus, parties engage in excessive discovery for the same reason firms pollute excessively: they are able to **externalize** a portion of the cost.

To illustrate, suppose a plaintiff is considering whether to take an additional deposition in a case with an expected trial award of $200,000. The deposition will cost each side $8000, and plaintiff expects it to yield evidence that would boost his likelihood of trial success by a 5% increment. On these assumptions, the plaintiff will take the deposition. The benefit to him is a gain in expected trial value of $10,000 (i.e., $0.05 \times 200,000 = $10,000$), and the cost is only $8000.

Now assume that the *social* benefit of the deposition is the same as the private benefit to the plaintiff: namely, a gain in expected trial value of $10,000. It is easy to see that taking the deposition is excessive from a social point of view. The total social cost of the deposition includes both the plaintiff's *and* the defendant's costs (ignoring the public cost of subsidizing the court system), which equals $16,000. Thus, cost exceeds benefit from a social point of view. The reason the plaintiff takes the deposition is that he pays only one-half of the total cost (his $8000 and not defendant's $8000).

Some commentators treat discovery as excessive whenever it goes beyond the break-even point where the total cost to the parties of an additional increment just begins to exceed the trial value.[24] There is a problem with this definition, however. The social benefit from additional discovery is not the same thing as the trial value to the parties; rather, it includes the deterrence gains to everyone made possible by a more accurate outcome. Therefore, additional discovery that is excessive in terms of trial value might not be excessive in terms of total deterrence benefits.[25] (On the other hand, a definition stated in terms of deterrence would be difficult to implement practically. It is hard to imagine how judges would go about estimating the social benefits from additional deterrence in the context of a specific case.)

Cost-externalization is not the only reason for excessive discovery. Agency problems also contribute. Suppose, for example, that clients have difficulty monitoring their attorneys, who as a result have considerable freedom to pursue their own self-interest. If the arrangement is fee-for-services, the attorney is prone to engage in excessive discovery in order to pad fees. We discussed this agency problem

24. *See* Cooter & Rubinfeld, *supra* note 15.

25. *See* Hay, *supra* note 10. As well as whatever additional deterrence benefits result from defendant's anticipating higher litigation costs.

in Section 2.4, where we examined its impact on settlement incentives. The same point applies to excessive discovery.

7.3.2 Abusive Discovery

"Abusive discovery" refers to discovery practices aimed at imposing costs on the other side and leveraging a favorable settlement. In this connection, it is useful to distinguish between "informational value" and "impositional value."[26] Discovery is abusive insofar as it is used, at least in part, for its impositional value, whatever informational value it might also possess.

7.3.2.1 Abuse by the Requesting Party

To illustrate one kind of abusive strategy, consider the following scenario. Suppose a plaintiff is deciding whether to serve an additional request for documents that the plaintiff expects will uncover nothing of informational value but will impose costs on the defendant. Suppose that the plaintiff must spend $1000 to prepare and serve the request and the defendant must spend $10,000 to respond. Suppose that both parties believe that plaintiff has a 60% chance of success, the expected trial award is $500,000, and litigation costs without the additional discovery are $50,000 for each side. The following summarizes these assumed facts:

26. *See* John K. Setear, *The Barrister and the Bomb: The Dynamics of Cooperation, Nuclear Deterrence, and Discovery Abuse*, 69 B.U. L. REV. 569, 581 (1989) (referring to these as "informational benefits" and "impositional benefits").

Abusive Discovery Example

p=0.6   w=$500,000

Plaintiff's cost of promulgating = $1000
Defendant's cost of responding = $10,000
Remaining litigation costs per party = $50,000

If the plaintiff does not serve the document request, her minimum demand is 0.6 × 500,000 − 50,000 = $250,000, and defendant's maximum offer is 0.6 × 500,000 + 50,000 = $350,000. Therefore, assuming equal bargaining power, the parties should split the surplus evenly and settle for $300,000.

The settlement picture changes if plaintiff serves the document request and the defendant believes the plaintiff will actually enforce it. Under these circumstances, the defendant will increase his maximum offer by $10,000, the expected cost of responding to the request. The new settlement range is between $250,000 and $360,000. Assuming equal bargaining power, the predicted settlement is now $305,000. Thus, plaintiff pays $1000 for preparing and serving a document request and gets $5000 in return, for a net gain of $4000—all by threatening discovery with no informational value.

The key to plaintiff's success in this example is the asymmetry of discovery costs. The plaintiff is able to leverage an advantage because she can threaten to impose much greater costs on the defendant than it costs her to make the threat. The defendant might simply refuse to respond in the hope that plaintiff will back down rather than follow through with enforcement. But this strategy is likely to backfire when the plaintiff anticipates future litigation and has something to gain by developing a reputation as an aggressive enforcer of discovery requests.

This example highlights the different social costs that abusive discovery creates. The plaintiff incurs the cost of preparing and filing the discovery request.[27] More significantly, settlements end up skewed in favor of the party with the discovery cost advantage and this creates error costs. (In a more complete analysis, we might denominate errors in plaintiff's favor as "false positives" and errors in defendant's favor as "false negatives.") Finally, in order for the plaintiff to make a credible threat, the defendant must actually believe that the plaintiff will follow through and pursue the discovery if the parties fail to settle. But for defendants to believe this, plaintiffs must actually enforce their requests in those cases where settlement negotiations fail.

7.3.2.2 Abuse by the Responding Party

It is also possible for a responding party to use abusive tactics. He can simply refuse to comply or

---

27. Plaintiff's threat alone might be sufficient, but defendant is likely to wait for a formal request to be served because the formal request bolsters the credibility of the threat and also provides a clearer basis for estimating response costs.

comply only partially in order to make the other side invest in enforcement. So long as the cost to the responding party of resisting is less than the cost to the requesting party of enforcing, the responding party has a cost advantage that he can use to leverage a better settlement.

Indeed, this possibility creates a Prisoners' Dilemma, in which both parties withhold information from one another and both invest in motions to compel.[28] In Chapter Two and again in Chapter Five, we saw the effect of the Prisoners' Dilemma Game. The players are driven to a noncooperative equilibrium that makes them both worse off, because neither can trust the other to stick with a promise to cooperate. In the discovery situation, cooperation involves fully disclosing information in response to a discovery request. Neither side cooperates because it is too tempting to defect and too disastrous to be the only one who cooperates.

To illustrate, suppose that the plaintiff and the defendant serve discovery requests on each other in a case with $400,000 at stake, a probability of success of 50%, and $40,000 in litigation costs for each side unrelated to discovery. Suppose as well that if a party withholds, it costs each side $4000 to litigate a motion to compel and that these motions succeed in obtaining disclosure 80% of the time (in other words, courts make mistakes and deny the motions 20% of the time). Finally, suppose that the

28. *See, e.g.,* Ronald J. Gilson & Robert H. Mnookin, *Disputing Through Agents: Cooperation and Conflict Between Lawyers in Litigation,* 94 COLUM. L. REV. 509, 514–15 (1994).

withheld information, if known by the other side, would increase the other side's likelihood of success by an increment of 10%.

On these assumptions, it is rational for each side to enforce a discovery request if the other side withholds.[29] Given that the parties will enforce their discovery requests, the payoff matrix is as follows (the plaintiff's expected gain is in the upper left corner of each cell and the defendant's expected loss, with a negative sign to show it is a loss, is in the lower right corner):[30]

29. Since the information increases the probability of obtaining the $400,000 trial award by 10%, its expected trial value is $0.1 \times 400,000 = \$40,000$. And since there is an 80% chance of success on a motion to compel, the expected gain from enforcing the discovery request is $32,000—in other words, 0.8 (the chance of compelling disclosure) $\times$ 40,000 (the value of the information if disclosed) = $32,000—which is much greater than the enforcement cost of $4000.

30. The payoffs are calculated in the same way as in Chapter Two. For example, if both parties disclose (the upper left hand cell of the matrix), then the probability of success remains at 50% because each side's information offsets the other side's. Therefore, plaintiff's expected gain from trial is $0.5 \times 400,000 - 40,000 = \$160,000$, and defendant's expected loss is $0.5 \times 400,000 + 40,000 = \$240,000$. If both parties withhold, then both parties will spend $4000 to enforce their requests and end up symmetrically advantaged and disadvantaged. Once again, the advantages and disadvantages offset one another, so the parties remain with a 50% chance of success. Therefore, plaintiff's expected trial gain is reduced and defendant's expected loss is increased by $8000, the extra cost each party incurs in enforcing his own request and countering his opponent's.

DEFENDANT

		Disclose	Withhold
PLAINTIFF	Disclose	$160,000 − $240,000	$148,000 − $236,000
	Withhold	$164,000 − $252,000	$152,000 − $248,000

By inspecting the payoffs, it is easy to see that each party is better off withholding no matter what the other party does. Therefore, both parties will withhold in equilibrium even though each would be better off if he could commit to disclosure. As is typical of a Prisoners' Dilemma, the parties are forced into the perverse equilibrium by fear of being the only one to disclose and ending up a "sucker" and by the irresistible temptation to "sucker" their opponent should he decide to cooperate.[31]

31. Moreover, there is a chance that only one side will succeed in compelling disclosure, in which case the trial outcome will be distorted by the asymmetric result. In the text example, the probability that plaintiff succeeds is 0.8, and the probability that defendant fails is 0.2, so the probability of both is 0.8 × 0.2 = 0.16. Since the situation is symmetric, the probability that defendant succeeds and plaintiff fails is also 0.16. Therefore, the total probability of a distorted outcome is 0.32. In other words, the trial result will deviate from the full information outcome roughly one-third of the time.

7.4 DISCOVERY REFORMS

The following discussion briefly examines three proposals to deal with discovery costs: mandatory disclosure, discovery limits, and cost-shifting.

7.4.1 Mandatory Disclosure

"Mandatory disclosure" requires parties at the outset of a lawsuit to exchange certain core information "voluntarily," that is, without formal requests. The idea is to supplement regular discovery with a preliminary exchange that (hopefully) reduces the need to use formal requests later on. For example, Rule 26(c)(1) of the Federal Rules of Civil Procedure requires that parties exchange the names of witnesses and provide copies or descriptions of documents at the beginning of the suit, and Rules 26(g)(3) and 37(c)(1) impose sanctions for failing to comply. The parties are free to make use of formal discovery tools after the initial disclosure phase is completed. While the federal rule limits mandatory disclosure to favorable evidence—that is, witnesses and documents that "the disclosing party may use to support its claims or defenses"—there is no reason why a rule could not cover unfavorable evidence as well.

Supporters of mandatory disclosure argue that it will increase the likelihood of early settlement.[32] The argument is strongest for an approach, like the

32. They also argue that the "voluntary" nature of mandatory disclosure nurtures a cooperative spirit from the outset, which promotes cooperation at later stages, reduces the abuse of formal

one embodied in Rule 26, that limits the disclosure obligation to favorable evidence. As we noted previously, the exchange of evidence favorable to the disclosing party tends to counteract mutual optimism by making the parties more pessimistic about their own success. However, it is not clear how much mandatory disclosure is needed to achieve this result. To be sure, a disclosure obligation might accelerate the exchange of information in those few cases where parties have strong reasons to delay, but in most cases favorable information will be disclosed early without the pressure of discovery rules.

Mandatory disclosure could be expanded to require exchange of unfavorable as well as favorable evidence. When *all* evidence is disclosed, the parties' estimates should come closer together, making settlement more likely and driving the settlement amount closer to the full information outcome. There is a problem, however. This happy result obtains only when the parties fully comply with their mandatory disclosure obligations. But there is no reason to believe they will fully comply any more than they already do with formal discovery. In other words, parties willing to abuse formal discovery should be willing to abuse mandatory disclosure as well.[33]

discovery, and facilitates settlement bargaining. Critics question how realistic this claim is, given the adversary nature of litigation, the numerous opportunities for conflict, and the availability of traditional discovery later in the suit.

33. In one study of mandatory disclosure, 37% of attorneys surveyed reported problems and 19% cited the source of the

Furthermore, whatever positive effect mandatory disclosure has in aligning party estimates of case strength is offset to some extent by its negative effect in reducing the size of the settlement surplus through the sunk-cost effect. When settlement negotiations take place after mandatory disclosure, the disclosures in effect reduce the size of the surplus by reducing the need to resort to formal discovery later on. With less need for formal discovery, parties expect to spend less on the litigation and therefore have less to save by settling. In general, a reduction in the size of the settlement surplus reduces the frequency of settlement.

There are other potential problems as well. Parties have incentives to over-comply with mandatory disclosure by providing a lot of irrelevant information mixed in with relevant material. This strategy forces the opposing party to separate the wheat from the chaff and increases his costs. Moreover, mandatory disclosure does nothing to cure the problem of excessive discovery because it does nothing to force the requesting party to pay the costs he externalizes. And when parties have access to traditional discovery tools, the opportunity to engage in discovery abuse remains strong. Thus, the case for mandatory disclosure does not seem terribly persuasive from an economic point of view.[34]

problem as incomplete disclosure. *See, e.g.,* Willging et al, DISCOVERY AND DISCLOSURE, *supra* note 22, at 6. However, the same study reported a correlation between mandatory disclosure and reduced time to disposition, although not reduced costs.

34. Mandatory disclosure might have benefits for relatively small cases that present little need for discovery in any event.

7.4.2 Discovery Limits

A second reform proposal involves limiting the scope of formal discovery. One way to do this is to limit the kind of information that can be discovered, such as allowing discovery of only directly relevant evidence. Another way is to put upper limits on the use of specific discovery tools. As an example, Rule 30 of the Federal Rules of Civil Procedure limits each party to ten depositions.

One problem with strict limits is that they are insensitive to the specific discovery needs of particular cases. When the case is complicated, the amount at stake is large, and there is a great deal of valuable information, the efficient level of discovery can end up exceeding the limit.[35] For this reason, discovery limits are usually presumptive rather than strict; parties can exceed the limit with the court's approval. However, making limits presumptive undermines their ability to reduce costs and control strategic abuse. When the additional information is valuable enough, parties will seek court permission to exceed the limits, triggering a poten-

The lawyers in such cases might be happy to exchange evidence without having to draft discovery requests. But these are not the cases with serious discovery problems. Indeed, the Federal Judicial Center study surveying lawyers, *see id.*, reported that most attorneys were reasonably satisfied with mandatory disclosure and that the bulk of the problems occurred in high stakes, complex cases.

35. For example, if the defendant has much more information than the plaintiff, a strict discovery limit is likely to increase the error risk for large and complex cases and thus produce error costs.

tially costly battle over exceptions.[36]

Furthermore, presumptive limits create new opportunities for strategic abuse. A party wishing to impose costs on his opponent can engage in discovery up to the presumptive limit and then threaten to drag the opponent through a costly adversarial battle for judicial permission to exceed the limit. Depending on how costs are distributed between the parties, this strategy could reproduce some of the same settlement problems that formal discovery creates.

From an economic perspective, the challenge is to design a system of limits that strikes the best balance between the benefit of reducing discovery excess and abuse and the cost of depriving parties of valuable information. Strict limits increase the benefit but also increase the cost. Allowing exceptions reduces the cost but also undermines the benefit.

7.4.3 Cost Shifting

The third proposal is to shift response costs to the requesting party.[37] The justification for this approach is straightforward. If parties have incentives

36. To decide whether an exception is justified, judges must determine the value of the additional discovery, but verifying that value is bound to be difficult in the absence of precise knowledge of what the discovery will reveal. If judges respond to this uncertainty by erring in the direction of granting exceptions, then parties will have even stronger incentives to seek exceptions in the first place.

37. For a discussion of this proposal and the switching point idea, *see* Cooter & Rubinfeld, *supra* note 15; Daniel L. Rubinfeld, "Discovery" *in* 1 THE NEW PALGRAVE DICTIONARY OF ECONOMICS AND THE LAW 609, 612–14 (Peter Newman, ed. 1998).

to engage in excessive discovery because they can externalize some of the cost, then the obvious solution is to make them pay for that cost. Just as nuisance law deters pollution by forcing the polluter to internalize pollution costs, so too a cost-shifting rule deters excessive discovery by forcing a requesting party to internalize discovery costs.[38] Moreover, cost-internalization is likely to have a salutary effect not only on excessive discovery but also on some types of abusive discovery. For example, a strategy of threatening discovery for its impositional value backfires when the abuser must pay the additional costs it threatens to create.

One problem with this proposal is that it gives responding parties an incentive to inflate response costs in order to shift more costs to the requesting party and deter discovery requests. As a result, courts will have to review expense claims to make sure they are reasonable and this will increase process costs.

There is an even more serious problem. If information is asymmetrically distributed between the parties, the party with the greater need for information will make more use of discovery and incur higher costs than his opponent under a cost-shifting rule. The resulting asymmetry is likely to skew

38. Recall the example in which a deposition with an expected trial value of $10,000 cost each side $8000. The deposing party will take the deposition if all he has to pay is his own costs, but he will not do so if he also must pay the defendant's response costs.

settlements in favor of the party with the cost advantage.[39]

Supporters propose to handle this problem by creating a switching point where liability for response costs switches back to the responding party. The idea is to choose the switching point so discovery costs end up equally distributed between the two sides. The requesting party pays all costs up to the switching point, and, beyond that point, the responding party pays its own response costs. There are complications defining the switching point and controlling for strategic abuse, but supporters of cost-shifting claim that these complications can be addressed.[40]

39. To illustrate, suppose the plaintiff expects to spend $55,000 and the defendant expects to spend $5000 on discovery necessary to disclose all information. Suppose each side estimates the plaintiff's likely success at 50%, the expected trial award at $200,000, and the rest of the trial costs at $20,000 each. Plaintiff's minimum demand is $25,000 and defendant's maximum offer is $125,000. With equal bargaining power, the parties will settle at $75,000, which, if 50% is also the full information estimate, is $25,000 less than the ideal outcome.

40. Also, the additional cost of conducting discovery up to the switching point might discourage plaintiffs from filing low-probability suits. This could be a problem for areas of litigation such as civil rights where low-probability suits can have substantial social value. One way to handle this problem is to exempt these categories of litigation from the rule.

CHAPTER EIGHT:

PRECLUSION

```
┌─────────────────────────────────────────┐
│                                         │
│          CONCEPTS AND TOOLS             │
│                                         │
│     • Claim Preclusion                  │
│         · Error Costs                   │
│         · Transaction Costs             │
│     • Issue Preclusion                  │
│         · Nonmutual                     │
│         · Nonparty                      │
│                                         │
└─────────────────────────────────────────┘
```

The law of preclusion deals with the effects that a judgment in one suit has on future litigation.[41] It has two branches: claim preclusion and issue preclusion. Claim preclusion (also known as "merger and bar" or "res judicata") prevents a party from suing twice for the same transaction or occurrence, even if she modifies her legal theory and seeks different remedies the second time around. For example, a plaintiff who sues her doctor for negli-

---

41. For a good discussion of the legal framework and some of the historical background of preclusion law, *see* Professor David Shapiro's volume for this series. David L. Shapiro, PRECLUSION IN CIVIL ACTIONS (Foundation Press 2001).

gence in surgery and loses cannot turn around and file a second suit for breach of contract seeking relief for the same surgical procedure. Even if she wins her negligence suit, claim preclusion still prevents her from suing again to recover more.

The second branch, issue preclusion (also known as "collateral estoppel"), prevents relitigation of identical issues in different suits. For example, if the defendant loses against one plaintiff on the general causation issue in a products liability suit, future plaintiffs can bind the defendant to the adverse determination.

Whereas claim preclusion bars litigation of new legal theories and prayers for relief that were never actually litigated but should have been, issue preclusion bars litigation of issues only if they have already been litigated and decided. This difference follows from the different functions of the two doctrines. The function of claim preclusion is to encourage plaintiffs to bring all related legal theories and factual matters in a single suit, while the function of issue preclusion is to prevent relitigation of identical issues.

According to the standard account, the values served by preclusion include judicial economy, repose, and decisional consistency. Preventing the splitting up of suits and the relitigation of issues saves litigation resources. It also allows parties to rely on a single adjudication to resolve a matter once and for all and in this way furthers the repose values of predictability and certainty. And by preventing relitigation of the same dispute or issue, preclusion reduces the costs of decisional inconsistency.

There are a number of exceptions to preclusion. One of the most important is the rule of nonparty preclusion, which holds that persons who were not parties or in privity with parties to the first suit are not precluded. The idea of "privity" is not clearly defined. Examples of cases in which nonparties are bound include those in which the nonparty actually controls the first suit and those in which the nonparty is a member of a properly certified class action or is otherwise represented by a party to the first suit. This is not the place to describe these rules in detail.[42] The important point is that nonparties are precluded only in exceptional cases. For example, in a mass tort case, each of tens of thousands of injured parties can relitigate all the common issues (such as general causation or defendant's knowledge) in their separate suits because none is in privity with any other (assuming no class action). Each has a right to her own personal "day in court," so it is said, and this right guarantees an individual opportunity to control the litigation choices that affect the common issues.

This chapter first examines claim preclusion from an economic perspective and then turns to issue preclusion. The discussion of issue preclusion focuses on two important doctrines: nonmutual issue preclusion and nonparty preclusion.

42. For a more detailed account of the rules, *see id*. at 74–118.

8.1 THE ECONOMICS OF CLAIM PRECLUSION

8.1.1 Benefits of Claim Preclusion

The standard account of the policies served by claim preclusion—judicial economy, repose, and decisional consistency—assumes that parties would relitigate the same dispute over and over again if preclusion law did not prevent them. But this is highly unlikely. Parties faced with the risk of costly relitigation are likely to settle and, as part of the settlement, agree not to sue again.[43]

To see this point more clearly, imagine a procedural system with no claim preclusion rules. A losing plaintiff is allowed to bring the exact same lawsuit over again, and a losing defendant is allowed to initiate a second lawsuit to set aside the judgment and obtain a declaration of nonliability.[44] Assume, for simplicity, that all the suits are mutually independent, so the outcome in one does not affect any of the others (this is obviously somewhat unrealistic in a system of *stare decisis*).[45] To make

43. The following discussion relies heavily on the work of Professor Bruce Hay. *See* Bruce Hay, *Some Settlement Effects of Preclusion*, 1993 U. ILL. L. REV. 21, 24–41.

44. Each party must have the ability to relitigate; otherwise, the party without the ability would be at a considerable disadvantage and systematically suffer inadequate outcomes.

45. The example also assumes that parties do not revise their estimates of likely success based on information learned in previous suits. While unrealistic, the assumption is unrealistic in the right way—it makes it harder to argue against the need for

matters more concrete, suppose Doris Delano, a surgeon, operated on Pablo Prentice, and Pablo believes that his paralyzed leg is due to Doris's negligence. Pablo files suit against Doris seeking damages for medical malpractice.

Both Pablo and Doris know that whoever loses the first suit can sue again, and whoever loses the second suit can sue yet again—and so on indefinitely. If Pablo is willing to sue once, he should be willing to sue again, and if Doris is willing to litigate once, she should be willing to litigate again. But if each party anticipates repeated rounds of litigation, then both parties should anticipate high litigation costs, and the expected burden should create enormous pressure to settle the first suit and agree not to initiate any future litigation. The agreement not to sue in effect creates a private law of claim preclusion.

To illustrate, suppose Pablo's probability of success is 60% and the expected trial award is $200,000. Also suppose that in each round of litigation, the parties expect to spend $20,000 in litigation costs.[46] Pablo and Doris know that if Pablo

formal preclusion rules. If a party who lost a previous round revised its estimate of success downward for a subsequent round, that party would be less inclined to relitigate. Ignoring this possibility therefore makes the strongest case for formal preclusion rules.

46. This assumption is somewhat unrealistic. One would expect litigation costs to be less in the second round because a lot of the discovery and investigative work would already have been done in the first round. However, these cost savings simply make

loses the first suit, he will sue again, since his expected value from bringing the second suit is the same as the first (i.e., $0.6 \times 200{,}000 - 20{,}000 = \$100{,}000$). If Doris loses the first suit, she will also sue again, since her chance of winning the second suit and therefore not having to pay the $200,000 judgment is 40%, so her potential gain is $80,000, compared to a litigation cost of $20,000. Therefore, Pablo and Doris anticipate that if they do not settle the first suit, they will spend $20,000 on that suit and another $20,000 litigating a second round. By settling in the first round, they each save $40,000 in litigation costs, for a total saving and thus a surplus of $80,000.[47]

One can repeat this logic over and over again for third, fourth, and later rounds. Each round would add $20,000 more to litigation costs. But if the litigation could proceed indefinitely, then Pablo would never sue because he could never be confident that he would actually obtain any relief. In fact, however, the outcome is more complicated because the interaction is a strategic game. What each party will do in the first round depends on what he thinks his opponent will do in future rounds, knowing all the while that his opponent is thinking the same thing about him. In deciding on a strategy, a party does not simply assume that her opponent will relitigate indefinitely absent a settle-

relitigation more likely. And the parties still must invest in motions, follow-up discovery, pre-trial preparation, and trial.

47. The knowledgeable reader will note that I am ignoring the effects of discounting; that is, I am assuming that the discount factor is 1.

ment agreement. Instead, each side tries to predict the "staying power" of his opponent; that is, the number of rounds his opponent is willing to litigate. The party with more staying power is able to extract a favorable settlement.

The technicalities of the analysis are not important. What is important is that the parties will not relitigate indefinitely in the absence of a claim preclusion rule. The pressure to settle is too great. Settlement obstacles might frustrate agreement in the first round and the parties might end up litigating one or more rounds before succeeding with their negotiations. But the prospect of paying litigation costs in each subsequent round should apply substantial pressure toward settlement in the first round. Therefore, the case for claim preclusion must rely on something other than judicial economy, repose or decisional consistency, all of which depend on lawsuits actually being repeatedly litigated.

There are two economic arguments for adopting a formal claim preclusion rule. First, claim preclusion reduces error costs. The settlement pressure created by the relitigation threat is not always symmetrically distributed between the parties, and when it is not, the side with more leverage can obtain a settlement skewed in its favor.[48] Claim preclusion re-

48.   For example, suppose one side has enough at stake and sufficient resources to credibly threaten in round one to relitigate for ten rounds, while the other side is only able to threaten eight rounds. The party who can go ten rounds has greater staying power and thus a substantial advantage in round-one settlement negotiations.

duces this source of error by eliminating a party's ability to threaten future litigation.

The second reason for a claim preclusion rule is to save the transaction costs involved in negotiating a private preclusion arrangement. Crafting a settlement provision that effectively prevents relitigation can be a tricky matter in a judicial system without a formal preclusion law. The problem involves figuring out some way to prevent the second suit from turning into litigation over the validity of the settlement agreement. For example, if the plaintiff settles but sues again and the defendant defends with the settlement agreement, the plaintiff might respond by challenging the agreement's validity. In that event, the parties would simply end up litigating enforceability in the second suit. And if the parties entered into another settlement agreement settling the second suit, the plaintiff (or defendant) might just sue again and challenge the validity of the second settlement agreement. [49]

There are ways to minimize this risk, but all of them require careful drafting and negotiation. For example, the settlement agreement might include a requirement that each party post a bond that is forfeited if the party files a subsequent suit. The amount of the bond could be set at a level that deters subsequent filings even with a small chance that a second court might invalidate the settlement

[49] Since it is costly to sue, parties are unlikely to repeat these challenges too many times if they lose consistently. In a system of *stare decisis*, the probability of winning another challenge will diminish with the number of adverse determinations already made.

agreement. The details are not important. What is important is that a formal claim preclusion rule that substitutes for private agreement saves the costs of negotiating these complicated provisions.[50]

Transaction cost savings will be substantial, however, only if the preclusion rule matches what most parties would agree to if they actually negotiated a private preclusion clause. If the rule fits the preferences of only a few parties, then most will negotiate for something different (assuming that they are allowed to contract around the rule) and very little in the way of transaction costs will be saved. It seems reasonable, however, that parties in most cases would prefer only one round of litigation over a single dispute, so current claim preclusion rules that limit the parties to one round seem correct.[51]

In sum, none of the standard justifications for claim preclusion—judicial economy, repose, and decisional consistency—make much sense on economic grounds when settlement is part of the picture. Rather, the principal benefits of the doctrine appear to lie in error cost reduction and savings in settlement transaction costs.

50. A formal rule might also make settlement more likely by reducing the number of issues that need to be negotiated and thus the number of opportunities for conflict.

51. This is not to say that it fits party preferences in every case. For example, in a very complex case with a lot at stake and high risk of trial error, the parties might agree to litigate two rounds and accept the average of the two trial awards if there were no claim preclusion rule. The average of two awards is likely to be more accurate than a single award. If so, then the parties might bargain around a claim preclusion rule that allowed only one round of litigation.

8.1.2 The Costs of Claim Preclusion

Claim preclusion rules also generate their own costs. Enforcing the rules, through motions to dismiss and for summary judgment, requires litigation and administrative resources, which add to process costs. These costs might be greater than the costs required to enforce agreements not to relitigate in a world without claim preclusion, but they might also be less.

Furthermore, costs are affected by the scope of what is precluded. Claim preclusion rules differ according to how closely related the legal matters need be to fall within the prohibition against splitting. The current law recognizes a narrow and a broad approach.

The narrow approach requires the joinder in one suit of only those matters that involve a single "legal right." For example, a copyright owner might be able to bring a breach of contract claim against a licensee who violates the conditions of the license, and then turn around and sue again for copyright infringement if he loses. This would be possible if the claim preclusion law treated breach of contract as a different legal right than copyright infringement even when the two claims seek damages for the same acts.

The broader approach requires parties to include everything that is transactionally related in one suit. Roughly speaking, this includes all legal theories, remedies, and factual matters that involve the same transaction or series of related transactions.

On this view, the copyright owner in the previous example would have to litigate his copyright infringement claim together with his breach of contract claim.

If the parties settle the first suit, not much turns on which claim preclusion rule applies because parties are likely to settle all transactionally related matters in any event.[52] But the rule does matter if the case goes to trial. A broader preclusion rule creates more complicated lawsuits by pressuring parties to include more legal matters in one suit. In general, the more complicated the suit, the more costly the trial and the more likely a jury or judge will get confused and commit an error. These process and error costs must be compared to the benefit of avoiding duplicative litigation and redundant presentation of evidence.[53]

As it turns out, this cost-benefit balance does not always favor a broader preclusion rule over a narrower one. The reason is easy to see. Return to our copyright example and assume that the narrow rule is in force. Suppose the copyright owner brings the copyright infringement claim in the first suit. If the case goes to trial and the plaintiff wins and recovers all the relief to which he is entitled, there will be no second suit. The entire dispute is resolved in only

---

52. Although it is possible that the scope of claim preclusion might affect the likelihood of a settlement.

53. The trial judge has discretion to sever pieces of the more complex whole for separate trials if he believes that a single trial will be unmanageable or create confusion, but doing so replicates the duplicative litigation costs that a broad preclusion rule is meant to avoid.

one lawsuit and that lawsuit is simpler and less expensive than a suit with both claims tried together.[54] Therefore, duplicative litigation of common issues and redundant presentation of evidence are problems only if the plaintiff loses the first suit (and the parties do not settle the second suit). It follows that if the probability of plaintiff losing is low enough and the cost advantage of trying the claims together is not too great, a narrow preclusion rule can be better than a broad one.

This example illustrates a more general point. There is a limit to how broad a claim preclusion rule should be. In general, the optimal scope of claim preclusion depends on the likelihood of settlement, the probability of plaintiff's trial success, and the amount of the litigation cost savings from joinder.[55]

8.2 THE ECONOMICS OF ISSUE PRECLUSION

The previous analysis does not transfer readily to issue preclusion. It is possible that parties would agree in a private settlement to be bound by the

54. This result assumes that the claim brought in the first suit is capable of providing all the relief to which the plaintiff is entitled under either claim. This is a plausible assumption for many cases because the plaintiff has an incentive to bring the broader claim first.

55. An even broader rule might be justified by the social benefits of repose (predictability and certainty), but marginal repose benefits are likely to diminish with increasing scope.

determination of any factual or legal issue in the first suit. But whether they would do so depends on how much future litigation involving the same issue they anticipate. In lots of cases, parties do not expect to be involved in future litigation between them, and even when they do, they expect the litigation to involve different matters. More precisely, it is difficult to predict future disputes and the issues that are likely to arise in them. As a result, it would be hard for parties to value the gains from a private preclusion agreement and thus hard for them to agree.

Therefore, the law of issue preclusion is easier to justify than the law of claim preclusion. Formal rules save the costs of relitigation in circumstances where parties are unlikely to reach private agreements that accomplish the same result. Furthermore, any such agreement can bind only those persons who are parties to it. Therefore, formal preclusion rules are needed to extend preclusive effects to nonparties.

The following discussion focuses on two situations in which issue preclusion has been extended to nonparties: cases in which the nonparty is the person doing the precluding, and cases in which the nonparty is the person being precluded.

8.2.1   Nonparty Precluding: Nonmutual Issue Preclusion and the Mutuality Rule

Traditionally, the availability of issue preclusion was limited by the so-called "mutuality rule." The mutuality rule holds that A can use issue preclusion against B *only* if B could have used issue preclusion against A had the decision of the issue turned out the other way. In effect, mutuality requires a kind of symmetry across the party line—the person using preclusion and the person being precluded must both have faced preclusion risks from the first suit.

The mutuality rule has been heavily criticized for producing a great deal of wasteful relitigation. The federal courts and the courts of many (though not all) states have abolished the rule and allow nonmutual issue preclusion. Nonmutual preclusion can be used defensively or offensively. Defensive use involves a defendant using it to defend against a second suit. Offensive use involves a plaintiff using it to secure relief in a second suit.

For example, suppose a patent owner (P) sues an alleged infringer (D-1). Suppose D-1 wins the suit by proving that P's patent is invalid. P then sues a second infringer (D-2) and D-2 argues that P should be bound to the determination of patent invalidity. Under the mutuality rule, P would not be bound because D-2 would not have been bound had the first court decided that the patent was valid. D-2 would not have been bound because D-2 was not a party or in privity with a party to the first suit (we examine these narrow nonparty preclusion rules in Section 8.2.2, below). However, in jurisdictions that have abolished the mutuality rule, P can be bound, and D-2 can get summary judgment on the patent infringement claim. This is an example of the *defensive* use of nonmutual issue preclusion: D-2 is using preclusion to defend against P's suit.

To illustrate offensive use, consider a mass tort in which the defendant (D) sold a drug that caused widespread injury. An injured party (P–1) sues D and the jury finds that D should have warned the public of the drug's risks. A second injured party (P–2) then sues D on the same legal theory and argues the D should be bound to this determination because it had a full and fair opportunity to litigate the warning issue in P–1's suit. Under the mutuality rule, D would not be bound because P–2 would not have been bound had the jury found the other way. In those jurisdictions that have abolished mutuality, however, P–2 can preclude D on the warning issue, at least if D had reason to litigate the issue vigorously in P–1's suit and P–2 had no reason to intervene. This is an example of *offensive* use: P–2 is using preclusion to secure relief in the second suit.

The critics of mutuality claim that there is absolutely no justification for a blanket rule that tolerates costly relitigation when the party to be bound has already had a full and fair opportunity to litigate. The rest of this section examines this claim critically and asks whether there are any benefits to a mutuality rule. From an economic perspective, the mutuality rule can serve two possible functions: it can help to avoid asymmetric stakes, and it can help to control strategic abuse.

8.2.1.1 Asymmetric Stakes

Abolishing mutuality runs the risk of increasing litigation costs and producing systematic error by creating asymmetric stakes.[56] To illustrate, consider the mass tort hypothetical involving D's drug and P-1's lawsuit. Suppose that P-1 expects a trial award of $500,000 if he wins on liability, and that for P-1 to win, the jury must decide that D breached its duty to warn. Also assume that D expects another 1000 lawsuits, each seeking $500,000 in damages.

Under the mutuality rule, D does not need to worry about being bound to an adverse decision of the duty to warn issue in P-1's suit. As a result, D's stakes are the same as P-1's: D stands to lose $500,000 and no more. Compare this to the situation facing D in a litigation system that has abolished mutuality. If P-1's suit goes to trial, D has to worry not only about losing P-1's suit but also about being bound to an adverse decision in 1000 subsequent suits. P-1, on the other hand, need only worry about the $500,000 in his suit.

Therefore, nonmutual preclusion creates an asymmetry of stakes. D has much more to lose than P-1 has to gain. Since rational parties are likely to spend more on litigation the more they have at stake, D should spend more on litigating P-1's suit than P-1 does. For example, D might invest more in discovery and trial preparation, call more witnesses, hire a better lawyer, and more readily appeal an adverse result.

56. For a formal analysis of the effect of different issue preclusion rules on stakes, litigation investment, probability of success, and trial error, *see* Stephen J. Spurr, *An Economic Analysis of Collateral Estoppel*, 11 INT'L REV. L. & ECON. 48 (1991).

D's greater investment in P-1's suit increases process costs, of course, but it also has another adverse effect. It increases the risk of trial error in D's favor. In general, a party that invests more in litigation is more likely to win. It follows that when a defendant invests more than a plaintiff, the defendant's chances of winning should increase and the plaintiff's decline. Even a case that is very strong for the plaintiff on the objective merits might be difficult for the plaintiff to win because of the difference in investment incentives produced by asymmetric stakes.[57]

This hypothetical is idealized, of course. In real litigation, there are several factors that mitigate the adverse effects. For one thing, litigation investment is subject to diminishing returns. As parties invest more, the same amount of additional investment makes less of an impact on likelihood of success. As long as P-1 has serious damages, he is likely to invest a great deal in litigating the suit, and it is not clear how much of a comparative advantage D gets from investing more.

Moreover, in mass tort cases, one of the areas where the adverse effects of asymmetric stakes are likely to be very serious, it is quite common for a single lawyer or law firm to represent large numbers of similarly situated plaintiffs under contingency fee arrangements. In these circumstances, it is not just the defendant who will consider future

57. *See* Stephen J. Spurr, "Collateral Estoppel" *in* 1 THE NEW PALGRAVE DICTIONARY OF ECONOMICS AND THE LAW 289, 289–90 (Peter Newman, ed. 1998).

suits. P–1's lawyer also has something to gain from nonmutual issue preclusion if he wins on the warning issue. He can use preclusion to improve his chances of winning and getting his contingency fee in future litigation. Therefore, P–1's lawyer is likely to invest at a level that reflects the future benefit, and this will help reduce the distortion caused by asymmetric stakes.

8.2.1.2 Strategic Settlement Leveraging

The mutuality rule also helps to prevent strategic use of preclusion to leverage socially undesirable settlements.[58] The analysis in the previous section assumed that P–1's suit would go to trial. But this is unlikely. The availability of nonmutual preclusion puts the defendant under considerable pressure to settle, and this pressure can produce systematically skewed settlement outcomes.

To see this point, consider P–1's suit against D with 1000 other suits waiting in the wings. For purposes of this analysis, ignore the effects of asymmetric stakes. Assume that P–1 and all the other 1000 plaintiffs have a 60% chance of winning, an expected trial award of $200,000, and litigation costs of $20,000. With nonmutual issue preclusion, D knows that if it suffers an adverse ruling on the duty to warn issue, all subsequent plaintiffs will be able to use that decision in their suits. Let us

58. For a formal analysis of this effect, *see* Note, *Exposing the Extortion Gap: An Economic Analysis of the Rules of Collateral Estoppel*, 105 HARV. L. REV. 1940 (1992).

assume that preclusion on this issue increases the likelihood of success in later suits from 60% to 80%.

The key to the analysis is that D can escape these preclusive effects by settling P–1's suit. Settlement, after all, avoids a decision on the duty to warn issue. Given this additional benefit, D calculates its maximum settlement offer as follows. D's expected trial loss in P–1's suit is $140,000.[59] But this is not all D has to lose from going to trial. D also faces a risk of nonmutual preclusion in later suits based on an adverse decision in P–1's suit. Therefore, D should be willing to pay P–1 a premium to avoid this risk and the premium should be substantial, given the fact that there are 1000 future suits.[60] As a result, D's maximum offer will exceed $140,000 by a significant amount.[61]

On the other hand, since P–1 has only his own lawsuit to worry about, his minimum demand is $100,000.[62] Therefore, the settlement range lies be-

59. $0.6 \times 200,000 + 20,000 = \$140,000$.

60. Nonmutual issue preclusion also increases the defendant's risk at trial. If D is risk-averse, the additional risk-bearing costs will also inflate the maximum offer.

61. Because D can still be precluded by decisions in later suits, settling P–1's suit eliminates only one source of preclusive effect. This makes it difficult to calculate the precise amount of the premium. For example, suppose that access to preclusion in a later suit increases the plaintiff's likelihood of success in that suit by an increment of 20%—from 60% to 80%. If D could avoid preclusion in all 1000 future suits, D would expect to save a total of $0.2 \times 200,000 \times 1000 = \$40,000,000$. D saves part of this by settling P–1's suit, and this is what D is willing to pay as a premium.

62. $0.6 \times 200,000 - 20,000 = \$100,000$.

tween $100,000 and an amount significantly larger than $140,000. Assuming equal bargaining power, the parties will settle for much more than $120,000, the amount of the settlement in the absence of nonmutual preclusion. So P–1 reaps a windfall and the outcome ends up systematically skewed in his favor.

However, it is not just P–1 who reaps a windfall. The same reasoning applies to P–2, although the preclusion-related benefit to D from settling is less because there are only 999 suits left. Furthermore, the same reasoning applies to P–3, P–4 and all subsequent plaintiffs up to P–1000. Each plaintiff is able to leverage the risk of nonmutual issue preclusion into a windfall settlement. The amount of the advantage drops as the number of remaining suits declines. However, even P–1000 gets a benefit, since D should be willing to pay a premium to avoid the preclusive effect in P–1001's suit.[63] When all the skewed settlements are added together, the total can greatly exceed what D is supposed to pay under the substantive law.

63. This extra amount is easy to calculate in P–1000's suit. Assume that if P–1001 can use issue preclusion, his chance of success increases by an increment of 20%. If D settles P–1000's suit, D avoids the expected trial loss of $140,000 and also saves giving P–1001 an additional 20% chance if D loses P–1000's suit. Therefore, P–1000's advantage traceable to nonmutual issue preclusion is 0.6 (D's probability of losing) × 0.2 (P–1001's improved chance if D loses) × 200,000 (P–1001's expected trial award) = $24,000. So D should be willing to settle for as high as $164,000. P–1000's minimum demand is $100,000, so with equal bargaining power, the parties should settle for $132,000.

Requiring mutuality corrects for this distortion. Because the mutuality rule confines the preclusive effects of P-1's suit to that suit alone, D need not worry about future litigation and will settle P-1's suit on its own terms. The same is true for every subsequent suit; each such suit will be settled without concern about future effects. The result is a total settlement for D that comes closer to what the substantive law demands.

This analysis ignores the effect of asymmetric stakes discussed in the previous section. Asymmetric stakes give D an advantage, which counteracts to some extent the leveraging advantage of the plaintiffs.[64] Moreover, the stylized hypothetical exaggerates the actual difference between mutuality and nonmutual preclusion. Even with a mutuality rule, D must worry about *stare decisis* effects in future suits. Furthermore, by settling P-1's suit, D avoids revealing its trial strategy to P-2 and subsequent plaintiffs. Therefore, there are ways for plaintiffs to leverage a higher settlement even with a mutuality rule, but they are probably not as strong.

There is another important qualification. In real litigation, the windfall from nonmutual preclusion is likely to be much less than in our idealized

64. In fact, the precise effect is unclear. On the one hand, the fact that asymmetry of stakes reduces plaintiff's likelihood of success means that all plaintiffs receive less benefit from leveraging preclusion, so D will reduce its maximum offer. On the other hand, the fact that D invests more in the litigation if the case goes to trial means that D will increase its maximum offer. The net result is uncertain, although it seems reasonable to assume that settlements will be for less.

hypothetical. As we shall see in Chapter Nine, P–1 and the other 1000 plaintiffs in our example are likely to end up being joined together in a class action or some other aggregation and all or most of their suits resolved together. When this happens, there are many fewer sequential suits to create a preclusion risk. Furthermore, in mass tort litigation, a few attorneys tend to collect large inventories of clients and settle all the individual cases en masse. So in our example, it is very likely that large groups of plaintiffs will share the same attorney and that this attorney will settle all the suits for a total lump sum. This aggregate approach makes it much more difficult to mount a credible threat to use issue preclusion strategically.

In sum, a mutuality rule has potential benefits in reducing litigation costs and preventing systematic trial and settlement error. At the same time, mutuality creates substantial costs of its own by requiring the relitigation of issues that have already been vigorously litigated and carefully determined in previous suits. It is not possible to determine how the balance comes out without more empirical information and a more careful analysis. Furthermore, even if the balance strikes in favor of nonmutual issue preclusion, there are other potential costs that should be considered in determining the rule's scope and application.[65]

65. For example, special concerns about limiting the development of law arise when offensive issue preclusion is used against the government, concerns that convinced the United States Supreme Court to limit such use in United States v. Mendoza, 464 U.S. 154 (1984). Also, in Parklane Hosiery Co. v. Shore, 439 U.S.

8.2.2 Nonparty Precluded: The Right to a "Day in Court"

Courts feel relatively comfortable making inroads on the mutuality rule partly because the party being precluded has already had a full and fair opportunity to litigate the issue. However, courts balk at extending issue preclusion to bind parties who have not had a chance to litigate. Everyone is said to have a right to her own "day in court" and this right guarantees a personal opportunity to make one's own litigation choices. Precluding a nonparty on the basis of litigation conducted by someone else is thought to violate this right, even if the issue is identical in both suits, one of the parties to the first suit shared the same litigation goals, and the parties litigated the issue vigorously.

It is extremely difficult to justify this narrow approach to nonparty preclusion on economic grounds. If the issue was vigorously litigated and carefully decided in the first suit, there is no reason to think that relitigation will produce a more accurate result. The first decision could be erroneous, but relitigation is just as likely to introduce a new error as correct an error already made. To be sure, the nonparty would like to relitigate the issue and might even win if allowed to do so. But the fact that relitigation is good for the nonparty does not mean that it is also good for society.

322 (1979), the Supreme Court limited the use of offensive nonmutual preclusion in order to address particular strategic costs in that setting.

To see these points, consider the following hypothetical. Suppose that there are 100 lawsuits in which a purely factual issue or a mixed issue of law and fact arise. Suppose that the probability of a correct decision in any given suit is 80% and that each suit is independent of the others in the sense that a decision in one does not influence the decision in any other. Under these circumstances, the expected number of correct decisions is the same with or without nonparty preclusion. With preclusion, the chance of a correct decision in the first suit is 0.8 and that decision will then apply over all 100 suits for an expectation of 80 correct decisions (i.e., $0.8 \times 100 = 80$). Without preclusion, the issue will be relitigated in all 100 suits and each time the chance of a correct decision is 80%, for an expected total of 80 correct decisions.

Even though the expected number of correct decisions is the same, the variance of the distribution of decisions is different. In particular, a preclusion system creates higher variance by making all 100 decisions turn on the result in one case. Higher variance means greater risk, which produces more risk-bearing costs for risk-averse actors.[66] Still, at some point, the social cost of relitigation exceeds any benefit associated with risk-reduction.

66. In most situations of interest, like the mass tort, the nonparty will be a plaintiff. When the nonparty is a plaintiff, the defendant already faces high risk-bearing costs as a result of nonmutual issue preclusion, and it is not clear how much a nonparty preclusion rule adds on defendant's side. Still, nonparty preclusion might increase the risk-bearing costs of plaintiff's lawyer if the lawyer represents lots of additional plaintiffs with suits raising the same issue.

There are special circumstances that might justify a limited amount of relitigation. Sometimes in mass tort cases involving complex scientific evidence and novel issues, the evidence and argument get better over time as the science improves and lawyers learn from earlier suits. Therefore, decisions in later cases might be more accurate than decisions in earlier ones. Furthermore, if earlier decisions correlate with or influence later ones (i.e., the assumption of mutual independence is relaxed), relitigation can improve later settlements by generating a baseline of decisions to guide estimates of trial value. Especially if cases are numerous and involve high stakes, such as in mass torts, it might make sense on balance to tolerate some relitigation in return for more accurate settlements.

The main argument against broad nonparty preclusion has to do with the adverse effect of asymmetric stakes.[67] Consider a mass tort in which P–1 sues D and there are 1000 additional plaintiffs who will sue in the future. If D can bind all 1000 plaintiffs to a favorable jury determination in P–1's suit, D's stakes are much greater than P–1's. As we saw in Section 8.2.1.1, a difference in stakes is likely to produce a difference in litigation investment and an error risk skewed in the defendant's favor.

67. *See* Richard A. Posner, ECONOMIC ANALYSIS OF LAW § 21.11, at 635–37 (5th ed. 1998). Posner argues as well that when a single plaintiff precludes multiple defendants, the plaintiff can select the weakest defendant to sue first, thereby magnifying the asymmetry and exacerbating the error effects.

However, the same factors discussed in Section 8.2.1.1 should mitigate the adverse impact here as well. Plaintiffs with large damages are likely to invest at a high level anyway, and this fact limits defendant's advantage when litigation investment reaps diminishing returns. Furthermore, when a single attorney represents lots of plaintiffs on a contingency fee basis, the attorney's level of investment is also affected by the risk of preclusion in later suits, and the asymmetry is reduced.

In addition, if a system already has nonmutual preclusion, adding nonparty preclusion can help to correct some of the distortions associated with nonmutuality. Nonparty preclusion gives the defendant a reason to litigate and obtain a judicial determination, and this helps to counteract defendant's incentive under nonmutuality to avoid decision, an incentive that we saw in the previous section supports plaintiffs' strategy of settlement leveraging.

In sum, it is difficult to defend current nonparty preclusion law on economic grounds. Precluding nonparties yields such large savings in relitigation costs that its social benefits are likely to outweigh its costs, at least in those situations like mass torts where there is a huge amount of relitigation. This conclusion strongly suggests that the rationale for current rules must be based on something other than economic efficiency. As a matter of fact, those rules seem to be based on a process-oriented, rights-based theory of participation.[68] Chapter Six discussed this theory briefly. In the end, whether the theory can justify the high social costs of relitigation depends on how coherent it is and how strong a participation right it supports.

68. *See* Robert G. Bone, *Rethinking the "Day in Court" Ideal and Nonparty Preclusion*, 67 N.Y.U. L. Rev. 193, 212–32 (1992).

CHAPTER NINE:

THE CLASS ACTION

CONCEPTS AND TOOLS

- Non-cost-justified versus Cost-justified
  Individual Suits
- Free-riding
- Agency Costs
- Adverse Selection
- Collective Action Problems

The class action is a device for resolving a large number of similar claims in one proceeding. It works by allowing representative parties to litigate on behalf of a much larger group. For representatives to bring a class action in federal court, they must file a motion to certify the suit as a class action and demonstrate that all the requirements of Rule 23 of the Federal Rules of Civil Procedure are satisfied. In some types of class actions—so-called "opt out classes"—absent class members are allowed to remove themselves from the class ("opt out") and litigate on their own. In other types of class actions—so-called "mandatory classes"—no one is allowed to opt out.

The idea behind a class action is to bind the entire class to the final judgment as if each member had litigated an individual suit on his own. If a class action settles, as almost all do, the trial judge must review the settlement for fairness and reasonableness, and if the settlement is approved, all class members are bound.

The complexity of the class action stems mainly from the large number of actors involved and the wide range of strategic opportunities that the device opens up. In a large class action, there are lots of interested persons, including: (1) representative parties, (2) class attorneys, (3) absent class members with interests that may differ from one another, (4) attorneys for individual class members or groups of class members, (5) defendants, and (6) the judge. All of these persons have their own particular interests in the class action and the conflict and competition among them can produce high social costs.

The literature on the economics of the class action is extensive, and the issues addressed are complex.[69] The following discussion explores the economics in a general way, drawing on federal class action practice for concrete examples. The first sec-

69. I cite some of the important sources at various points in the following discussion. For a partial bibliography, *see* Geoffrey P. Miller, "Class Actions" *in* 1 THE NEW PALGRAVE DICTIONARY OF LAW AND ECONOMICS 257 (Peter Newman, ed. 1998). For an overview of the class action from a legal, policy, and doctrinal perspective, *see* Deborah R. Hensler et al, CLASS ACTION DILEMMAS: PURSUING PUBLIC GOALS FOR PRIVATE GAIN (RAND 2000). Also most major articles in the legal field list the primary sources in footnotes.

tion recounts the benefits of the class action, the second section describes the costs, and the third section examines some proposed reforms. A word of caution at the outset. The class action is more complex than many of the other topics addressed in this book and certainly more complicated than discovery or preclusion. Thus, it is even more necessary in this chapter than it was in the others to pitch the discussion at a relatively general level. With a general background, the interested reader should be in a good position to explore the details on his or her own.

9.1 THE BENEFITS OF THE CLASS ACTION

To identify the main benefits of the class action, it is useful to distinguish between two paradigmatic cases: class actions in which each class member has enough at stake to bring an individual suit, and class actions in which each class member has too little at stake to bring an individual suit. Many class actions are hybrids, embracing both cost-justified (i.e., positive expected value) and non-cost-justified (i.e., negative expected value) individual suits. Nevertheless, focusing on the two paradigms usefully illustrates the different reasons for class treatment.

9.1.1 The First Paradigm: Cost–Justified Individual Suits

When individual suits are cost-justified, the class action serves at least three important functions: it saves litigation costs, achieves economies of scale, and avoids serious externalities associated with individual litigation.[70] The first function is the most obvious. By adjudicating lots of otherwise separate suits in one proceeding, the class action avoids the high social costs of relitigating issues common to the different suits. To be sure, individual issues must still be adjudicated, at least if the class action fails to settle. But there is considerable benefit in being able to litigate the common issues only once, and that benefit increases with the size of the class and the number of common issues.

Second, class members enjoy economies of scale by litigating as a group. The large potential recovery in the class action can attract a better lawyer than would be interested in an individual suit and the efficiencies of group litigation make possible a higher level of investment in discovery and trial preparation. Some commentators believe that this is one of the *main* benefits of the class action for cost-justified claims.[71] They argue that individual litigation gives the defendant a substantial advantage,

70. It might serve a fourth function as well. When the federal class action rule was completely revised in 1966, subdivision 23(b)(2) was included to ensure that civil rights cases seeking injunctive and declaratory relief could proceed as class actions. In these cases, the class action not only avoids the costly scenario of different courts ordering conflicting forms of injunctive relief, but also facilitates the participation of a wide range of interested parties and makes it easier for a judge to invite outside input into the formulation of a complex decree.

71. *See* Bruce Hay & David Rosenberg, *"Sweetheart" and "Blackmail" Settlements in Class Actions: Reality and Remedy*, 75 NOTRE DAME L. REV. 1377 (2000) (hereinafter, "Hay & Rosenberg, *Sweetheart Settlements*").

which the scale economies of class action litigation help to counteract. When deciding how much to invest in litigating common questions, a rational defendant will consider its total expected loss to all plaintiffs and invest more than any single plaintiff's attorney. This argument is similar to the asymmetric stakes argument discussed in Section 8.2.1.1 of Chapter 8, and the concern is the same: when the defendant invests more, its chance of success is greater than the plaintiff's. By aggregating all the individual suits together in one proceeding, the class action helps align investment incentives and restore parity across the party line.

It is true that class members could achieve these same benefits by organizing voluntarily. However, the transaction costs of organizing a large group are simply too high. A few individuals would have to be willing to assume the burden of identifying and contacting all potential class members, explaining the plan to each of them, and obtaining their approval. The cost of doing this for a large class would be prohibitive. Thus, the class action reduces the costs of organizing the class by allowing a few individuals to bring suit on behalf of everyone else and enlisting the court's aid to protect the interests of the absentees.

The third function of the class action for cost-justified suits is to prevent serious externalities from individual litigation. To illustrate, suppose that 100,000 persons claim injuries from taking a drug manufactured by the defendant drug company (D). Each of the injured parties brings an individual suit, and each seeks $6 million in compensatory and punitive damages. Suppose each suit has a 60% chance of success. Also, suppose that D's liability insurance is capped at $50 million and its corporate assets are worth another $50 million.

The total expected liability of all 100,000 injured parties is 0.6 × 100,000 × 6 million = $360 billion. The total amount available to satisfy all the judgments is $100 million, which is nowhere near the $360 billion expected liability even allowing for individual judgments to be spaced out over time. Under these circumstances, the first few plaintiffs are likely to exhaust all the available resources, leaving the rest with nothing to satisfy their judgments.

This situation is often referred to as a "limited fund." [72] When there is a limited fund, each plaintiff imposes an external cost on other plaintiffs by increasing the risk they will recover nothing. The class action aggregates all 100,000 plaintiffs together in a single suit, eliminates the externalities, and makes it possible to distribute the limited fund equitably among all claimants.

From an economic perspective, this result has at least two benefits. First, it reduces plaintiffs' risk-bearing costs by eliminating the extremes of no

72. However, the Supreme Court, in Ortiz v. Fibreboard, 527 U.S. 815 (1999), placed restrictions on what could qualify technically as a "limited fund" supporting federal class action treatment under Rule 23(b)(1)(B), and it is not clear that my example in the text would satisfy those restrictions. Nevertheless, the "limited fund" label is still useful as a descriptive term to denote any situation in which the total amount available for satisfying judgments is inadequate.

recovery or full recovery and smoothing out the possible trial outcomes. Second, it maximizes the limited fund for distribution by reducing the amount that the defendant has to invest in defending individual suits.[73]

9.1.2 The Second Paradigm: Non–Cost–Justified Individual Suits

When class members have too little at stake to justify individual suits, the economic rationale for the class action has nothing to do with litigation cost savings or limited funds. Without a class action, there would be no individual suits and therefore no duplicative litigation and no externalities.

The reason for allowing a class action in these cases—often called a "small claim class action"—is to promote private enforcement of the substantive law.[74] What these cases—typically securities fraud, antitrust, and consumer protection suits—have in

73. There are other types of externalities as well. Consider asbestos litigation. The docket congestion created by thousands of pending asbestos cases produces extremely high delay costs for cases that happen to end up late in the trial queue, delay costs that can eat up much of the plaintiff's recovery. Under these circumstances, cases early in the trial queue in effect create delay externalities for later cases. This is one of the arguments made for aggregative treatment of asbestos cases in the form of large class actions. But courts, while receptive to the concerns, have not yet been willing to recognize this kind of externality as a reason by itself for class certification.

74. For a thorough discussion of the economics of these class actions, *see* Jonathan R. Macey & Geoffrey P. Miller, *The Plaintiffs' Attorney's Role in Class Action and Derivative Litigation: Economic Analysis and Recommendations for Reform*, 58 U. CHI.

common is a high probability that wrongful conduct will produce very small individual harms to a large number of geographically dispersed persons. For example, many, perhaps most, investor members of a securities fraud class action will have suffered only small losses when a company's stock price plummets. The same is true for consumers forced to pay inflated prices because of violations of antitrust or consumer protection laws.

The class action collects all the small claims together in a single lawsuit with a large aggregate expected recovery. This gives an attorney a strong incentive to take the case and earn a fee based on the results he achieves for the class as a whole. For example, suppose each member of a securities fraud class suffers an average loss of $100 and suppose the expected cost of litigating the securities fraud claims through trial is $1 million. Suppose as well that the likelihood of success on liability is 60%. Obviously no one in the class would bring an individual suit for $100. But if there are 100,000 class members, the expected class recovery is $6 million,[75] which is large enough to interest an attorney who expects to get, say, 20% of the total recovery (or $1.2 million) as his fee.

Individuals could accomplish the same result by organizing a group.[76] However, as noted in the

L. REV. 1 (1991) (hereinafter "Macey & Miller, *Plaintiffs' Attorney's Role*").

75. $0.6 \times 100,000 \times 100 = \$6$ million.

76. The class action is not always necessary to vindicate the interests of members of a group. For example, when a corpora-

previous section, the transaction costs are far too high to make this a feasible strategy. Moreover, there is an additional obstacle in the small claim setting: no one has enough at stake to make it personally worthwhile even to try organizing a group.

From an economic point of view, the main benefit of the small claim class action is deterrence. Without the class action, defendants could avoid paying for the harm caused by their wrongdoing whenever that harm was dispersed in small amounts over a large number of persons. The small claim class action also provides compensation to class members, but this benefit is not likely to be great, at least in economic terms, if individual losses are small. It is true that small claim class actions can include some class members with large losses; an example is a pension fund or other large institutional investor in a securities fraud class action. However, these large claimants do not need the class action to sue; they can litigate individually. And they can also achieve some economies of scale by joining together voluntarily in a single suit.

The deterrence argument for the small claim class action rests on two important assumptions. First, it assumes that statutory remedies do not already take account of the under-enforcement problem. For example, the federal antitrust statutes allow for recovery of treble damages. The effect is to

tion sues, the resulting lawsuit can be thought of as a group suit, in which the corporation as an entity seeks relief for a group consisting of its shareholders.

make more individual suits cost-justified and to multiply the deterrent impact of each suit. If the treble damage provision were intended, in part, to compensate for some degree of under-enforcement due to small claims, then using the class action to overcome the under-enforcement problem might lead to *over-enforcement* and chill socially useful activity.[77]

Second, the argument assumes that private enforcement of the substantive law is a socially desirable supplement to whatever public enforcement already exists. For example, the Securities Exchange Commission has statutory authority to sue firms for securities violations and the U.S. Attorney's Office has power to seek criminal penalties. Given these alternatives, the choice is not between private enforcement and no enforcement, but rather between private *plus* public enforcement and public enforcement alone. The usual justification for choosing private plus public enforcement has to do with resource limitations, political pressures, and other impediments to effective public enforcement and with the incentives private parties have to investigate wrongdoing and litigate vigorously.

9.2　THE COSTS OF THE CLASS ACTION

The costs of the class action include the process costs of managing and litigating a complex lawsuit

77. If, on the other hand, the treble damage provision was designed mainly to deal with the difficulty of detecting wrongdoing or some other under-enforcement problem unrelated to filing incentives, then the class action would not necessarily create a risk of over-enforcement.

and the error costs associated with adjudicating claims in a group setting. Some special features of the class action exacerbate these problems. For example, agency costs are especially severe, and many of the collective action problems familiar to economists, such as adverse selection effects, compound the error risk. In addition, the settlement pressure of a large aggregation can make frivolous litigation attractive.

9.2.1 Process Costs

Process costs include the costs of litigating and managing a class action, trying a complex case if the class action goes to trial, and negotiating and reviewing a complicated settlement if the class action settles. These costs can be substantial. For example, at the beginning of the suit, the judge must decide whether to certify a class. Certification motions are usually heavily contested because the certification decision makes a big difference for relative bargaining power at the settlement stage. In addition, for most damage class actions, class counsel must send notice to the class informing members of their right to opt out. Sending this notice is expensive and adds to the process costs of litigating the suit.

Process costs get even larger later in the litigation. If the judge certifies a class, she must find some way to coordinate multiple attorneys. In large claim class actions like those involving mass torts, it is often the case that, before certification, class members will already have retained their own attorneys and filed suit. Moreover, in small claim (and large claim) class actions, it is not uncommon for different attorneys to file overlapping class actions. Consolidating these cases into a single proceeding brings together multiple attorneys in the same litigation (in some large class actions, more than one hundred lawyers).[78] Multiple attorneys cannot all control their own litigation separately without undermining the benefits of the class action. Therefore, coordination is imperative, and it is usually achieved by creating a litigation steering committee and appointing lead counsel to be in charge. Choosing the committee and lead counsel can be a costly undertaking, depending on how it is done.[79]

Furthermore, if the class action goes to trial, the judge must manage what is bound to be a highly complex trial process, oversee distribution of any trial award, and review the fee requests of class counsel. The trial might adjudicate only the common questions or it might adjudicate common and individual questions, such as damages, in a bifurcated proceeding. It might also involve even more sophisticated trial plans with multiple phases adju-

78. Although all these attorneys may not be entitled as a legal matter to represent their clients in the class action, there is a strong incentive to include them all in order to minimize the risk that one of them will object to a class settlement down the road. *See* Sections 9.2.2.3 and 9.2.4, *infra* (discussing some of these settlement incentives).

79. Whoever is appointed lead counsel has broad control over the litigation and the allocation of work, and thus has considerable power to shape the fee award that other lawyers receive. As a result, competition for lead counsel is often quite intense.

dicating distinct sets of issues. All of this complexity adds process costs to the action.

The prospect of settlement reduces the costs of trial and sometimes even the cost of organizing a litigation committee. This is important because most class actions settle. Sometimes, class attorneys even work out a settlement with the defendants before certification, and the defendant then joins with the attorneys in asking the court to certify for the purpose of binding everyone to the settlement. (See the discussion of the settlement class in Section 9.2.4, below.)

Still, the costs of negotiating a complex class settlement can be very high. Furthermore, the trial judge must approve any settlement based on a review of its terms for fairness and reasonableness. As part of this review process, the court must hold a hearing, give notice to class members, and allow objectors to appear and present their objections. In cases involving particularly complex agreements, judges sometimes even appoint lawyers, law professors, or even other judges to assist in the review process.

In sum, the expected process costs associated with the class action are substantial. Of course, these costs must be compared to the process costs of litigating individual suits and the comparison is likely to favor the class action when the class is large and lots of common questions are involved. However, process costs are not the only problem. Class litigation also produces error costs by creating especially severe agency problems, adverse selection effects, and settlement leverage in weak cases.

9.2.2   Agency Problems

The primary locus of agency problems in the class setting is the relationship between the class attorney and the class.[80] To be sure, individual litigation can also produce agency costs. But the problems are likely to be more severe in the class setting for several reasons.

9.2.2.1   Small Claim Class Actions

In class actions with only small claims, no class member has enough at stake to justify the cost of monitoring the class attorney. Indeed, few class members are likely to be more than fleetingly aware that there is a class action, even with formal notice, because few are likely to read the notice carefully or understand its terms. Not even the named representatives care enough about the action to pay much attention to what the attorney is doing. One might expect that representatives would have some

---

80. For extensive discussions of these agency problems in small claim and large claim class actions, *see* Macey & Miller, *Plaintiffs' Attorney's Role, supra* note 74; John C. Coffee, Jr., *The Regulation of Entrepreneurial Litigation: Balancing Fairness and Efficiency in the Large Class Action*, 54 U. CHI. L. REV. 877 (1987) (hereinafter "Coffee, *Entrepreneurial Litigation*"); John C. Coffee, Jr., *Class Action Accountability: Reconciling Exit, Voice, and Loyalty in Representative Litigation*, 100 COLUM. L. REV. 370 (2000) (hereinafter "Coffee, *Class Action Accountability*"); John C. Coffee, Jr., *Class Wars: The Dilemma of the Mass Tort Class Action*, 195 COLUM. L. REV. 1343 (1995) (hereinafter "Coffee, *Class Wars*").

interest in monitoring the litigation based on the fact that they appear as named plaintiffs, but this is rarely the case. It is customary for the class attorney to seek out class representatives rather than the other way around (despite ethical rules against client solicitation). Indeed, before passage of the Private Securities Litigation Reform Act in 1995, attorneys specializing in federal securities fraud class actions often kept names of "professional plaintiffs"—individuals with a few shares in many different companies who could serve as named plaintiffs in many different class actions.[81]

Furthermore, when class members have very little at stake, they have little reason to report a class attorney's inadequate representation or violation of ethical rules even if they happen to notice. Nor does reputation work as a disciplining force. For it does not pay for class action lawyers to cultivate a reputation for loyal advocacy when there is no actual client to impress. In other words, it is class counsel, acting as an "entrepreneurial" attorney,[82] who initiates and drives the lawsuit; the named representative "operates almost always as a mere figurehead."[83]

81. In fact, some observers believe that this practice is still prevalent despite the statutory reforms.

82. *See* Coffee, *Entrepreneurial Litigation*, *supra* note 80, at 882.

83. Macey & Miller, *Plaintiffs' Attorney's Role*, *supra* note 74, at 5.

9.2.2.2 Large Claim Class Actions

Agency problems are also severe in large claim class actions, such as mass tort cases. Although many class members have enough at stake to justify some monitoring of the class attorney, most of them lack the sophistication necessary to do an effective job. Also, information about an attorney's litigation conduct is hard to obtain. The attorney is not likely to be forthcoming with this information, and there is no readily available public source or easy access to formal tools like discovery to force disclosure. Some of these concerns are also present in individual suits, but the broad reach of the class action makes them more troubling. With individual suits, there are more opportunities for chance events to bring attorney misconduct to the attention of a client.[84]

Furthermore, class members have incentives to free ride on the monitoring efforts of others in the class. The **free-rider problem** is endemic to all types of collective action. The problem arises when each member of a group would rather that others in the group bear the burden of group tasks. More precisely, because all members of a group benefit from any efforts that improve the prospects for the group as a whole, each member has an incentive to

---

84. Furthermore, the attorney for the class owes a duty to the class as a whole rather than to individual class members. As a result, she can defend against legitimate criticism by claiming that the criticism serves the private interests of the objecting class member and not the interests of the class as whole. Under these circumstances, it would be difficult for a third party to sort out the truth of the competing claims.

leave those efforts to others, since by doing so he benefits without having to incur any cost.

In addition, most absent class members do not have enough direct involvement or feeling of a stake in the litigation to pay much attention to the attorney's litigation activity. Many are also likely to take some comfort in knowing that there are other injured parties acting as their representatives. What they do not know is that, in many cases, the class representatives have been hand-picked by the class attorney.

9.2.2.3 Consequences

Because of these agency problems, class attorneys have a great deal of latitude to run the class litigation in their own self-interest. What adverse consequences are likely to flow to the class? To answer this question, it is important to begin with an explanation of how fees are awarded in class actions, since the attorney's interest usually lies in maximizing his fee.[85]

A class attorney cannot be paid on the basis of a contract with the class, because there is no way to enter into individual fee agreements with each class member. If a class action actually goes to trial, the court determines a reasonable fee in light of the benefit that the attorney confers on the class. In

85. This motivational assumption holds for damages class actions like the small claim and mass tort actions that we have been discussing. However, it does not apply universally. For example, an attorney for a civil rights class is likely to be more interested in furthering his own view of the public interest or possibly advancing his own reputation than maximizing his fee.

complex class actions with a litigation committee, the largest fraction of this fee almost always goes to lead counsel. On the other hand, if a class action settles, as most do, the parties usually agree on a fee as part of the settlement. But the trial judge is still supposed to review the fee when reviewing the settlement.

There are two ways to calculate a reasonable fee, either for determining the fee award in a litigated case or for reviewing the fee provision of a settlement. The so-called "lodestar method" follows the pattern of a fee-for-services arrangement. The attorney files a record of the hours worked and the judge multiplies those hours by a reasonable hourly rate. This generates the "lodestar" figure, which the judge then adjusts to take account of special factors, such as unusual risk. The "percentage of recovery" method follows the pattern of a contingency fee arrangement. The judge decides what fraction of the total recovery to award the attorney based on an evaluation of the attorney's efforts, the value of the recovery to the class, and the nature of the case.

It follows that the class attorney's incentives should parallel those of attorneys in ordinary fee-for-services and contingency fee representation. Chapter Two discussed some of these incentives. If the class attorney expects to be paid according to the lodestar method, he has an incentive to prolong the litigation in order to run up total hours worked. If he expects to be paid on a percentage-of-recovery basis, he has an incentive to settle early or on the eve of trial, and for less than the expected trial value of the class claims.

But these are not the most serious problems. The most serious problem, in the view of most critics of the class action, is the so-called "sweetheart settlement," in which the class attorney sells out the class by trading a high fee for a low class recovery. While there is some disagreement about the extent of this problem, many observers of the class action believe that it is serious. They cite as examples cases like *Kamilewicz v. Bank of Boston Corp.*, in which the class attorneys received millions of dollars in fees while most of their class clients ended up with a net loss.[86]

Judicial review at the settlement stage is supposed to catch this abuse, but judicial review works poorly, especially when the trial judge has a strong interest in approving the settlement to clear his docket of a complicated case. Moreover, even if the judge wants to conduct a thorough review, he will have considerable difficulty finding anyone to pres-

86. *See* Kamilewicz v. Bank of Boston Corp., 92 F.3d 506 (7th Cir.1996). In *Kamilewicz*, a class of 715,000 mortgagees, whose mortgages were serviced by BankBoston Mortgage Corp., sued for damages in an Alabama state court, alleging that the bank improperly calculated the surplus that the mortgagees had to maintain in their escrow accounts. The parties settled, with the class attorneys receiving somewhere between 8.5 and 14 million dollars in fees and class members receiving one-time interest payments between $0 and $8.76. The settlement provided that BankBoston could deduct the attorney's fees from each mortgagee's escrow account, and in most cases this deduction exceeded the interest payment, with the result that most class members suffered a net loss from the litigation.

ent the opposing case effectively. Neither class counsel nor the defendant has an interest in doing so. Some class members might take on the task, but experience shows that few bother and those who do are likely to be inadequate. This is especially problematic because class settlements can be crafted in complicated ways that make them difficult to evaluate without expert analysis.[87]

Indeed, when a class member intervenes to raise objections, it is often the lawyer representing the class member, rather than the class member himself, who is interested in blocking the settlement. This lawyer might have lost the competition for lead counsel and expects to receive a higher fee if he scuttles the settlement and pushes forward with a parallel and overlapping class action. More likely, he has no intention of exiting the class but is simply using the threat of exit to get a larger share of the settlement and fee award. When this happens, the objector cannot be trusted to have the best interests

---

87. For example, one of the most controversial types of settlement, frequently used in small claim class actions, involves providing class members with in-kind compensation, such as coupons that go toward future purchases of defendant's products. Not all class members are likely to use the coupons or other forms of non-monetary compensation and this makes it extremely difficult to estimate the true benefit to the class. Another example is the reversionary fund settlement, in which the defendant establishes a fund to compensate class members, the class attorney receives a fee based on the fund, and anything left unclaimed after a period of time reverts back to the defendant. Here too it is difficult to estimate exactly how much benefit the class will enjoy, since the class attorney and the defendant have incentives to create a large fund and discourage class members from making claims on it.

of the class in mind. Furthermore, the class attorney and the defendant have incentives to "buy off" the objector. They do this by making a side deal that settles the attorney's individual claims for a premium, or by making slight adjustments to the settlement so the attorney can argue that he benefited the class and thus deserves a higher fee.

In sum, there are many opportunities to enter into sweetheart settlements that shortchange the class and end up systematically skewing recovery below the substantive entitlements of class members. To evaluate the social cost of these errors, one must consider the purposes of the class action.[88]

Given the deterrence purpose of the small claim class action, it makes sense to evaluate the settlement and fee award not by how much compensation class members receive, but instead by how much the defendant pays. Who gets the payment, whether the attorney or class members, is not particularly important. Nor does it matter that the settlement falls short of the expected value of the class claims insofar as public enforcement is available to fill the deterrence gap. This means that the cost of error due to sweetheart settlements depends on the residual deterrence loss when public enforcement is insufficient.

---

[88]. There are potential costs other than error costs, such as damage to the moral authority or legitimacy of the court system. While some of these additional costs might fit within an economic approach, those that rely on a moral metric unrelated to economic welfare cannot be assimilated to economics. For useful background, see the introduction to Part II and Chapter Six.

The cost of sweetheart settlements is likely to be much higher in the large claim setting because compensation figures more prominently. When large amounts are at stake, compensation is valuable from an economic perspective because it reduces the risk-bearing costs of class members, encourages efficient investment in primary activity, and facilitates socially optimal insurance choices. Still, before condemning the class action for creating error costs, one must also consider the risk of sweetheart settlements in individual suits. Mass tort attorneys, for example, routinely assemble huge inventories of clients (often in the tens of thousands) and settle en masse for a lump sum. Neither the settlement nor the attorney's contingency fee is subject to any court review or approval. It should be obvious that this arrangement is also vulnerable to agency problems and creates incentives for settlements that sell out clients. While the magnitude of the risk might well differ between these two situations, it is important to recognize that individual litigation can create similar problems.

9.2.3 Adverse Selection and Opt Outs

9.2.3.1 Intra–Class Wealth Transfers

Class attorneys have an incentive to include in the class as many injured parties as possible, no matter how weak their individual cases happen to be. For example, in a mass tort class action, the more individual clients a lawyer has, the more influence he wields and the more leverage he can exercise over the fee award. The problem is that there are just so many injured parties with strong claims, so the inventory of known class members represented by lawyers will end up heavily stacked with plaintiffs who have moderate or weak claims. Since it is difficult to distinguish weak from strong claims without investigating the merits of each individual case, plaintiffs with weak claims—or more precisely, their attorneys—can pretend to have strong claims.[89]

This result is an example of what economists call **adverse selection**.[90] The class action "adversely selects" for weak claims that end up pooled together with strong ones because the two cannot be easily distinguished. From this description, it should be clear that adverse selection is an application of the pooling strategy described in Section 1.2.3.2.3 of Chapter One. A familiar example out-

89. This is a particular problem in mass tort cases because the individual issues (different exposure scenarios, different facts on specific causation, and the like) create high variance within the plaintiff group and thus wide divergence between the strongest and weakest cases. Indeed, mass tort law firms tend to separate into "boutique firms" that screen cases carefully for strong suits and "wholesale firms" that are far less discriminating and take lots of weak cases. *See* Coffee, *Class Wars*, *supra* note 80, at 1365. This might provide some signaling benefit that could help to some extent to separate strong from weak suits.

90. The adverse selection problem in the class action setting is discussed in Coffee, *Entrepreneurial Litigation*, *supra* note 80. There is a different dynamic, unrelated to adverse selection, which can also end up stacking the class with weak claims. The defendant and class counsel sometimes have an interest in creating as large a class as possible—and thus including weak claims in the class—in order to persuade the trial judge to accept a large class counsel fee as part of a settlement.

side the litigation setting is the tendency of insurance policies to attract poor insurance risks. Suppose an insurance company wants to offer a life insurance policy at a low premium to healthy individuals. If the company relies exclusively on self-disclosure, applicants will lie about their health in order to buy at the low premium. The company knows this, so it conducts medical exams and asks for health records. However, this adds costs to the policy and these costs are passed on to customers through higher premiums. Moreover, medical tests and health histories do not screen perfectly, so the company still charges a somewhat higher premium to cover the higher risk.

This example illustrates two points. First, adverse selection operates under conditions of asymmetric information where it is costly for one party to determine what type the other party is (e.g., a high or low health risk, a strong or weak plaintiff). Second, adverse selection creates social costs by pooling undesirable types with desirable ones and thus frustrating efforts to treat the different types according to their specific characteristics. If it were possible to distinguish the strong claims from the weak ones, a court could divide the large class into subclasses according to claim strength and designate a separate attorney to protect the interests of each subclass. This approach is unavailable, however, because of the information obstacles that support the pooling strategy.

In the class setting, therefore, adverse selection attracts plaintiffs with weak claims. The defendant expects this and therefore sets a lower estimate of expected class recovery and offers a lower settlement to the class as a whole. Since claims cannot be distinguished by strength, the total class settlement is usually distributed on a pro-rata basis (often by disease category). As a result, class members with strong claims get less than the expected trial value of their claims and class members with weak claims get more. In effect, class action settlements transfer wealth from above-average to below-average plaintiffs, thereby producing errors of both types—high-end plaintiffs receive less than their substantive entitlements and low-end plaintiffs receive more. The errors become more numerous and the wealth transfers more pronounced as the adverse selection problems increase.[91]

9.2.3.2 Opt Out by High–End Plaintiffs

Adverse selection also gives plaintiffs with large claims a reason to exit an opt-out class. As the average expected recovery falls due to the influx of

91. To illustrate, suppose a class of 10,000 members includes plaintiffs with weak, moderate, and strong claims. The weak claims comprise 50% and the moderate claims 30% of the class. Suppose the weak claims have an expected trial value of $10,000 on average, the moderate claims have an expected trial value of $200,000, and the strong claims have an expected trial value of $500,000. Assuming symmetric litigation costs and equal bargaining power, the settlement should be 5000 × 10,000 + 3000 × 200,000 + 2000 × 500,000 = $1.65 billion. If this total is distributed on a pro rata basis, each class member will receive $165,000. Plaintiffs with weak claims get a windfall of $155,000 at the expense of plaintiffs with strong and moderate claims. Moreover, plaintiffs with strong claims receive only about one-third of the true value of their claims.

weak claims, individual litigation becomes more attractive to high-end plaintiffs. At some point, the difference between expected class recovery and individual recovery gets so large that the class member does better opting out despite the higher cost of individual litigation. And as more plaintiffs opt out, the relative proportion of high-end plaintiffs remaining in the class falls and the defendant reduces its settlement offer further, thereby triggering even more opt outs.

Another factor contributes to the attractiveness of opt out. A class member who opts out will usually have his individual case transferred to the court where the class action is pending and consolidated with it. This gives the class member an opportunity to free ride on the research, discovery and other work done by class attorneys, while still avoiding the class settlement and protecting his ability to litigate individually.

Theoretically, the class action could unravel completely, leaving only the weakest claims in the class. However, complete unraveling is unlikely as a practical matter because not all high-end plaintiffs know they have strong cases or fully appreciate the value of opting out. Still, individual litigation by opt outs undermines the efficiency of the class action, especially when the class ends up stacked with weak claims that would not be litigated vigorously (if at all) in individual suits. Agency problems are also exacerbated by opt outs, since high-end plaintiffs are the ones most likely to monitor the class attorney.

To make matters even worse, opting out can be in the attorney's and not the class member's best interest. When a lawyer is not chosen for the litigation committee and has only a minor role in the class suit, he can expect only a small fraction of the class action fee award. Sometimes in a situation like this the attorney does better by exiting the class even when the class members he represents do worse. The attorney might leave the class, for example, because he has more control in an individual suit and is guaranteed his full contingency without risk of court adjustment to reflect hours worked. Also, he might leave to litigate his own parallel class action in the hope of getting the defendant to settle with him and pay a larger fee.

One way to prevent opt-outs is to deny an opt-out right; in other words, to make all damage class actions into mandatory class actions. But locking high-end plaintiffs into the class forces them to accept wealth transfers that give them less than they deserve under the substantive law and less than they could obtain from individual litigation. Whether this result is seriously inefficient depends on how its prospect affects party incentives in the real world before any litigation arises.[92] Neverthe-

92. High-end plaintiffs would receive less than their substantive entitlements and low-end plaintiffs would receive more, but these errors might not be all that costly from an economic point of view. Since a plaintiff has no way to know for sure whether he will have a strong or a weak case, he will take an expectation over all future contingencies and therefore average between the high and the low. Because averaging smoothes out the high-end and low-end distortions, it might produce optimal decisions ex ante, at least for risk-neutral plaintiffs. However, wealth trans-

less, even if it is not seriously inefficient, it is, in the opinion of many, seriously *unfair*.[93]

9.2.4 The Special Case of the "Settlement Class Action"

The agency cost and adverse selection problems take a somewhat different, and possibly more serious form, in the mass tort "settlement class action."[94] The most controversial use of the settlement class involves defendants negotiating a "global settlement" with lawyers representing injured parties *before* suit is filed. While global settlements need not resolve all possible claims, the kind of global settlement that has attracted the

fers can create risk-bearing costs for risk-averse individuals, although it is not clear how serious these costs are.

93. Some class action supporters rely on an argument from hypothetical consent to explain why wealth transfers in mandatory class actions are compatible with individual justice and fairness. *See* Bruce Hay & David Rosenberg, *The Individual Justice of Averaging, http://papers.ssrn.com/paper.taf?abstract_id.* They claim that everyone who might be a future class member would, if they could, agree before any injury or lawsuit occurs to bind themselves to a mandatory class action because of the substantial savings in litigation costs and other private benefits. Thus, a formal rule requiring a mandatory class action simply gives the parties what they would have consented to if they could have entered into a binding agreement ex ante. Whether hypothetical consent can carry this much moral weight, however, is controversial. After all, hypothetical consent is not the same thing as real consent, and ordinarily consent must be real in order to have moral force.

94. For more on the settlement class action, see Coffee, *Class Action Accountability, supra* note 80; Coffee, *Class Wars, supra* note 80; Richard A. Nagareda, *Autonomy, Peace, and Put Options in the Mass Tort Class Action*, 115 Harv. L. Rev. 747 (2002).

most controversy in fact concludes *all* of defendants' potential liability—liability not only to persons having present injuries but also to all persons exposed but not yet manifesting injury who might sue in the future (so-called "future claimants").

With settlement in hand, the parties file a class action complaint, attach a copy of the settlement, and press a motion for certification. The idea is to get the trial judge to certify a class, approve the settlement, and bind all class members to its terms. If the judge grants the certification motion, he does so conditional on approving the proposed settlement. If the judge ultimately rejects the settlement, the certification lapses.

The settlement class action is extremely attractive to mass tort defendants because it settles their liabilities to both present and future claimants in one fell swoop and thus buys "global peace." Mass tort injuries are characterized by long latency periods. This means that the defendant has to worry about thousands of future cases and potentially massive and possibly bankrupting liability to future claimants. Moreover, there is good reason for defendants to think that these future claimants will sue. Mass torts spawn specialized plaintiffs' firms that have strong interests in identifying as many future claimants as possible when their injuries become manifest. For these reasons, mass tort defendants tend to be more concerned about future liability than about liability to current plaintiffs. The settlement class gives them a way to manage this future liability without jeopardizing the viability of the company.

According to critics, what makes the settlement class action so attractive to defendants is also what makes it unusually susceptible to lawyer opportunism and sweetheart settlements. Two factors are important: the rational apathy of future claimants, and the comprehensive, all-or-nothing quality of the global settlement. Future claimants who are perfectly healthy at the time of the class action have little incentive to monitor class attorneys, object at the settlement stage, or opt out of the class. Moreover, because a global resolution eliminates all possibility of future litigation and lucrative settlements, it puts enormous pressure on the mass tort law firms to maximize the settlement class fee and secure a piece of it for themselves—even at the expense of the class. These two factors, combined with judicial receptivity to broad settlements that clear congested dockets, create conditions ripe for abuse—or so the critics claim.

To illustrate, consider the standard critical account of asbestos litigation. As asbestos claims soared and more companies faced bankruptcy, defendants searched for ways to manage the risk of future liability and keep their companies intact. In the 1990s, they seized on the settlement class action. Defendants shopped around for plaintiff lawyers willing to negotiate a global settlement on favorable terms. The fact that this was the endgame guaranteed lots of interested parties. In fact, the defendants were able to take advantage of a "reverse auction," in which mass tort firms competed with one another to be the most pro-defendant so they would be chosen to negotiate and serve as class counsel.

The negotiating parties structured global settlements to take maximum advantage of the rational apathy of future claimants, to minimize objectors, and to maximize the likelihood of judicial approval. A popular strategy involved two steps. The defendant first settled current claims separately from the class action, and then arranged a global settlement class to resolve all future claims. This two-step approach had several advantages. When the defendant settled current claims, it settled not just with the law firm serving as class counsel, but with all law firms having inventories of asbestos clients. The defendant agreed to pay premium lump sum settlements for these inventory claims with the understanding that the law firm would not oppose the global class settlement. Thus, these side agreements made it possible to limit the class definition at the second stage to future claimants, the group most likely to be rationally apathetic.

This account simplifies a complex phenomenon. Moreover, it is a critical account and might not be accepted in full by all class action supporters. Nevertheless, it explains why many observers of the class action worry especially about the settlement class. The United States Supreme Court has expressed concern as well and in two opinions imposed some limits on use of the device.[95] At the same time, the settlement class, if properly regulated, can create substantial social benefits. The challenge is to develop an appropriate set of legal controls.

9.2.5   Settlement Leverage

Some observers of the class action worry that the settlement leverage created by class certification attracts frivolous and weak class action suits.[96] Although people disagree about the precise scope of the problem, those who believe the risk is serious point to three features of class litigation that can play a role in enhancing settlement leverage and attracting frivolous suits: first, the class action magnifies the stakes through aggregation; second, it increases the risk-bearing, litigation, and reputation costs of the defendant, and third, it enlists the trial judge in the settlement process.

The first factor, large stakes, can turn a class action consisting only of frivolous suits into a positive expected value suit in the aggregate, even with a very small risk of trial error. If the class attorney expects a large enough fraction of the total recovery as a fee, he will be willing to file suit and make a credible threat to take the case all the way through trial. For example, suppose that courts make mistakes and find liability in a frivolous suit 2% of the

95. *See* Amchem Products, Inc. v. Windsor, 521 U.S. 591 (1997); Ortiz v. Fibreboard, 527 U.S. 815 (1999).

96. For a discussion of these concerns, see Robert G. Bone & David S. Evans, *Class Certification and the Substantive Merits,* 51 Duke L. J. 1251 (2002) (hereinafter, "Bone & Evans, *Class Certification*").

time. Suppose that a class includes 10,000 members, each of whom has a frivolous suit but could prove $500,000 in damages if the court mistakenly found liability. Also suppose that the attorney's fee is 20% of the class recovery. Under these circumstances, an attorney will expect a fee of $20 million,[97] and therefore should be willing to litigate the class action even if the expected cost is in the millions.[98]

The second and third factors—high defendant costs and judicial involvement in settlement—make frivolous class action suits more likely even when class litigation has negative expected value. In Chapter One, we studied cost-based and information-based models of frivolous litigation. When these models are applied to the class setting, they predict even more serious frivolous suit problems than in individual suits because of higher litigation, risk-bearing and reputation costs and judicial pressure to settle.[99] For example, since the defendant settles in the information-based models in order to avoid the cost of litigating, the higher those costs and the more aggressive the judge is in pushing for

[97]. $0.20 \times 10,000 \times 0.02 \times 500,000 = \$20$ million.

[98]. If the attorney maintains a highly diversified portfolio of cases and can spread the risk of loss efficiently, he should be risk-neutral and willing to take the case even if the expected litigation cost is only slightly less than $20 million. However, if the attorney is risk-averse, he will take the case only if the cost is substantially lower (how much lower depends on how risk-averse he is).

[99]. Risk-bearing costs can be substantial even for corporate defendants in the class action setting because of the high stakes and the all-or-nothing nature of the class action gamble. And the adverse publicity that sometimes accompanies a class action compounds a defendant's reputation costs.

settlement, the greater the settlement pressure and the more leverage frivolous plaintiffs enjoy.[100]

9.3   REFORM PROPOSALS

There are many proposals to reform class action law, and they differ according to what aspect of the problem they target: fee awards, client monitoring, sweetheart settlements, or frivolous suits. This final section briefly surveys some of the most salient. Its goal is strictly descriptive; no effort is made to offer a critical evaluation.

9.3.1   Fee Awards

On the assumption that agency problems are best handled by linking the agent's payoff to the benefit he bestows on the principal, some proposals aim to link attorney fee awards more closely to the actual benefits that the attorney confers on the class. One such proposal recommends calculating fees exclusively by a percentage-of-recovery method.[101] The idea is that the attorney will do a better job of maximizing class recovery if he expects a higher fee when he obtains a larger recovery. A further refinement on this proposal would adjust the percentage

100. Recall that in the asymmetric information models, it is the defendant's fear of having to try a meritorious suit that creates pressure to settle frivolous suits. Therefore, whatever adds to the cost of going to trial in a meritorious suit will increase settlement leverage in a frivolous suit.

101. *See* Macey & Miller, *Plaintiffs' Attorney's Role, supra* note 74.

multiplier so that the attorney expects the same fee award from settling as from litigating to final judgment.[102] If the attorney expects to do no better by settling than by going to trial, he will be less inclined to accept a sweetheart settlement.

One of the most controversial fee-based reforms, one that has actually been implemented in some small claim class actions, involves auctioning the position of lead counsel. The judge invites bids proposing different fee schedules and chooses the bid with the lowest fee, subject to quality constraints. The goal is to control excessive fees by approximating the conditions of a competitive market for legal services.

Yet another proposal is to use fee awards to discourage strategic opt outs in large claim class actions; that is, opt-outs that are in the attorney's interest but not the class member's.[103] The idea is to make fee awards in individual suits depend on the difference between the plaintiff's individual recovery and the average recovery of the class. The attorney gets a fee only if his decision to opt out ends up benefiting the class member by giving her more than she would have received had she remained in the class.

9.3.2 Monitoring

A second approach to agency problems focuses on strengthening client monitoring. For example, the

102. *See* Hay & Rosenberg, *Sweetheart Settlements*, *supra* note 71.

103. *See* Coffee, *Entrepreneurial Litigation*, *supra* note 80.

Private Securities Litigation Reform Act of 1995 ("PSLRA") requires that the party filing a securities fraud class action in federal court publish notice inviting members to apply for appointment as representatives.[104] The court selects the representative parties from the applicant pool, with a strong presumption in favor of the candidate with the largest amount at stake. Once selected, the representative party then chooses a lawyer for the class.

The purpose of this procedure is to select large institutional investors to take the role of the class representative. An attorney who files a securities fraud class action is not likely to choose an institutional investor voluntarily because of the cost of locating a willing party and because institutional investors are capable of evaluating the attorney's performance and more likely to monitor. The PSLRA approach assumes that when the judge appoints an institutional investor and the institutional investor selects class counsel, monitoring is more likely to take place. Also, institutional investors are repeat players in securities fraud litigation. Therefore, selecting them as class representatives and empowering them to choose the class attorney gives securities fraud lawyers an incentive to develop reputations for fair settlements in order to be chosen as class counsel in future suits.[105]

104. *See* 15 U.S.C. §§ 78u–4(a)(3)(B)(i), 78u–4(a)(3)(B)(iii)(I).

105. In fact, the PSLRA provision has had mixed success in practice. One problem is that judges object to obstacles in the way of class settlements and therefore condone the creative ways class attorneys circumvent the provision. For a discussion of

9.3.3 Sweetheart Settlements

A third approach targets settlements directly. One proposal focuses on elements usually associated with sweetheart settlements. For example, the Class Action Fairness Bill, which is pending in Congress as of this writing, regulates the use of coupons and other non-cash settlements[106] and prohibits side deals with selected class members.[107] Other approaches focus on different elements, but all share in common the assumption that regulating typical features of sweetheart settlements will make those settlements more difficult to negotiate and to get approved.

Another proposal seeks to bolster judicial screening at the settlement stage. The idea is to encourage objections, create more of an adversarial contest, and improve the information available to contesting parties and the court. For example, amendments to Federal Rule 23, which are pending as of the time of this writing, require more detail in the notice to potential objectors, encourage more exacting judicial review, and require disclosure of information about any side agreements.[108] Other proposals along

some of these problems, *see* Coffee, *Class Action Accountability*, *supra* note 80, at 413–17.

106. For the Senate version of this bill, see S.1712 (107th Cong. 1st Sess.) and in particular, section 1712 of the bill.

107. *See id.* §§ 1714, 1715.

108. Particularly relevant are the proposed amendments to Rules 23(c)(2) and 23(e). *See* CIVIL RULES ADVISORY COMMITTEE, JUDICIAL CONFERENCE OF THE UNITED STATES, REPORT OF THE CIVIL RULES ADVISORY COMMITTEE 93–104 (Admin. Office of the U.S. Courts, May 20, 2002).

the same lines include appointment of a guardian ad litem to advocate the interests of the class and greater use of special masters to review the terms of complicated settlements.[109]

A third proposal is to give absent class members an opportunity to opt out of the class at the time of the settlement, or in the case of mass tort settlements covering persons exposed but not yet suffering injury, at the time serious injury is manifested.[110] Different proposals structure these "back end opt out rights" differently. For example, one commentator would have trial judges, as part of reviewing a proposed settlement, invite offers by competing attorneys proposing better terms to class members who opt out and join a competing class action.[111] One purpose is to give class members a chance to protect themselves by exiting an

109. In general, a "guardian ad litem" is an attorney or other person appointed to protect the interests of someone, such as a minor or mentally incompetent, who is unable to protect himself. The proposal would have the court appoint an attorney to serve as a guardian ad litem for the class and advocate the interests of the class at the settlement stage. A "special master" is a person appointed by the judge to act in effect as the judge's assistant. In the class action setting, the special master is likely to be a lawyer or law school professor with more time and possibly greater expertise to devote to the complicated and lengthy settlement review process than the federal court judge.

110. Proposed amendments to Rule 23(e) would give the trial judge discretion to allow class members in an opt-out class action to opt out at the time of a settlement as well as at the time of original certification. *See id.*

111. *See* Coffee, *Class Action Accountability, supra* note 80; *see also* Nagareda, *supra* note 94 (arguing for a settlement structure in which class members get to choose at the time an injury manifests itself whether to take advantage of the class

inadequate settlement. But another purpose is to create incentives for class attorneys to negotiate fair settlements attractive enough to discourage opt out.

9.3.4 Frivolous Class Actions

A fourth reform area targets the problem of frivolous class action suits. One approach, adopted by the Private Securities Litigation Reform Act, is to strengthen sanctions for frivolous filings.[112] Another approach is to apply a version of the British Rule on attorney fees to the class action and shift some portion of the winner's fees to the losing side.[113]

A third option is to screen the merits at the certification stage. Under this approach, the trial judge would review the substantive merits of the class action and certify a class only if the suit had a significant probability of success.[114] In addition, a merits review could be aided by litigation of some individual suits before a class is certified. With a track record of individual judgments and settlements, the judge (and the parties) would have an easier time evaluating the merits of the class claims. Although incorporating a merits review at

settlement or opt out and pursue individual litigation—on condition of waiving punitive damages in the case of an opt out).

112. *See* 15 U.S.C. § 78u–4(c).

113. For a tentative, exploratory suggestion along these lines, see Deborah R. Hensler & Thomas D. Rowe, Jr., *Beyond "It Just Ain't Worth It": Alternative Strategies for Damage Class Action Reform*, 64 L. & CONTEMP. PROBS. 137 (Spring/Summer 2001).

114. *See* Bone & Evans, *Class Certification, supra* note 96.

the certification stage is likely to increase process costs and erroneous certification denials, it reduces erroneous grants and, supporters claim, creates more benefits than costs.

Conclusion

We began our journey with a fundamental point about procedure. Procedure is much more than a set of rules or a technical exercise in litigation management. The design of a procedural system implicates complicated questions of prediction and evaluation and at times deep philosophical puzzles. This book's nine chapters confirm this basic point.

The discussion of positive tools in Part One showed how important—and how difficult—prediction is in the setting of litigation. The strategic nature of the environment makes simple predictions highly unreliable. The economic models and game-theoretic tools that we explored are useful for probing some of the complexity, but these positive tools also have limits. And they rest on assumptions about the way people behave that may need to be modified in light of the bounded rationality insights discussed in Chapter Three.

The normative tools described in Part Two remind us that costs must always be considered along with benefits. It is not possible to design a procedural system that gives everyone the relief they deserve. Even avoidable error has to be tolerated in a world of scarce resources. At some point, individuals must suffer their losses despite their substantive entitlements so that enough resources are left to pursue other worthy social goals. For the economist, this is a matter of balancing costs and benefits, although the balance can be very difficult to strike when incentives are involved—as we saw in Chapter Five. For those who focus on fairness and recognize strong procedural rights, the problem is, in some ways, even more difficult. We saw in Chapter Six that one of the trickiest aspects is how to reconcile protecting rights as utility trumps with limiting social costs.

Part Three applied the economic tools of Parts One and Two to three procedural topics: discovery, preclusion, and the class action. These three topics were chosen for their current interest. Yet many more could have been discussed. Economics can be used to analyze every facet of procedural law.

This book will have succeeded if for some readers it opens up a new perspective on procedural law. It will have succeeded even more if it sparks interest in the economic approach and equips the reader to explore this fascinating area on his or her own.

TABLE OF CASES

References are to Pages.

*

INDEX

References are to pages.

---

†